"*To the Promised Land* helps us to remember King as a prophet for poor and working-class people, as we carry on that campaign against racism and poverty in our own times. A terrific book."
—Timothy B. Tyson, author of *The Blood of Emmett Till*

"Dr. Martin Luther King, Jr., was a revolutionary, a dangerous man. . . . Michael Honey tells a compelling story of militant, revolutionary love in action. This is a dangerous book."
—Robin D. G. Kelley, author of *Freedom Dreams: The Black Radical Imagination*

"Michael Honey's important and timely new book recovers the fullness of King's social Christian vision. More than just Jim Crow's most formidable detractor, he was one of capitalism's most insistent and incisive critics. Honey leaves no doubt that, in our new Gilded Age, King's dream, marked by a longing for both racial and economic justice, remains as relevant as ever."
—Heath W. Carter, author of *Union Made: Working People and the Rise of Social Christianity in Chicago*

"Honey's book offers a lively, inspiring, and carefully researched study of King's efforts for economic justice, reminding readers of this seldom-documented but crucial aspect of King's legacy. . . . *To the Promised Land* is especially timely and revelatory as we struggle still with racism, militarism, poverty, and extreme economic inequality 50 years after the death of King."
—Robin Lindley, *History News Network*

"Michael Honey's very cogent book shows that King intended from the start of his public career to work to end racial discrimination and poverty for all Americans. . . . *To the Promised Land*'s thorough treatment of King's efforts to support black unionism and to forge an alliance between the black and the white working classes reveals the arduous effort that he put into this project, most heartbreakingly in his final years."

—Annette Gordon-Reed, *New York Review of Books*

"Civil rights buffs will enjoy this book." —*St. Louis Post-Dispatch*

"Honey writes to each margin of the civil-rights era and clarifies it with a deep understanding of King's true significance. . . . [*To the Promised Land*] reveals and raises up the many thousands of people who took King's advice to commit to 'dangerous unselfishness' directly to heart." —*Providence Journal*

"King the economic radical has renewed relevance, and Honey's work helps to shift him from static icon to dynamic thinker whose vision can guide us in taking on the grossly unfair aspects of American capitalism."

—Lynn Parramore, Institute for New Economic Thinking

OTHER WORKS BY MICHAEL K. HONEY

Books

Sharecropper's Troubadour:
John L. Handcox, the Southern Tenant Farmers Union,
and the African American Song Tradition

Going Down Jericho Road:
The Memphis Strike, Martin Luther King's Last Campaign

Black Workers Remember:
An Oral History of Segregation, Unionism, and
the Freedom Struggle

Southern Labor and Black Civil Rights:
Organizing Memphis Workers

Film

Love and Solidarity:
James M. Lawson and Nonviolence in the
Search for Workers' Rights

Edited Work

Martin Luther King, Jr., *"All Labor Has Dignity"*

"We can all get more together than we can apart."

MARTIN LUTHER KING, JR., AT MASON TEMPLE, MEMPHIS, MARCH 18, 1968

TO THE PROMISED LAND

*Martin Luther King
and the Fight
for Economic Justice*

Michael K. Honey

W. W. NORTON & COMPANY
Independent Publishers Since 1923
New York London

For information about permission to reproduce selections from this book, write to Permissions, W. W. Norton & Company, Inc., 500 Fifth Avenue, New York, NY 10110

For information about special discounts for bulk purchases, please contact W. W. Norton Special Sales at specialsales@wwnorton.com or 800-233-4830

Manufacturing by LSC Communications Harrisonburg
Book design by Lovedog Studio
Production manager: Julia Druskin

Library of Congress Cataloging-in-Publication Data

Names: Honey, Michael K., author.
Title: To the promised land : Martin Luther King and the fight for economic justice / Michael K. Honey.
Description: New York : W.W. Norton & Company, 2018. | Includes bibliographical references and index.
Identifiers: LCCN 2017060268 | ISBN 9780393651263 (hardcover)
Subjects: LCSH: King, Martin Luther, Jr., 1929–1968. | Equality—Economic aspects—United States—History—20th century. | African Americans—Economic conditions—20th century. | African Americans—Civil rights—History—20th century. | Poor People's Campaign. | Discrimination in employment—United States—History—20th century. | Right to labor—United States—History—20th century. | Civil rights movements—United States—History—20th century. | African Americans—Biography. | Civil rights workers—United States—Biography.
Classification: LCC E185.97.K5 H59 2018 | DDC 323.029—dc23
LC record available at https://lccn.loc.gov/2017060268

ISBN 978-0-393-35673-1 pbk

W. W. Norton & Company, Inc., 500 Fifth Avenue, New York, N.Y. 10110
www.wwnorton.com

W. W. Norton & Company Ltd., 15 Carlisle Street, London W1D 3BS

1 2 3 4 5 6 7 8 9 0

To family, friends, colleagues, students, and fellow workers seeking a better world.

I never intend to adjust myself to the evils of segregation and the crippling effects of discrimination. I never intend to adjust myself to the tragic inequalities of an economic system which takes necessities from the masses to give luxuries to the classes. I never intend to become adjusted to the madness of militarism and the self-defeating method of physical violence. I call upon you to be maladjusted.

—KING AT HIGHLANDER FOLK SCHOOL,
SEPTEMBER 2, 1957

* * *

Whether it be the ultra-right wing in the form of Birch societies or the alliance which former President Eisenhower denounced, the alliance between big military and big business, or the coalition of southern Dixiecrats and northern reactionaries, whatever the form, these menaces now threaten everything decent and fair in American life. . . . As we struggle to make racial and economic justice a reality, let us maintain faith in the future. At times we confront difficult and frustrating moments in the struggle to make justice a reality, but we must believe somehow that these problems can be solved.

—KING AT THE AFL-CIO CONVENTION,
DECEMBER 3, 1961

* * *

You are reminding, not only Memphis, but you are reminding the nation that it is a crime for people to live in this rich nation and receive starvation wages. . . .

—KING AT MEMPHIS SANITATION STRIKE RALLY,
MARCH 18, 1968

CONTENTS

Introduction

PROMISED LAND

> *Be concerned about your brother. You may not*
> *be on strike. But either we go up together or we*
> *go down together.*
>
> —Martin Luther King, Jr.,
> April 3, 1968, Memphis

O N April 3, 1968, Martin Luther King, Jr., swayed
at the pulpit in a late night gathering at Mason Temple in
Memphis, Tennessee. At age thirty-nine, King sometimes looked
like an older man, tired, worn, and discouraged. Exhausted from
constant travel, often making four or five speeches a day and sleeping only a few hours per night, King had a sore throat and slight
fever. His companion, Rev. Ralph David Abernathy, said King had
those symptoms whenever he felt premonitions of death. Thunder
and lightning rent the air, and when a ceiling fan made a banging
sound it startled King as if it were a rifle shot. Memphis that night
experienced one of the drenching downpours that regularly swept
through the Mississippi Delta, as a storm outside turned into a tor-
nado that wreaked havoc on neighboring towns and killed several
people. King had at first stayed in his hotel, but when told that the
news media and hundreds of his supporters demanded his presence,
he had made his way to the temple through a driving rain.

King and his organization, the Southern Christian Leadership
Conference (SCLC), had fought since 1957 to "redeem the soul of
America" by seeking equality before the law, integration, and voting
rights for all. The country's adoption of the Civil Rights Act of 1964
and the Voting Rights Act of 1965 had completed a "first phase"

of the freedom movement, King said. Now he wanted a "second phase" struggle for "economic equality," so that everyone could have a well-paying job or a basic level of income, along with decent levels of health care, education, and housing. Along with the A. Philip Randolph Institute, King had promoted a detailed document called an "Economic Bill of Rights for All Americans." Before coming to Memphis, he had been crisscrossing the country for weeks, promoting a multiracial coalition to pressure Congress to reallocate money for war to money for human needs. King called it the Poor People's Campaign, a "last ditch" effort to save America from the interrelated evils of racism, poverty, and war. Urban rebellions of the last four summers, and the wanton destruction of human life and waste of America's economic resources in the escalating Vietnam War, he feared, would lead to escalating racism and repressive, authoritarian government.

Time magazine in 1957 had declared him "no radical," but America's segregationists and right wing saw King as just that. Federal Bureau of Investigation (FBI) director J. Edgar Hoover publicly called him a liar in 1964 and in March 1967 ordered a counterintelligence (COINTELPRO) campaign by his field agents to prevent the rise of a "black messiah," and redoubled efforts to counteract King. From the 1963 March on Washington onward, Hoover's agents followed King, wiretapped his office, his hotel rooms, his house. They even sent an anonymous letter that urged King to take his own life or else have his private life exposed. Hoover's FBI leaked fake news and distorted reports to journalists, presidents Kennedy and Johnson, the heads of all major departments of government, the military, and the CIA. FBI secret agents paid agents provocateurs to stir up dissension and conflict among King's followers and within the Black Power and New Left movements.

Southern segregationists and the ultraright John Birch Society sent out pamphlets and postcards, and mounted billboards on southern highways, claiming to picture "King at a Communist Training School"—in fact, a picture of King and Rosa Parks and Myles Horton at the nonsectarian Highlander Folk School, the one institution in the South where blacks and whites were encouraged to frankly discuss issues. A right-wing campaign by neo-Nazis and promilitary, anticommunist groups painted the famous Baptist preacher as Communist.

By 1968, King had suffered a bombing of his home and his hotel room; body blows by a neo-Nazi in the South; stoning by whites armed with baseball bats wanting to kill him in a suburb of Chicago; a raucous anticommunist shout-down in Grosse Point, Michigan, largely due to his stand against the Vietnam War. Death threats plagued King and his family. Some saw him as a dangerous radical troublemaker, others thought King wasn't radical or militant enough. King's philosophy of love and nonviolence looked like old-fashioned sentimentalism unsuited to violent American realities. H. Rap Brown of the Student Nonviolent Coordinating Committee (SNCC) said, "Violence is as American as cherry pie," and it was true. Most Americans did not understand nonviolence as a philosophy or strategy for social change. Many in the business and political classes also opposed King's strong support for unions as a way to obtain a greater degree of racial and economic justice. Although today many have come to see King as an icon for American values, in his own time he was often reviled, physically attacked, and dismissed as a false prophet. In 1968, he was struggling to survive.

Yet to most African Americans, and certainly to his audience in Memphis, King offered extraordinary inspiration, dedication, book learning, and gifts of oratory. On this evening in Bishop Mason Temple of the Church of God in Christ, hundreds of striking black sanitation workers, their families, and community activists knew King understood the plight of the working poor. They were now in the sixth week of a desperate struggle and King came to support them in their efforts to raise their families above the poverty level through unionization. In December 1964, after receiving the Nobel Peace Prize in Oslo, Norway, King had returned to his hometown of Atlanta to join picket lines and declare an economic boycott to support some six hundred black women on strike, declaring, "We have decided that now is the time to closely identify our movement very closely with labor." King told a reporter "many more" alliances between civil rights and labor movements would follow. Memphis became one of those efforts, along with his dozens of speeches to union rallies, picket lines, and conventions in the years to come.

Some in his audience in Mason Temple thought King looked exhausted, but he soon proved otherwise. Speaking without notes, he started quietly, slowly. King imagined himself moving from the beginning of time to have a "panoramic view of the whole of human history up to now." He took his audience back to the struggles against slavery in Egypt and Greece, back to the Civil War and slave emancipation, and to President Franklin D. Roosevelt's vow that "we have nothing to fear but fear itself" during the Great Depression. King described the past as a mighty movement for human freedom. But he said if the Almighty asked him when he would most want to live he would answer, "If you allow me to live just a few years in the second half of the twentieth century, I will be happy."

Why? In 1968, he lived in a climate of left-right political polarization, white racial backlash, and massive carnage by and against the U.S. military in Indochina. He admitted, "The world is all messed up. The nation is sick. Trouble is in the land. Confusion all around." Yet he saw 1968 as a time of great social change. His voice rising, King cried out, "Something is happening in Memphis, something is happening in our world!" From South Africa to Memphis, "the masses of people are rising up." And their demand "is always the same: we want to be free." Humanity's difficulties had accumulated, so that all problems had to be solved together, creating an opportunity for what King called "the human rights revolution."

King had only been to Memphis a few times, yet he seemed to know his audience and their issues well. Conditions in Memphis exemplified the country's failure to move beyond civil rights to economic justice. African Americans, many of them recent migrants from the collapsing cotton economy, suffered from high unemployment, low wages, and soaring poverty. Perhaps half of the population of young black men had no jobs at all. Of those who had jobs, some 80 percent of black women worked in the homes of whites, with no labor law protections, and 80 percent of employed black men did unskilled labor. For black women and men in factory, service, laboring, or municipal jobs, a union provided their only hope for a better life.

The conditions of Memphis sanitation workers exemplified the plight of the working poor. They suffered from low wages, abuse by white supervisors, unsafe conditions, and systemic poverty. Through their union organizing, they protested being dismissed from work by white supervisors for the slightest infraction; being forced to carry leaking garbage tubs on their heads; eating their lunches in the shade of the garbage truck; being hurt and even killed on the job; reeking of garbage when they came home because they had no access to washing facilities. They sought an end to wages so low that men worked full time but their families lived in poverty. The all-male group demanded union recognition, collective bargaining rights, and deduction of union dues from their paychecks to make it possible to pay for a union staff person to represent them and operate a union effectively. Getting the city of Memphis to recognize their right to belong to a union with collective bargaining rights became the single most important point of conflict, and gave rise to the worker slogan, "I *Am* a Man."

Some 1,300 workers had endured six weeks of unemployment, hunger, and foreclosures on cars and homes. White police had attacked strikers, ministers, and civil rights activists with tear gas, the chemical Mace, and clubs; the police and FBI had infiltrated the ranks; the mayor had hired strikebreakers and threatened to fire strikers. The black community, women and men alike, understood and rallied behind their "I *Am* a Man" picket signs as a cry for recognition, of their union and their human dignity.

Some saw the strike of garbage and street and sewer workers as a small story, but, as he had done during the Montgomery bus boycott thirteen years earlier, King elevated it as part of an epochal movement for human freedom. "We mean business now, and we are determined to gain our rightful place in God's world," he said, to shouts of affirmation. "We are saying that we are determined to be men. We are determined to be people. We are saying . . . that we are God's children and we don't have to live like we are forced to live." In good Baptist-preacher style, he speeded up his cadence and intensity as the audience response gave him power and energy.

King's staff had strongly opposed going to Memphis. Sanitation worker Taylor Rogers recalled, "He was planning this big march to Washington. All his staff thought it was outrageous of him to stop and come to Memphis. But he went where he was needed, where he could help poor people. That's why he dropped everything, regardless of what all his staff people told him. Even if it had been poor white workers, King would have done the same thing," he recalled. "That's just the kind of person he was." But on April 3, King was in a crisis.

He had given a rousing and powerful speech at a mass rally for striking workers in Memphis on March 18, and vowed to come back to lead a mass march and a general strike of workers, students, and teachers. When he returned on March 28, everything went wrong. King had tried to lead a solidarity march, but black teenagers and possibly agents provocateurs broke out store windows after a Black Power *lumpen* proletariat group called the Invaders had egged them on. Its leader, Charles Cabbage, told me his group deliberately set out to discredit King's nonviolence strategy through disruptive street actions. Black ministers led King out of the march while James Lawson tried to halt it. Police officers charged, beating everyone in sight and sending many marchers to the hospital. It was a brutal police riot as much as anything, but mass-media news stories depicted King as a instigator and a coward running from the melee. Hostile congressmen and news outlets charged that King could not mount a nonviolent march in Washington, D.C. King had seen Memphis as a natural starting place for his Poor People's Campaign, in which African Americans, Mexican Americans, Puerto Ricans, Native Americans, and poor and working-class whites would besiege Congress to demand acceptable standards of housing, health care, education, and meaningful employment—economic justice for all. The richest country in the world, he said, had the means to end poverty; it only lacked the will to do so.

Memphis put all that in jeopardy. King felt he had to return to lead a nonviolent mass march or an image of movement disunity around nonviolent tactics would destroy his credibility to launch the Poor People's Campaign. In this emotionally charged atmosphere, King called on his audience at Mason Temple "to stay together and maintain unity," to not fall prey to what the Pharaoh had done during slavery. "He kept the slaves fighting among themselves," he said, but "when the slaves get together, that's the beginning of getting out of slavery." In his last days, King spoke repeatedly about the legacy of slavery and the need to overturn it through solidarity.

King insisted, "We've got to march again, in order to put the issue where it is supposed to be . . . that there are thirteen hundred of God's children here suffering, sometimes going hungry, going through dark and dreary nights, wondering how this thing is going to come out. That's the issue." King's return to Memphis was a faith act: buffeted by opposition from outside and inside the freedom movement, King refused to back off. Often on the road for three hundred days a year, he declared, "The preacher must have a kind of fire shut up in his bones. And whenever injustice is around, he must tell it." King still had the fire.

In this extemporaneous speech, King drew on the seemingly impossible victories of the past for strength: the student sit-ins and freedom rides of the early 1960s; black children standing up to fire hoses and police dogs in Birmingham, Alabama; civil rights and labor mobilizations that successfully pressured Congress to pass the Civil Rights Act of 1964 guaranteeing equal access to the law, to public facilities, and to jobs; the sacrifice of lives in Mississippi and in Alabama to obtain the federal Voting Rights Act of 1965.

People often called the civil- and voting-rights campaigns from 1955 to 1965 the Second Reconstruction, an effort to bring back the rights crushed by violence after slave emancipation and Reconstruction following the Civil War. But King now sought yet another phase of struggle, beyond civil and voting rights, for economic justice. In "these powerful days," he said, an interracial coalition could "make America what it ought to be."

In King's last speech he reminded his audience of the collective power they had as consumers and workers. If employers and politicians would not do right by the sanitation workers, he warned them, "We do have an agenda that we must follow. . . . And our agenda calls for withdrawing economic support from you." A boycott of Memphis downtown businesses—and of the *Commercial Appeal* newspaper that had distorted the issues and misled much of the white community—had already proved the power of economic withdrawal, a tried and true method of labor and civil rights movements.

In making his appeal for solidarity, King relied on black southern familiarity with the gospel of Jesus and his role as a prophet demanding economic justice. "God has commanded us to be concerned about the slums down here, and his children can't eat three square meals a day," King said. He drew on the Good Samaritan parable told by Jesus to his disciples to drive home his point. He painted a word picture of the desolate, curving, dangerous road between Jerusalem and Jericho, and told the story of the Samaritan who stopped to help a man of a different race who had been beaten, robbed, and left for dead. The wealthy and religious Levites had passed him by, but the lowly Good Samaritan risked his safety to save another man's life. Virtually all of the people in Mason Temple that night knew this story and its meaning. King's last speech was part of a biblical epic that they heard from the pulpit and sang about almost weekly.

King's lesson was, "Let us develop a kind of dangerous unselfishness." He thought the parallel to Memphis was obvious. "The question is not, 'If I stop to help this man in need, what will happen to me?' Rather, 'If I do not stop to help the sanitation workers, what will happen to them.' That is the question." Going down the Jericho Road, King had said many times, required "dangerous altruism"—being willing to sacrifice for others. That belief remained at the core of his religion and his life.

True to form, as King neared the end of his speech he became as one with an electrified and uplifted audience. Against the powerful winds and crackling lightning outside, people shouted "Tell it!," "Go ahead on!" and rose from their seats. King took them beyond the petty tyrannies they lived with day in and day out: ministers attacked by police, strikers whose children were hungry, students who had walked out of school—they all shared a vision of more noble human relationships. People may be poor, they may be tired, King told them, "but whenever men and women straighten their backs up, they're going somewhere. Because a man can't ride your back unless it is bent."

King then turned to his premonitions of death. He recalled the mentally ill black woman who stabbed him through the chest with a letter opener in 1958. That dagger lodged against his aorta, and would have killed him if he had merely sneezed. He gave thanks that he did not sneeze, so that he could be a part of the great changes brought about by the freedom movement. Starting with the bombing of his home in Montgomery in 1956, King had counted his days as numbered. When an assassin murdered President John F. Kennedy with a rifle bullet on November 22, 1963, King had told his wife Coretta that this is how he too would die.

King recounted that when he and his aides got on the plane in Atlanta that morning, "The pilot said over the public address system, 'We are sorry for the delay, but we have Dr. Martin Luther King on the plane. And to be sure that all of the bags were checked, and to be sure that nothing would be wrong with on the plane, we had to check out everything carefully. And we've had the plane protected and guarded all night.' "

King was a toxic figure to racists and the extreme right, to the FBI, and to the police and many white public officials. The commander of the Memphis Police publicly warned that King could be killed if he returned to Memphis. King said, "And then I got into Memphis. And some began to say the threats, or talk about the threats that were out. What would happen to me from some of our sick white brothers? Well, I don't know what will happen now." King's voice trembling, he asserted, "We've got some difficult days ahead. But it really doesn't matter with me now. Because I've been to the mountaintop."

From his parable of the Good Samaritan on the road from Jerusalem to Jericho, King had moved to the image of Moses leading the oppressed Hebrew slaves out of Egypt, looking out from Mount Pisgah across to Jericho and seeing Canaan, the land the Lord promised as a land of freedom for the Jews. Black preachers for generations had used the Exodus as a story of hope for liberation from slavery. King's audience knew the story well. They also knew that according to scripture, after he saw the Promised Land, Moses died.

Raising his voice, King concluded, "I may not get there with you, but I want you to know tonight that we as a people will get to the promised land!" He shouted out a verse from the Battle Hymn of the Republic, an anthem written to end slavery, "Mine eyes have seen the glory of the coming of the Lord!" King turned, almost in a trance, and nearly collapsed into the arms of Ralph Abernathy, surrounded by James Lawson and his other colleagues.

Pandemonium swept Mason Temple. King's last speech came at a hard-won moment of spiritual triumph. He had frequently said, "I would like to live a long life; longevity has its place." But King spoke of something more valuable than life itself. People with a common history of slavery, barbaric lynching, daily oppression in public places, police brutality, incarceration, poverty and labor exploitation, employer and white worker discrimination, the unimaginable humiliation of black women raped with no consequences for the rapist—yes, these people could quickly understand this moment.

In Mason Temple a community deeply wronged by injustice called upon its collective resources and sense of solidarity. This is what the Movement was all about: creating hope out of despair, taking action instead of giving in to fear, finding joy and speaking of love rather than succumbing to hatred. While some recalled the foreboding of King's last speech, Rev. James Lawson, who had brought King to Memphis, remembered the uplifting power of King's speech that night. He took it not as a sign of darkness to come but as a ray of light breaking through the clouds, a promise of freedom that inspired them all. Some who were there also felt a deadly chill mixed with King's ecstatic prophecy. Clarence Coe, a black member of the United Rubber Workers Union, whose union hall provided the launch pad for strike activities, commented, "I mean, if you listen to King's last speech, he could see it, but he had just gone to the point that he couldn't turn around. And he knew it was going to happen. He knew it was going to happen." Despite concern for King's life, Coe felt King's message of hope.

In contrast to his "I Have a Dream" speech in 1963, witnessed by over 200,000 people at the Lincoln Memorial and broadcast live across the nation, King's "Promised Land" speech came at an almost private moment, among a small, beleaguered group of people and a community in turmoil. It burned deeply into the consciousness of those present, solidifying resolve and strength to move forward. This moment displayed King's prophetic role in building alliances and solidarity. Because of Memphis, he would be remembered not only as a civil rights icon but also as a labor hero.

With a Bible in one hand and the Constitution and Bill of Rights in the other, King had played a key role in the struggle for freedom and economic justice for thirteen years. He was thirty-nine years old. He would be assassinated the next day.

* * *

MORE THAN FIFTY years since Memphis, how should we remember King? People know of him as a civil rights advocate, but do they know about his lifelong struggle for economic justice and the empowerment of poor and working-class people of all colors? How we remember King matters. It helps us to see where we have been and to understand King's unfinished agenda for our own times.

James Lawson, perhaps the person closest to King's philosophical framework, told me that most Americans don't fully understand King because they don't understand nonviolence. An advocate of nonviolence "has made a major decision and a major analysis about violence that is all-encompassing," seeing life's "cruelty systems" as interrelated parts of the same problem. A failing in how we remember King, said Lawson, "is our typing of him as a civil rights leader. We do not type him as a pastor, prophet, theologian, scholar, preacher . . . and that allows conventional minds across the country to thereby stereotype him and eliminate him from an over-all analysis of our society." Beyond King's dream of civil and voting rights lay a demand that every person have adequate food, education, housing, a decent job and income, and a more revolutionary quest for a nonviolent society beyond racism, poverty, and war.

Popular treatments primarily portray King through his magnificent speech given at the Lincoln Memorial in 1963, in which King called on America to live up to its historic ideals of equal rights in which all people would be defined by the "content of their character" and not the color of their skin. Congress declared King's birthday a national holiday in 1986, the first one added to the calendar since Memorial Day in 1947. Since then, school assemblies and civic gatherings have often remembered King as a symbol of color-blind democracy. This way of remembering King appeals to a politically diverse audience, including advertisers, educators, the mass media, and elected officials. The King holiday helps us to imagine the best kind of country we could be and makes us proud to be Americans.

Yet most people misremember King's historical context. In 1963, King was calling on President John F. Kennedy to honor the emancipation of African Americans from slavery one hundred years before with a new freedom agenda. Historian Will Jones helps us to remember that this agenda was not only about civil rights. August 28 was publicized as a "March for Jobs and Freedom," and it resulted from many years of organizing by black workers and their unions. In his speech, King said the nation had given former slaves a "bad check"—a promise of freedom that had not materialized. Generations later, his dream was not only for equal rights but also for a substantive change in people's economic and social conditions.

At various times, as part of his larger discourse from civil to human rights, King often used the phrases "economic justice" and "economic equality." What did he mean? In 1961, he explained it to the American Federation of Labor and Congress of Industrial Organizations (AFL-CIO). "There is no intrinsic difference" between workers—skin color and ethnicity should not divide those who work for a living—he said. "Economic justice" would require "a land where men will not take necessities to give luxuries to the few," and "where all our gifts and resources are held not for ourselves alone but as instruments of service for the rest of humanity." In our own time, when "everything decent and fair in American life" is under threat, as King said it was in his time, we might do well to remember his fight for economic justice as part of his dream for a better America.

Although public awareness often focuses on his "first phase" of the movement for civil and voting rights, we now have a plethora of scholarship that sees the "radical" King as "an inconvenient hero" who led a movement beyond civil rights to more fundamental economic and social change. Stanford University's Martin Luther King, Jr., Research and Education Institute and the King Papers Project, led by senior editor and historian Clayborne Carson, has given us a deep understanding of King's life and thought. In 1997, Coretta Scott King took Clay and Susan Carson into her basement and introduced them to a box of over two hundred folders of King's early letters and sermons. Drawing on these documents, volume 6 of the King Papers, edited at Stanford University, helps us to see that King's criticisms of American capitalism and his search for economic justice did not just appear in his last tumultuous years. Rather, King early on described himself as a "profound advocator of the Social Gospel" who decried a capitalist system that put profits and property rights ahead of basic human rights. The King Papers also allow us to better understand King's ancestors, who lived in slavery and segregation and fought for economic justice and human rights, guided by the black church and the Christian Social Gospel.

A generation of freedom-movement scholarship puts King in a broad context and goes against the "great man" theory that views history as motivated mainly by leaders that too often surrounds popular memories of King. Historical accounts show that he existed in a milieu of many people working for change, including other preachers and church people, labor organizers, peace advocates, socialists, communists, civil rights organizers, and nonviolence advocates going back many years. Historians write today of the "long civil rights movement" stretching back to the 1930s and forward into the present. That movement was part of an even longer black freedom struggle that began when Europeans brought the first slaves from Africa to the North American continent in 1619. Labor history documents slavery and slave resistance, and the long struggles of working-class women and men to make a better world. Movement scholarship sees King as one extremely important actor in a complex of individuals and movements at the grass roots.

Freedom history documents generations of people struggling against slavery and segregation: military veterans and rural residents protecting their families with force of arms against police and vigilante violence; the Black Power movement building on the work of Malcolm X to organize cultural, artistic, economic, and political power; younger people in our own era struggling against mass incarceration, police brutality, and economic impoverishment; and continuing protests against the most pernicious aspects of both Jim Crow capitalism in the South and racial capitalism in the North. Ordinary people picked up the themes of economic justice and civil rights. As one example, in October 1963, in Homewood, Pennsylvania, a suburb of Pittsburgh, a local coalition called the United Negro Protest Committee led by black men and women picketed a company employing 1,200 workers but almost no black people. Their effort to open up skilled and unskilled jobs for African Americans (pictured on the cover of this book) also led them to picket the local plumber's union that had kept blacks out. Their efforts were among the hundreds of struggles for economic justice inspired by local organizers as well as King's leadership and eloquent speeches.

Freedom-movement scholarship especially remembers King's leadership in the context of black women, including Coretta Scott King, Ella Baker, Septima Clark, Dorothy Cotton, Fannie Lou Hamer, Rosa Parks, Diane Nash, and so many others who built families, communities, and movements. In the South, women filled the pews, sang the songs, boycotted the buses, sheltered freedom fighters in their homes, went on strike, and went to jail by the thousands to build the movement that King represented through his oratory and strategic leadership. From slavery onward, black women did much of the work and bore disproportionate burdens in making America a wealthy nation, and in the modern era fought for welfare rights and family and community development. One finds little writing about King by women authors in part because they have been busy restoring the role of women to their rightful place in history.

* * *

TO THE PROMISED LAND does not provide a King biography or an overview of freedom-movement history, but rather seeks to bring to a larger audience a different memory of King. It focuses on his struggle to achieve a greater degree of economic justice, a struggle especially relevant to our own times. My own work grows out of both research and personal experience. I followed King's leadership as a young person—as a conscientious objector to war, as a participant in the Poor People's Campaign, and as a civil liberties organizer in Memphis and the South in the years after his death, from 1970 to 1976. Since that time, as a scholar trained at Howard University and other institutions of higher learning, I have traced how black and white workers, men and women, challenged slavery, Jim Crow, white supremacy, and economic injustice. My research continues to benefit greatly from interviews graciously granted to me by scores of workers and civil rights activists who improved their lives through union organizing and whose lives traced back to the 1920s and forward to the present.

A signal moment in how I remember King occurred in April 1994, when I found a file of King's labor speeches in the Martin Luther King, Jr., Center for Nonviolent Social Change library in Atlanta. These speeches, some in typescript written by King's labor advisers and others in King's own handwriting, gave me a different view of King and made me wonder how he and his colleagues built alliances with workers and organized labor. This book delves into that story. In addition, my numerous interviews with and study of James Lawson, the ministerial leader of the Memphis sanitation strike whose life and teachings more closely parallel that of King's than any other person, also greatly influenced my perspective.

Historians constantly search for and reshape our knowledge of the past, often based on the challenges they face in their own times. This book is part of that search. It is my hope that remembering King's unfinished fight for economic justice, broadly conceived, might help us to better understand the relevance of his legacy to us today. It might help us to realize that King's moral discourse about the gap between haves and have-nots resulted from his role in the labor movement as well as in the civil rights movement. In addition to remembering the eloquent man in a suit and tie at the Lincoln Memorial in 1963, we could also remember King as a man sometimes dressed in blue jeans marching on the streets and sitting in jail cells, or rousing workers at union conventions and on union picket lines. We must also remember him as a man of nonviolence often surrounded by violent police and screaming mobs, and at times physically assaulted by white racists. The nation may honor him now, but we should also remember the right-wing crusade against him in his own time as he sought just alternatives to America's exploitative racial capitalism.

Montgomery Bus Boycott, by Burton Silverman. African Americans, predominantly working class, ended bus segregation in Montgomery, Alabama, after 381 days of nonviolent economic withdrawal.

Chapter 1

"We the Disinherited of This Land"

Kinship with the Poor, 1929-1956

> Let us continue to hope, work, and pray that in the
> future we will live to see a warless world, a better
> distribution of wealth, and a brotherhood that
> transcends race or color. This is the gospel that I
> will preach to the world.
>
> — KING TO CORETTA SCOTT, 1952

I N 1967, AT A BAPTIST CHURCH IN CHICAGO CALLED MT.
Pisgah, Martin Luther King, Jr., commented, "It is the black man
who to a large extent produced the wealth of this nation . . . the
black man made America wealthy." Although some talked of going
back to Africa, he said, "I'm not going anywhere. . . . My grandfather and my great-grandfather did too much to build this nation for
me to be talking about getting away from it." When he preached,
King drew upon knowledge of the slave ancestors and sharecroppers from whom he was less than two generations removed. This
history may be unknown to many whites, but it provided a basic
framework for King. We typically remember him as a well-dressed,
seemingly middle-class proponent of the "American dream," but in
fact he came from African American and Irish dirt-poor people who
lived the American nightmare.

At union conventions and in churches King continually linked
slavery as part of an exploitative economic and racial system that
needed fundamental transformation. "Segregation is wrong because

it is nothing but a new form of slavery covered up with certain nice-ties of complexity," he told a union convention on September 8, 1962. The sermons and spirituals he grew up with linked King back to centuries of striving and to ancestors he never met.

Willis Williams, King's great-grandfather (b. 1810) lived as a slave for over fifty years in Greene County, Georgia, seventy miles east of Atlanta. In theory, he gained his freedom on January 1, 1863, when President Abraham Lincoln issued the Emancipation Proclamation in the Civil War the North was losing. Lincoln's enlistment of black soldiers and the withdrawal of labor by slaves helped bring down the Confederacy. The day after the proclamation, Willis's partner Lucrecia (Creecy) gave birth to Martin's maternal grandfather, Adam Daniel Williams. Slaves on the other side of King's family tree included Martin's paternal grandfather, Jim Long (b. 1842), used by his owner to "breed" other slaves. The history of King's ancestors had a basic labor component: slavery more than any other system of production used labor exploitation to make some people rich.

Along with the theft of Native American lands, the exploited labor of millions of slaves served as a basic building block of white wealth. Karl Marx aptly called slavery, along with piracy and the stealing of peasant and Native American lands, sources of the "primitive accu-mulation" of capital. Unpaid black labor fueled the rise of slaveholders in the South and the profits of mercantile and banking capitalists in the North, who invested in the slave trade and in cotton, which before the Civil War became America's major export to the world economy. Most slaves at the bottom of this economy of racial cap-italism worked without wages and had no control over their labor, their families, or their conditions of life. Indentured servants and poor whites suffered similarly but were not consigned to poverty for life by their skin color. In places like Memphis, Tennessee, the larg-est slave-trading depot between Cairo, Illinois, and New Orleans, Louisiana, whites rationalized an evolving system of cheap labor by creating a hierarchy of "races," with European whites at the top and African Americans, Indians, Asians, and Mexican Americans at the bottom. We now know that all humans are part of the same species originating in Africa, but racial ideology and markers throughout history have provided powerful ways to separate people into competing groups. As anthropologist Ashley Montague documented, the false idea of race is "man's most dangerous myth."

For workers, racism had devastating effects, undermining any notion of labor solidarity. White supremacy laws and practices separated workers and farmers by skin color, making interracial marriages illegal and even requiring nonslaveholding whites to serve in slave patrols to capture escaped slaves. As W. E. B. Du Bois wrote in *Black Reconstruction*, dividing poor and working-class people called "white" from people called "black" made it very difficult to organize labor in the South or anywhere else. The "wages of whiteness" provided some perceived and some real advantages, but the labor of most workers designated as "white" accumulated capital for someone other than themselves. During his Poor People's Campaign in 1968, King repeatedly referred to the horrors of slavery to explain the origins of the black freedom movement and its demands for economic justice. Africans did not come to the United States looking for a better life, as black conservative Ben Carson once ludicrously claimed; rather, slave traders stole a better life from them. Slaves went on a "general strike" and over 200,000 African Americans joined Union Army regiments that helped to win the Civil War, yet one hundred years later, King would have to fight for civil rights and economic justice to redress the nation's failure to bring full freedom.

Sometime after the Civil War, Martin Luther King, Jr.'s great-grandfather James Albert King moved to Georgia from Pennsylvania hoping to obtain land and economic independence. The son of an Irish father and an African American mother, he married Delia Long, and the couple had ten children. The second of them, Martin's father Michael, was born in 1897. It was one year after the Supreme Court supported the fiction of "separate but equal" as the law of the land in *Plessy v. Ferguson*. Ex-Confederate states by the end of the century, through voter-suppression laws and violent white-supremacy campaigns, wiped out black elected officials and the right to vote. White-supremacy campaigns repeatedly destroyed biracial struggles for greater economic justice by workers and farmers in unions, Populist, and "fusion" movements.

Instead of gaining economic independence, as the King family hoped, they became sharecroppers, working on land owned by whites. They earned only a small share of the crops they produced, while going into debt to landowners and merchants for food, seed, and fertilizer. Women lived lives of hard labor, and Martin's grandmother Delia worked for white folks washing and ironing. James moved from place to place working for crops and wages in Henry and Clay counties. Indebtedness, phony "vagrancy" arrests, imprisonment, and convict leasing plagued black women and men alike. Segregation, or Jim Crow, made it illegal for blacks to share the same restaurants, transportation, schools, or public facilities as whites. They could not sit on juries, hold office or vote, and were consigned to schools that received little public funding. Most whites sought to keep African Americans out of skilled labor, to hold down their wages, to limit black property holding, and to block access to trade unions and education. Driving too nice a vehicle, owning too good a mule or too much land, failing to step off the sidewalk when a white person came the other way—in the era of segregation, these and other supposed transgressions against white supremacy could get a black person killed.

This system of Jim Crow capitalism suppressed the economic aspirations of King's ancestors. Born December 19, 1899, in Stockbridge, Georgia, Michael King, Martin's father, experienced deep poverty in the countryside, where, in his words, an African American "wasn't nothin' but a nigger, a workhorse" denied formal training as a worker or a chance to learn to read and write. As an adolescent, he witnessed the dangers of walking while black. He saw a mob of white men taunting a black man, who tried smiling, turning his back and walking faster, pretending normality. The whites beat him bloody and then lynched him with his own belt. Michael later wrote that such white violence happened because white politicians constantly stirred "the passions of all potential voters by appealing to their sense of insecurity." Southern white politicians made a profession of distracting whites from their poor economic conditions by egging them on to racial violence. Neither the lynching of black men falsely charged with rape of white women or for insolence, nor the actual rape of black women, met with legal consequences. Black women and men could end up not only imprisoned but also forced to work under horrendous conditions on chain gangs, with their labor sold to private landowners or coal companies. Black women especially suffered from white sexual exploitation with no consequences for perpetrators.

In these perilous conditions, in another incident, a white mill owner beat young Michael bloody in front of a crowd of white men when he refused to drop a can of milk he was carrying for his mother and instead fetch water for him. When she found out about it, Michael's enraged mother knocked the white man down; in a separate incident, Michael's father James threatened the man with a gun. A mob of white vigilantes soon came after James, who escaped to the swamps. He returned home after several months of hiding out, despondent and alcoholic. Michael had to physically fight with his father to stop him from beating his mother. Rebellion with no hopes of success dragged the family down.

Martin's father went to a one-room school for only three to five months a year, where a lone black woman taught children in all grades, with no books or blackboards. He spent most of his time doing farm work for pennies an hour. In 1918, functionally illiterate, Michael left the rural district of Stockbridge, Georgia, and hiked to Atlanta, wearing his only pair of shoes and with nothing but ambition in his pockets. His dear mother died and he lost track of his father. He worked in a tire shop, loaded cotton, drove trucks, and did odd jobs. He seemed condemned to a working-class life of poverty, but religion, deeply inculcated in Michael by his mother, provided joy and inspiration. Michael preached and sang the gospel, and it saved him.

Martin's maternal grandfather, A. D. Williams, was born into slavery at the start of the Civil War in 1861, in Greene County, Georgia. During the 1880s he followed his father's struggle to be a preacher but experienced poverty in the countryside, working in low-wage jobs and losing his thumb in a sawmill accident. In 1893 he got to Atlanta with five dollars in his pocket. Like his slave father, Willis Williams, A. D. preached the gospel as a way to imagine something beyond the South's nightmare regime of labor and racial exploitation. In 1894, A. D. became the pastor of Ebenezer Baptist church, a congregation of former slaves with thirteen members. A. D. built the congregation that built the church that still stands in Atlanta. He attended Atlanta Baptist College (later named Morehouse), and on October 29, 1899, married former Spelman Seminary student Jennie C. Parks, whose father was a carpenter. They had one surviving child, Alberta Williams, born September 13, 1903. This was Martin King's mother.

For more than thirty years, A. D. and Jennie made Ebenezer a rock in a weary land for urban and working-class African Americans. The black church, scholar Cornel West wrote, provided the only institution "created, sustained, and controlled by black people." Sermons, songs and congregational meetings built a sense of community and the ability "to come to terms with death, with dread, with despair." Ebenezer's members survived a five-day white race riot in 1906 that left twenty-six black people in Atlanta dead. The King family and others fought back nonviolently, pressing for black schools, voting and legal rights, and jobs. Martin Luther King, Jr., would later receive his education in elementary and high schools that his grandfather helped to create with public funding through protest. He would also inherit his grandfather's and his father's commitment to the working class and poor. Ebenezer Baptist Church took care of poor families, orphans, and the ill, baptized and buried people, raised money for schools and civic institutions, and nurtured a sense of hope that kept people's spirits alive.

Martin's great-grandfather Willis Williams had been a Baptist exhorter as a slave, and every generation after that used Christianity to resist Jim Crow's hardships and humiliations with a religion of hope. Through the black church, Martin King, Jr., would learn, West explained, to relate his expansive ideas "to common, ordinary people and to remain ensconced and enmeshed in their world." And he would learn "such values as integrity, love, care, sacrifice, sincerity, and humility. . . ."

Through the church, the Williams and King families joined forces. Young Michael weighed over two hundred pounds, but at age twenty-one squeezed into a small desk in a class with fifth graders to learn to read and write. He married Alberta Williams, daughter of Jennie Parks and A. D. Williams, who convinced Morehouse College president John Hope to let Michael into its school of religion, from which he graduated. Alberta also got degrees from Spelman Seminary and Hampton Institute, and she and Michael married on Thanksgiving Day, 1926. In 1931, upon the death of Rev. Williams, Michael King took over leadership of Ebenezer Baptist Church. His family and his people in the church largely consisted of former slaves and sharecroppers, many of whom now worked as laborers and domestic workers. Rev. King put the concern of these poor and working-class people at the core of his ministry.

Historian Clayborne Carson identifies the King family ministry as part of a black Christian Social Gospel that "combined a belief in personal salvation with the need to apply the teachings of Jesus to the daily problems of their black congregations." Protestant reformers in the United States, in churches, immigrant settlement houses, and civic and labor reform organizations, undertook the Social Gospel tradition in the late nineteenth century in response to the evils of unregulated capitalism—gross inequities between the rich and poor, suppression of worker rights to unionize, mass slums for immigrants and workers, unemployment, prostitution, and destitution. The black church evolved its own version of the Social Gospel in response to both racism and economic injustice.

Michael King and his son would both take the gospel of Jesus as told to Luke (Luke 4:18) as their guide. Jesus told Luke to "preach the gospel to the poor," "to heal the brokenhearted, to preach deliverance to the captives," and "to set liberty those who are oppressed." Martin would say that the commandments of Jesus required society to not only help the poor, but to change the conditions that made them poor.

* * *

ON JANUARY 15, 1929, Michael King, Jr. (later renamed Martin Luther King, Jr., after his father changed his name to Martin Luther King, Sr.) was born, in a nicely built but modest home, surrounded by a largely poor neighborhood filled with shotgun shacks and poverty. Yet this district also consisted of the black churches and black-owned businesses for which Auburn Avenue would become famous. Martin Luther King, Jr., wrote in a 1950 college essay, "I have never experienced the feeling of not having the basic necessities of life." Despite the fact that the Great Depression followed hard on the heels of his birth, he recalled, "The first twenty-five years of my life were very comfortable years. If I had a problem I could always call Daddy. Things were solved. Life had been wrapped up for me in a Christmas package."

Yet the young Martin knew he had privileges others did not have. His father took him to see the unemployed standing in lines for food and taught him respect for the unemployed poor and working poor. "Daddy" King led campaigns and marched for black schools and teacher funding and voting rights. He disobeyed the rules of segregation, riding the "Whites only" elevator at city hall, refusing to step off the sidewalk to make way for whites, and resisting demeaning white attitudes. He taught his son by his own behavior. When a white police officer stopped the Kings in the car and referred to him as "boy," Daddy King pointed to his son and shot back, "This is a boy. I'm a man, and until you call me one, I will not listen to you."

Martin's father also marched them out of a shoe store when a white clerk refused to seat them in the same area as whites. He told his son, "I don't care how long I have to live with this system, I will never accept it." When Daddy King changed his name and that of his son from Michael to Martin Luther, he signified larger aspirations to take on the world.

Martin's mother Alberta King and his grandmother Jennie Williams also had a major impact on his personality and sense of the world. Martin's female ancestors had labored hard in their own households and in the fields, and suffered from low wages from white employers, while nurturing hope and shaping the black Social Gospel. In the King home in Atlanta, his mother and grandmother provided a forgiving and nurturing environment of love, kindness, and spirituality. Grandmother Jennie, Martin wrote, had a "saintly" aura, and "it is quite easy for me to think of a God of love mainly because I grew up in a family where love was central and where lovely relationships were ever present."

The power of the love that flowed so strongly from his mother and grandmother and the authority of his father engendered personality traits of compassion, kindness, and empathy that would make Martin King a special kind of leader. By contrast, the family of Malcolm Little (Malcolm X) was torn asunder by the Depression and poverty, by his father's murder by white vigilantes and his mother's incarceration in a mental institution. Racism and poverty destroyed many such families. Instead, Martin King developed an inspiring optimism born out of a supportive family environment and adopted the traditions of hope and struggle epitomized by church songs with lyrics such as "I'm so glad trouble don't last always," and "Keep your eyes on the prize, hold on."

The young King grew up in an all-black neighborhood and went to an all-black school, somewhat protected from the ravages of white supremacy. But he knew he could not vote or hold office or even pass whites on the sidewalk without fear. A white playmate's father no longer allowed him to be friends with his son; a white woman slapped him in the face in a shopping area for no reason; Martin witnessed a KKK beating of a black man; he passed sites where he knew blacks had been lynched. At age fourteen he won an oratorical contest in Dublin, Georgia, with his speech on equal rights, "The Negro and the Constitution," but a white bus driver made Martin and his teacher give up their seats to white passengers and stand in the aisle for ninety miles riding back to Atlanta. "It was the angriest I have ever been in my life," he recalled. In another incident, white conductors forced him behind a curtain in the rear of a segregated railroad dining car. "I felt as if the curtain had been dropped on my selfhood," he wrote, and recalled thinking, "One of these days I'm going to put my body up there where my mind is." He would easily see the logic of the Montgomery bus boycott.

In a college paper in 1950, King wrote, "The inseparable twin of racial injustice was economic injustice. Although I came from a home of economic security and relative comfort, I could never get out of my mind the economic insecurity of many of my playmates and the tragic poverty of those living around me." He believed "the numerous people standing in bread lines" contributed to "my present anti-capitalistic feelings." As a teenager, King briefly did manual labor in Atlanta, where he experienced racism as a worker. He also later wrote, "I saw economic injustice firsthand, and realized that the poor white was exploited just as much as the Negro."

King's associate and friend C. T. Vivian told me in an interview, "The whole relationship between blacks and labor was something that was everyday for any middle-class black person to understand." One could always find poor people, white or black, barely surviving on low wages and sometimes no wages at all.

King's education created a framework for understanding the inequalities he saw all around him. As a precocious student, at age fifteen Martin entered Morehouse College, where professors explained why black people were oppressed and most were poor, and taught him about his proud heritage as an African American. Morehouse president Dr. Benjamin Mays, a learned minister, educator, and author who met with and studied Gandhi, fused religion, academic knowledge, and activism on behalf of equal rights and social justice in weekly talks to Martin and other students. They studied sociology, history, philosophy, literature, and religion during World War II, a time when the NAACP launched a "double V for victory" campaign against fascism abroad and racism at home. By the time King left Morehouse, Vivian believed, he "already knew ninety percent" of what he needed to know in order to preach the black Social Gospel. He would do it better than anyone in the twentieth century.

As a bright and eclectic scholar at Crozier Theological Seminary in Chester, Pennsylvania, from 1948 to 1951, and at Boston University, where he received his PhD in systematic theology in 1955, King studied history, literature, and theology in the Judeo-Christian tradition. He appreciated the writings of Reinhold Niebuhr, who highlighted the twin injustices of racial discrimination and the unequal distribution of wealth under capitalism. King also paraphrased Walter Rauschenbusch's critique of Christianity, writing, "Any religion that professes to be concerned about the souls of men and is not concerned about the slums that damn them, the economic conditions that strangle them and the social conditions that cripple them is a spiritually moribund religion awaiting burial." King's philosophy stressed the importance of individual experience and one's relationship to a personal God. He also drew upon the Hegelian dialectical method that allowed him to synthesize truth from seemingly conflicting ideas such as Marxism and capitalism to find a "third way" to economic justice. However, as scholars Clayborne Carson and Keith Miller both document, King's powerful oratory came not from his academic studies but from the deep wellsprings of the African American church. Ordained as a preacher at Ebenezer Church at age eighteen, King from an early age drew heavily on the Exodus message of deliverance from slavery, the slave community's most well-known Bible story. As his learning progressed, he appropriated the phrases and ideas of theologians, poets, philosophers, historians. Like a jazz, gospel, or blues musician, and like the most popular of Protestant preachers, he arranged texts to speak age-old truths.

In graduate school King heard black theologian Howard Thurman speak about his meeting with Mohandas Gandhi, and also encountered the twentieth century's leading white pacifist, A. J. Muste. King added to his repertoire the idea that "nonviolent resistance was one of the most potent weapons available to oppressed people in their quest for social justice." But he recalled that at first "I had merely an intellectual understanding." King might have gone on to live a comfortable life. Instead, history led him into a life of struggle marked by his solidarity with working-class and poor people.

At Boston University King presented himself not as an activist but as the quintessential middle-class student: well dressed, well educated, with marvelous diction and a poetic use of the English language. He drove a new car and wore such nice suits that friends at Morehouse had called him "tweedy." He lacked only one thing in his quest to become a top preacher: a wife. Then he met the vivacious Coretta Scott, a student at the New England Conservatory of Music. She lacked Martin's family advantages. At age ten, she had picked two hundred pounds of cotton in a day for pennies per hour in rural Perry County, Alabama. The Scott family, with Irish, Native American, and African American ancestors, lived and worked on three hundred acres of land acquired as freed slaves after the Civil War. White vigilantes who thought the family was too prosperous burned down Coretta's father's sawmill and the family's home burned down under suspicious circumstances as well. In another incident, white men hanged Coretta's uncle from a tree outside his home and filled his corpse with bullets. Armed white men regularly confronted Coretta's father Obadia when he hauled lumber to the mill, and he carried a loaded pistol in his open glove compartment to let them know he could not be intimidated.

Coretta had already committed herself to political and social action by the time she met Martin in college. During World War II, she went to Lincoln High School in nearby Marion, Alabama, a private school founded after the Civil War by freed slaves and white abolitionists. White teachers encouraged her, and a Quaker teacher brought Bayard Rustin to speak about Gandhi's struggle against British imperialism through nonviolence. In 1945, when Antioch College in Yellow Springs, Ohio, recruited her as the school's second black student (her sister was the first), she found her "escape route" out of the segregated South.

In 1948 Coretta attended the national convention of the Progressive Party. Former Democratic vice president Henry Wallace ran for president on a peace platform calling for détente with the Soviet Union. The mass media red-baited all Progressives as part of a "Communist front." Howling mobs of whites attacked Wallace during his interracial speaking crusade through the South, accompanied by singers Paul Robeson and Pete Seeger. Even as the United States descended into Cold War anticommunism, before leaving undergraduate school Coretta sang on a program with Robeson. The U. S. congressional House Committee on Un-American Activities (HUAC), formed in 1938 and led by segregationists, hounded him, and the red scare drove him into unemployment and obscurity. HUAC would hold scores of "hearings" falsely linking "communism," labor, and civil rights from the 1940s through the 1960s.

Coretta Scott went north penniless and could stay in school at the New England Conservatory only with the help of white donors. Competing for the intellectual attention of this lovely young woman brought out Martin's political side. At first she thought he seemed presumptuous, but she was quickly impressed by his strong opinions on racism, capitalism, and economic injustice. While they were apart during the summer in 1952, she sent him a copy of Edward Bellamy's *Looking Backward*, a classic utopian socialist novel published in 1888. In a letter to Coretta, King mixed his admiration of her beauty and intellect with an appeal to her political consciousness. He noted, "I am much more socialistic in my economic theory than capitalistic," and surmised "capitalism has out-lived its usefulness. It has brought about a system that takes necessities from the masses to give luxuries to the classes."

During King's childhood, unprecedented uprisings by workers in industries and among the unemployed had led to President Franklin Roosevelt's New Deal, which ensured the right of workers to vote for a union of their choice and required employers to bargain with them in good faith. Employers resisted this in many places, but especially in the South. The old American Federation of Labor (AFL) was an amalgam of overwhelmingly white and male craft unions that typically barred blacks, other minorities, and women from apprenticeships and even from union membership. Yet some white southern unionists believed strongly in racial equality. Members of the Communist Party in particular made equal rights, advocacy for the legalization of interracial marriage, and bringing blacks and whites together the bedrock of their southern organizing. Not surprisingly, they experienced heavy repression.

In 1935, when Martin was six, United Mineworkers president John L. Lewis and a group of unions broke away from the AFL to form the Congress of Industrial Organizations (CIO), which took an unequivocal stand for racial equality. Black workers, consigned to the hottest, most dangerous jobs, came to play a key role in CIO advances in the steel, packinghouse, auto, and other industries. Communist and Socialist Party members and an assortment of anticapitalist radicals organized on behalf of racial equality and civil rights unionism—advocacy for labor and civil rights together. The Southern Tenant Farmers Union in the Southwest and the Sharecroppers' Union in Alabama came under ferocious attack for doing so.

Through CIO industrial organizing, during World War II the American labor movement expanded dramatically and even made inroads into the South. It also began to break down racial barriers. In 1941 A. Philip Randolph, president of the Brotherhood of Sleeping Car Porters, a black union, threatened a mass march on Washington demanding access to defense jobs. President Roosevelt issued an antidiscrimination executive order that helped remove racial barriers to industrial jobs, although it had few enforcement mechanisms. White reaction to black competition for jobs and housing precipitated the white race riot in Detroit in 1943, leading to the deaths of thirty-four people, twenty-five of them black, and the destruction of the black neighborhood called Paradise Alley. White reaction against black advances occurred in various other cities and workplaces.

Nonetheless, by 1944 millions of black and white workers, in the South as well as nationally, in AFL as well as CIO unions, had created a powerful labor movement. The basis for a civil rights–labor alliance existed: NAACP membership ballooned; the Southern Conference Educational Fund (SCEF) built an effective interracial popular front for unionization, integration, and electing better people to office. Highlander Folk School, independently formed by Social Gospel activists in the hill country of Tennessee in 1932, allowed adults to discuss their problems and decide for themselves how to solve them, without political or racial restrictions. At the end of the war, the CIO and other organizations seemed ready to move the South toward higher wages, better conditions, and away from Jim Crow capitalism.

In 1946 American workers undertook the largest strike wave in U.S. history, based on pent-up demand for increased wages after wage restrictions during the war. The CIO also began "Operation Dixie," an ambitious campaign to organize the millions of unorganized workers in the South. But in the 1946 congressional elections, voters put in place an overwhelmingly Republican Congress dead set against organized labor. It enacted the Taft-Hartley Act, an employer-drafted law weakening unions. Its provision 14(b) allowed states to ban a "closed shop," whereby everyone covered by a union contract had to pay membership dues to the union for representing them. Within a year, seven of thirteen southern states passed "Right to work" laws that allowed workers to get union benefits without paying union dues—so of course many chose that option. Taft-Hartley made secondary boycotts and picketing by unions supporting each other illegal; it limited union political contributions; excluded foremen and supervisors from labor-law coverage; tied unions up with massive legal requirements; and required union officers to take a legal oath that they did not belong to the CP. If they did not sign, their union could not get on the ballot in National Labor Relations Board–protected elections. It killed much of the labor organizing in the South, as intended by its Republican sponsors. To make matters worse in the postwar years, black soldiers returning from fighting a war against Hitler's white supremacy abroad found themselves subject to ugly hate crimes, racial discrimination, and lack of employment opportunities at home. The CIO's southern organizing drive ran into internal racial and left-right political divisions, antiunion violence, and Taft-Hartley's restrictions. Right-wing organizations, along with federal government "loyalty" oaths and investigations of "communism" in the body politic poisoned any discussion of unions and civil rights. Then, in 1948, the CIO leadership endorsed Harry Truman for president while many of the left-leaning unions endorsed Progressive Party peace- and civil-rights advocate Henry Wallace. After the surprise reelection of Truman, and in response to rising anticommunism, the CIO purged eleven left-led unions with nearly a million members, and CIO unions began competing to take over the memberships of those expelled unions. Under pressure of the growing red scare, the CIO also cut off ties and funding to Highlander and the Southern Conference, and some white CIO leaders in the South ignored their CIO international constitution that called for equal rights at work and in society.

Republican senator Joseph McCarthy, who replaced the progressive Democrat Robert La Follette, Jr., in Wisconsin, set the tone for the 1950s when he unleashed unfounded charges that Communists riddled the U.S. government, and undertook investigations that targeted labor and civil rights activists and anyone else he could think of to call a "red." Attorney Roy Cohn, McCarthy's aide, would go on to tutor real estate developer Donald Trump to continue in the art of the Big Lie and no-holds-barred attacks against anyone perceived to be an opponent. In Memphis, Mississippi senator James O. Eastland similarly used the Senate Internal Security Subcommittee (SISS) to condemn black and white leaders of Local 19 of the left-led Food, Tobacco, Agricultural, and Allied Workers (FTA) union, whose members had protested the frame-up and execution of Willie McGee, a black truck driver, in Eastland's state.

In an interview, Memphis black Local 19 member Leroy Boyd told me that when employers called a white union leader a communist, it meant integrationist. "They knew how white men felt about another white man speaking up for the Negro. He was just branded a Communist." He also said this did not deter most black workers, who supported integrationist CIO unions despite red-baiting.

The red scare helped to incite white worker and employer racism, however. In Birmingham, white Klansmen physically attacked members of the interracial (and left-led) Mine, Mill and Smelter Workers Union to defeat it. In Winston-Salem, North Carolina, HUAC hearings and a media red scare destroyed a thriving black-led tobacco workers' union, the FTA. Anticommunist hearings, accompanied by media publicity, often held on the verge of elections in local industries, helped to wipe out interracial unions.

In 1955, with some of its best organizers removed, the CIO merged with the more conservative and white male–dominated AFL. The new AFL-CIO federation excluded supposed Communists, many of whom had helped to create the explosion of industrial unions in the 1930s and 1940s. In the 1950s, many unions stopped organizing new constituencies and concentrated on servicing their existing members. These tragic developments of the Cold War era cut short hopes that civil rights and labor organizing would move forward together. A number of progressive southern white Democrats lost their reelection campaigns, and the South moved toward becoming a bastion of white Republican power and antiunionism. The postwar red scare and white voting patterns would make King's struggle for racial and economic justice much more difficult.

* * *

IN GRADUATE SCHOOL in the early 1950s, King wrote that he opposed communism as godless, and because it accepted violence and dictatorship, whereas nonviolence insisted that "the end is pre-existent in the mean." His position on that would never change: one could only reach peaceful and democratic ends through peaceful and democratic means. He opposed all forms of dictatorship, but he also opposed crippling anticommunism and championed liberation movements against capitalist colonialism in the developing world. He held fiercely to the Social Gospel view that Christianity should help to liberate the poor and the oppressed. King wrote to Coretta that capitalism would probably be around for a long while but "I would certainly welcome the day to come when there will be a nationalization of industry."

Coretta kept Martin's letters and early sermons in a box in her basement for over thirty years after he died. Clayborne Carson reasoned that she probably feared that his candid thoughts about capitalism would be used by the American right wing to tarnish his legacy. The Kings lived in an era of unreasoning anticommunism, as governments and employers blacklisted people from employment and teaching simply based on their political associations, letters to the editor, or because they merely expressed sympathy for economic and social justice. Right-wing politicians and organizations would crusade against King throughout his adult life.

King's powerful convictions and personal charms ultimately convinced Coretta to set aside her ambition to be a concert virtuoso. He insisted that she not go into the music or work world, but raise a family. In 1953 they married, and the next year King accepted a ministry at the relatively prosperous Dexter Avenue Baptist Church in Montgomery, Alabama. With Martin finishing his PhD in philosophy and religion, tending to his congregation, writing and memorizing sermons that would later provide a base for much of his preaching, and with a child on the way, the Kings had a full life. But in Montgomery they ran into an appalling climate of white supremacy. Former slaves had built Dexter Avenue Baptist Church on foundations that had been a slave auction block, adjacent to the state capitol, the former headquarters for the southern Confederacy. The city's black leadership was competitive and divided.

However, below the surface in Montgomery lurked a history of black resistance. King's predecessor at Dexter Avenue Baptist Church, Rev. Vernon Johns, had preached powerfully against segregation. King, like Johns, practically required his church members to join the NAACP and strongly supported the organization, but as a busy pastor he turned down a nomination as its chapter president. He said later that if someone had asked him to lead the Montgomery bus boycott he would have "run the other way." History had other plans, however. The direct action of working-class bus riders transformed King's kinship with the poor from a largely intellectual and family matter to a matter of lived faith.

The Montgomery movement erupted on December 1, 1955, with the arrest of Rosa Parks for refusing to give up her seat on a bus to a white man. Jeanne Theoharis, in *The Rebellious Life of Mrs. Rosa Parks*, documents how this modest seamstress, prompted early on by her husband's participation in a Communist-led campaign in the 1930s to free the Scottsboro Boys, victims of a racial rape frame-up, had worked for years with E. D. Nixon, a member of A. Philip Randolph's Pullman Porters Union and longtime civil rights activist, protesting the rape of black women, the lynching of blacks, and other atrocities. The grisly murder of fourteen-year-old African American Emmett Till in Money, Mississippi, on August 28, 1955, for supposedly "speaking fresh" to a white woman, and the all-white-jury acquittal of his admitted racist killers, enraged African Americans and civil rights supporters everywhere. Members of the United Packinghouse Union attended the trial of Till's killers and helped to organize huge protests in the North. Four days after attending a Montgomery protest of the Till lynching, and deeply affected by what she heard there, Parks defied the city's segregation laws. Transportation racism reminded black people in Montgomery on a daily basis of racial injustice. White bus drivers had insulted, beaten, and even killed African Americans who resisted Jim Crow on the buses. Black people had to sit behind whites and move back to another row or stand up if one white person sat down in a row of seats that blacks already occupied. They had to pay their fare at the front of the bus, then go back out in order to enter from the back of the bus. White bus drivers sometimes drove off and left them standing in the street.

For black workers and the black middle class of teachers and preachers, white supremacy in Montgomery blocked nearly all avenues to success. The humiliations and violence of bus segregation provided a daily insult. Two weeks before refusing to give up her seat, Parks had participated in an interracial discussion of how to organize resistance to segregation at Highlander Folk School. Her refusal to give up her seat was not a planned attempt to start a movement, but her calm courage touched off a remarkable, community-based movement that outlasted police violence, multiple bombings of churches and homes, and mass economic reprisals for 381 days.

Working-class people filled the ranks of the Montgomery movement. Eighty percent or more of black women in the wage economy were domestic workers. Black men did mostly janitorial and service work. Most working-class black people made too little to buy a car. Any possibility of a successful bus boycott depended on these workers. Preexisting organizations made a community boycott possible. During the boycott, Pullman porter E. D. Nixon through his union and connections to its president, A. Philip Randolph, saw to it that unions at the national level donated significant amounts of money to keep the movement alive. The black bricklayers' union provided an office and a meeting place for an alternative transportation system operated by black taxi drivers and car owners. Jo Ann Gibson Robinson and the Women's Political Council put out some 50,000 leaflets in the weekend after the arrest of Parks. The WPC had been building up a network of professional and working women who did much of the groundwork and organizing for the Montgomery protests. On Monday morning, December 5, 1955, when Coretta Scott and Martin King looked out their windows, they could see that no black people were riding the buses.

King explained several times during and after the Montgomery movement that he did not start it and it would have happened without him. But it is hard to imagine the movement in Montgomery without the galvanizing power of his preaching. According to volume three of the King Papers, in the Montgomery movement he "set forth the main themes of his subsequent public ministry: Social-Gospel Christianity and democratic idealism, combined with resolute advocacy of nonviolent protest." In his first speech to a mass meeting, with only a few minutes to prepare, King proclaimed, "We, the disinherited of this land," should "keep God at the forefront." But "it is not enough for us to talk about love. . . . There is another side called justice." King immediately identified this local struggle with larger issues and forces.

He cited the Supreme Court desegregation decision and used the leverage of the U.S. claim to be the leader of the "free world," contrasting communist and totalitarian societies to the United States, where "the great glory of American democracy is the right to protest for right." King also invoked the history of the labor movement: "When labor all over this nation came to see that it would be trampled over by capitalistic power, it was nothing wrong with labor getting together and organizing and protesting for its rights." King defined the struggle as not only about race, but about "justice and injustice." That would include the economic injustice that black Montgomery saw every day. King later would regularly emphasize the common roots and common tactics of the labor and civil rights movements.

The bus boycott began with a demand for simple courtesy within a segregated system, but the city's refusal to negotiate led the movement to demand complete desegregation of the buses and the hiring of black bus drivers. White authorities tried to silence King and crush the movement. KKK members infested some white union locals and joined with white politicians, police, and businesspeople in a violent campaign of bombings, arrests, firings, and intimidation. Mississippi senator James Eastland led a rally of 10,000 whites with hateful, violent rhetoric; all of the city council members promptly joined the White Citizens Council, founded by white-supremacist business and political leaders in Mississippi to resist the Supreme Court's 1954 *Brown v. Board of Education* school desegregation decision. George Wallace, a Populist who claimed he got "outniggered" in an election campaign in the 1950s, filled Alabama with divisive racist rhetoric, and as governor in 1963 would vow "Segregation now, segregation tomorrow, segregation forever."

In this brutal and racist climate, King and others experienced death threats, arrests, and bombings. On January 26, 1956, police arrested him for supposedly going five miles over the speed limit, and took him on a harrowing ride into a desolate part of town where he thought he was about to be "dropped off" and killed like so many others. On January 27, following a stint in a Montgomery jail and a midnight phone call threatening the lives of his family, King had a crisis of fear. In a moment that changed his life, he felt the power of the Lord promising "never to leave me alone." From then on, he vowed to always push on despite his fears.

On January 30, Coretta with her baby and her sister were sitting in the front room when they heard a noise outside and quickly moved away. Otherwise they would have been maimed or killed as a bomb blew off the front of the house. Famously, King returned from a mass meeting to find a group of angry, armed African Americans gathered outside his wrecked home, ready to fight, and in a remarkably calm voice dispersed the crowd by invoking love and nonviolence as more powerful than bombs. "We are not hurt and remember that if anything happens to me, there will be others to take my place," he told them.

Out of necessity King committed himself to nonviolent discipline. He saw that the use of weapons by supporters outside of King's home would have led to a massacre by the police and defeat for the movement. He also understood that black southerners on an individual level often had to protect their families and homes and that most black southerners did not accept nonviolence as a general principle. Many black male military veterans agreed with black activist Robert F. Williams in North Carolina that nonviolence was a form of suicide. As civil rights activist and writer Charles Cobb later put it, "That Nonviolent Stuff'l Get You Killed." The bombing of the home of Harry and Harriette Moore in Brevard County, Florida, on Christmas night 1951, killing both of them, was but one example of the violence inflicted on black people who agitated for voting and civil rights. King in theory did not oppose using arms to defend his family, and he didn't condemn others for doing so. The right to self-defense when personally attacked, he would later write, "has been guaranteed through the ages by common law." Few suggested that individuals should not protect themselves, but he would always argue that taking up arms in a mass movement would not work for a minority population against a heavily armed state and would drive away others who might otherwise support a movement for change.

On February 1 King and Ralph Abernathy tried to get pistol permits, but the county sheriff denied them. That night vigilantes exploded a bomb in the yard of E. D. Nixon. Unarmed black men guarded King's home each night. On February 10 white supremacists circulated a "Declaration of Segregation" at the White Citizens Council meeting, declaring, "When in the course of human events it become necessary to abolish the Negro race, proper methods should be used. Among these are guns, bow and arrows, sling shots and knives." But despite constant threats of violence against them, people in the Montgomery movement followed King's teaching that they should not take up arms, both for moral reasons and because the superior weaponry of the state and white vigilantes would surely crush them if they did.

On February 21, a grand jury indicted King and over one hundred other movement leaders under a state antiboycott law aimed at unions. The indictments created national media attention that drew increased donations and support from outside Montgomery. On the same day, Bayard Rustin arrived, to provide support and counsel to King on how to conduct a nonviolent campaign. Rustin was the African American Quaker nonviolence advocate who Coretta Scott King had heard speak while in college. Like many radicals of the era, Rustin had joined the Young Communist League in his youth, but he became an independent socialist aligned with the Fellowship of Reconciliation (FOR). Its leader was A. J. Muste, a man of conservative Dutch Reformed upbringing who organized strikes and labor education for unions in the 1920s and 1930s and remained one of the most militant advocates of nonviolent direct action. Rustin followed Muste's path and went to prison for sixteen months rather than fight in World War II. In 1947, Rustin participated in a "freedom ride" to challenge bus segregation in interstate commerce, ending up on a chain gang for a month in North Carolina. He had been protesting segregation and speaking about nonviolence long before Montgomery.

Rustin lived in New York City and had close ties with other leftist and labor activists there. One was A. Philip Randolph, the dean of labor and civil rights in America. Another was Stanley Levison, a well-to-do left-wing New York City businessman and attorney who had raised money for civic and social justice causes, some of them linked to the Communist Party. Rustin and Levison became fund-raisers, strategic advisers, and ghostwriters for King. Despite false accusations by the FBI, neither Rustin nor Levison at the time they met King belonged to the Communist Party. Rustin had left the Young Communist League years ago, and Levison said he never joined the CP although he supported left-wing causes. They both knew their way into the complicated world of American labor and would especially help King link up with unions and to construct his labor speeches. Levison and Rustin also linked King to Ella Baker, a veteran civil rights and community organizer on the left in New York City politics who had traveled the South building up the NAACP during the 1940s. In February 1956 Levison, Rustin, and Baker formed a group called In Friendship to raise funds for the southern civil rights movement, and they immediately began to raise funds to support the Montgomery boycott.

Historian Thomas Jackson writes that King early on became linked to a "vanguard of activists who were vigorously pushing a combined race-class agenda in the late fifties." Rustin, Levison, Baker, Randolph, and other civil rights and labor leftists in New York discussed the Montgomery movement in great detail and this group sent Rustin to meet King. But they feared that as a homosexual who spent time in jail for his sexuality and as a leftist radical, Rustin could damage King's reputation. Rustin counseled King on the ideas and principles of nonviolent direct action, as an alternative to the idea of "passive resistance," and secretly left town before white supremacists could discover his presence. Rustin wrote an article on behalf of King for an April issue of *Liberation* magazine, a journal of the left, and intermittently continued to provide guidance, writing, and organizing support, sometimes as a staff to King and sometimes as an unofficial advisor.

Although outside help from the New York left, donations, and mass media publicity helped to make a victory possible in

Montgomery, the people themselves provided the key to success. Black women, cooks and maids, walked miles to and from work, and sometimes took rides from white housewives who did not want to lose their labor. Over 381 days, African Americans in Montgomery carried on a nonviolent bus boycott. After many trials and tribulations, a U.S. Supreme Court decision finally outlawed bus segregation in Montgomery, and King and the movement declared the boycott over on December 26, 1956. After that victory, someone fired into the front door of the King home with a rifle. King told a mass meeting that night, "I would like to tell whoever did it that it won't do any good to kill me," because "we have just started our work."

Freedom riders would later desegregate transportation across the South; some would sacrifice their lives. The movement started and ended with the courage and persistence of everyday people walking many miles to and from work and standing up to persecution. The Montgomery boycott's economic demands included the right to go to work in dignity and for black workers to be employed as bus drivers. Virtually every major struggle of the era, James Lawson told me in an interview, embodied a demand for economic justice as well as civil and voting rights.

Over the course of the Montgomery campaign, King came to use the term "nonviolent resistance," a phrase adopted from Mohandas Gandhi. The idea was simple: that people could end their oppression by refusing to participate in the system that oppressed them. A 1957 *Christian Century* magazine article, drafted by Bayard Rustin and elaborated by King in his first book, *Stride Toward Freedom* (1957), explained the basic tenets of nonviolent struggle. King turned to history to explain that slavery and the failed promise of Reconstruction, followed by the imposition of Jim Crow, had created a "negative peace" based on the suppression of black personhood. When blacks no longer submitted to it, they gained a "new sense of self-respect and sense of dignity." He observed that this dynamic appeared throughout the former European colonies in Asia, Africa, and Latin America, where "the struggle will continue until freedom is a reality for all the oppressed peoples of the world." King always saw the freedom struggle as world wide.

The question was not *if* there would be change, but *how* oppressed people would wage the struggle. King provided the answer, based on Gandhi: "Someone must have sense enough and morality enough to cut off the chain of hate." King explained that nonviolent resistance was not passive but must be active, spiritually and physically, yet without inflicting harm on others: "The nonviolent resister seeks to attack the evil system rather than individuals who happen to be caught up in the system." While "the aftermath of violence is bitterness," he wrote, "the aftermath of nonviolence is reconciliation and the creation of a beloved community."

King said implementing nonviolence required the practice of agape love. As opposed to erotic or familial love, agape love "means understanding, redeeming good will . . . an overflowing love which seeks nothing in return," and the belief "that God is on the side of truth and justice." He wrote that a better way of human relations "comes down to us from the long tradition of our Christian faith," in which "Christ furnished the spirit and motivation," while "Gandhi furnished the method." People of many faiths—or no faith—could follow a philosophy and practice of nonviolent resistance to violence, oppression, and economic exploitation. King believed he had found a moral framework to guide a universal struggle for justice from which all people could benefit.

News of Montgomery electrified James Lawson, who was at that time on a mission for the Methodist Church in India. A conscientious objector to war who had spent time in prison during the early Korean War as a draft resister, Lawson realized that the Montgomery movement could be replicated in other places. Indeed, it set the stage for the next decade of locally based freedom struggles across the South, from Albany, Georgia, to St. Augustine, Florida, from Mississippi to Birmingham to Selma, from Chicago to Memphis. Lawson pointed out to me that "the great man" theory does not explain King's role in history; that leaders are made, not born, through interaction with people during social-movement organizing. Ella Baker, one of the most influential grassroots organizers of the era, likewise explained that King did not make the freedom movement, the movement made King. Indeed, it transformed him from an intellectual follower of the black Social Gospel and nonviolence into a dedicated social-movement leader.

In Montgomery, a blacklist forced an unemployed Rosa Parks and her husband to leave for Detroit, while King began to travel and speak all over the country. E. D. Nixon complained that while King became a famous speaker, the local movement fell apart. King would forevermore be accused of taking the limelight. Indeed, King could never fully meet the needs of a congregation and a local movement while also addressing a national audience. His fame and personal success led to contradictions. King had his limitations. But his gifts of oratory and insight would energize both the freedom movement and the labor movement, and leave an indelible imprint on American history.

From left to right: King, Pete Seeger, Charis Horton, Rosa Parks, and Ralph David Abernathy at Highlander Folk School in 1957.

Chapter 2

"WE HAVE A POWERFUL INSTRUMENT"

Civil Rights Unionism and the Cold War, 1957–1963

> *There are three major social evils that are alive in our world today . . . the evil of war, the evil of economic injustice, and the evil of racial injustice. . . .*
>
> —KING AT DISTRICT 65, RETAIL, WHOLESALE, AND DEPARTMENT STORE UNION (RWDSU) CONVENTION, SEPTEMBER 8, 1962

WHITE MASS MEDIA WRITERS PORTRAYED MARTIN Luther King, Jr., as a "civil rights" advocate whose success affirmed the progress of American democracy. On February 18, 1957, *Time* magazine put a picture of King on its front cover and characterized him as an "expert organizer" but "no radical." Scholar/activist W. E. B. Du Bois and singer/actor Paul Robeson both had their passports lifted and public lives destroyed because they had spoken out against American militarism and imperialism and for détente with the Soviet Union. King's beliefs were not so different, but his powerful appeals to Christian and American founding concepts of charity, love, fairness, freedom, and equality for a time allowed him to sidestep media and government attacks. Yet *Time* was wrong on both counts. King often proved to be better at articulating a larger vision than at organizing. And, based on his understanding of the Social Gospel, he was indeed a radical by American standards.

King did become a high-profile target of bigots of all stripes. By April 1960, as he wrote in an article titled "Suffering and Faith," he had already been arrested five times (he would later lose count), while white supremacists had bombed his home and constantly threatened his family with hate mail and phone calls. In Montgomery, whites fired repeatedly on black bus riders, destroyed the home of a white minister who had supported the movement, and bombed at least four churches as well as homes. The city put some of the bombers, who admitted their crimes, on trial, but an all-white jury acquitted them. On January 27, 1957, vigilantes planted twelve sticks of dynamite in front of King's parsonage but the lit fuse fizzled out. King responded by telling his church that "if I had to die tomorrow morning I would die happy because I've been to the mountaintop and I've seen the promised land and it's going to be here in Montgomery."

On September 20, 1958, a deranged black woman named Isola Ware Curry, who was armed with a pistol and tormented by fears of communism, had nearly stabbed him through the heart as he signed his first book, *Stride Toward Freedom*, in Harlem. After a delicate operation, King spent months recovering from the stabbing. Coretta Scott King later wrote that threats and "Martin's repeated, unwarranted arrests" at times "pushed me to the breaking point." As a way to cope, she and Martin clung to the Christian concept that "unearned suffering is redemptive." Dr. King called suffering "an opportunity to transform myself and heal the people involved in the tragic situation which now obtains." The atmosphere of violence or potential violence experienced by the Kings was experienced on a daily basis by African Americans across the South.

A willingness to suffer made it possible for Martin and Coretta King to continue to advocate for racial and economic justice at a dark time of repression, when the country had a crying need for moral leadership. Cold War anticommunism cast suspicion on anyone who criticized American capitalism and forced civil rights advocates to downplay economic issues. King's allies on the labor left were fired from jobs and run out of communities. Segregationists and anticommunists inculcated the false idea that unions, civil rights, and communism were all the same thing. King walked a fine line. He decried communist state systems that repressed human personality, but he also condemned capitalism's exploitation of workers and the poor, and demanded that the country live up to its stated goals of equality and equal economic opportunity.

On January 10 and 11, 1957, King and other black ministers met at Ebenezer Baptist Church in Atlanta hoping to replicate the Montgomery experience of mass-movement organizing through the black church. They started the Southern Christian Leadership Conference (SCLC) with a broad pledge to "redeem the soul of America." Bayard Rustin had drafted papers for the conference, and he and Ella Baker and Fred Shuttlesworth in Birmingham, and other black ministers across the South, thought SCLC would foster a new generation of movement activists. On February 7, 1957, King met Oberlin student James Lawson and asked him to come South. Lawson moved to Nashville to take up graduate studies in theology at Vanderbilt University and simultaneously to work as a field secretary for the Fellowship of Reconciliation. As school integration battles raged in Little Rock, Arkansas, and elsewhere, Lawson trained people in the philosophy and methods of nonviolent direct action. His workshops in Nashville developed an extraordinary cadre of nonviolence activists.

On September 2, King strengthened his connections with the union-based civil rights movement when he gave the closing talk at the twenty-fifth reunion of the Highlander Folk School. Rosa Parks, antiracist journalist Anne Braden, and a vanguard of black and white integrationists celebrated the school's singular role in bringing together southerners, and particularly workers, across the racial divide. Rosa Parks had attended the school before the Montgomery bus boycott. King's speech to the Highlander Folk School reunion, "A Look to the Future," voiced his optimistic view that industrialization would spawn unionization, that unionized black and white workers would join together to fight for voting rights and elect progressive leaders and break the back of low wages and racial repression in the

South. In hindsight, King and his labor allies may appear to have been naïve in hoping to transform working-class white southerners, but at that time organized labor was at its height of power and optimism. He declared, "Organized labor is one of the Negro's strongest allies in the struggle for freedom." Opposing Cold War orthodoxy with his Social Gospel critique of American capitalism, King also said, "I never intend to become adjusted to the madness of militarism and the self-defeating method of physical violence." Using a phrase he would often repeat, he called on his audience to be "maladjusted" to "the tragic inequalities of an economic system which takes necessities from the masses to give luxuries to the classes."

At Highlander, King was preaching to the choir, so to speak. The Highlander sessions closed with singer Pete Seeger leading a rousing version of "We Shall Overcome," a song first learned by Highlander's Zilphia Horton from Lucille Simmons and black women in the Food and Tobacco Workers union on strike in 1945–46 in Charleston, South Carolina. Seeger and Guy and Candie Carawan of Highlander would later spread that song throughout the southern movement and the world. As a labor and Communist Party activist named Red Davis from Memphis and Anne Braden of Louisville left the 1957 Highlander meeting together with King, they shared a buoyant feeling that they were on the cusp of momentous change. However, while the Highlander gathering moved King more strongly into alliances with labor and civil rights activists, it also inaugurated the right-wing crusade against him.

Unknown to the participants at Highlander's twenty-fifth reunion, Ed Friend had "infiltrated" (a favorite word usually used against supposed Communists) the meeting as an agent of Georgia's misnamed Commission on Education (GCE), which sought to prevent black and white students from attending school together. Friend photographed King sitting next to New Deal liberal Aubrey Williams and Highlander founder Myles Horton, a few seats away from Rosa Parks. A Communist Party *Daily Worker* reporter named Abner Berry, an African American, also sat near King. The Georgia Commission spread the photo far and wide under the caption, "King at a Communist Training

Segregationists and the John Birch Society portrayed King's
visit as a part of an integrated Communist plot.

School," and identified the men, some of whom did not know each other, as the " 'four horsemen' of racial agitation." The commission claimed these men had "brought tension, disturbance, strife and violence in their advancement of the Communist doctrine of 'racial nationalism.' " Groups with names like the "Defenders of State Sovereignty and Individual Liberties," in Virginia, and "Aryan Views and White Folks News" in Waco, Texas, would follow Georgia's line on King for years to come. The commission also published a pamphlet with this picture and others depicting blacks and whites dancing and swimming and eating together at Highlander. It named a raft of supposed "Communist fronts," and indicted integration as a communist doctrine.

The John Birch Society, one of the most paranoid anticommunist organizations of the era, put the picture and the slogan on a postcard and mailed it across the country. Among the Birch Society's eleven founders was Fred Koch, a sympathizer with Nazi Germany and southern segregationists and an opponent of civil rights groups and unions; he and his sons would go on to invest a fortune in right-wing causes. Koch promoted "right to work" legislation in Kansas that became law in 1958, and his successors continued to campaign everywhere for antiunion laws. The Birch Society paid to put the image of King at Highlander on billboards, one of which King and others passed in 1965 when they marched on Highway 80 from Selma to Montgomery for the right to vote. The Memphis *Commercial Appeal* carried the "King at a Communist Training School" photo and phrase, which reappeared in other newspapers and racist leaflets throughout the South. Investigating committees and the Federal Bureau of Investigation (FBI) would cite the photo with its false caption as evidence against King.

This ludicrous characterization of one of the world's great Baptist ministers as a Communist became a staple for government and police agencies that promoted what historian Jeff Woods calls a distinctive "southern red scare" designed to use anticommunism to frighten whites away from integration. The antiunion Southern States Industrial Union Council and segregationist groups had used anticommunism since the 1930s to divide workers and break up union organizing. James Lawson saw the red scare as part and parcel of racism: it dehumanized the "enemy" and created an "other" to victimize. When I interviewed Myles Horton some years later, he cautioned me against thinking that the red scare was really about Communists, because there were very few of them in the South. Rather, he said, anti-communism was used as a means to close the minds of white southerners to needed change.

Some have analyzed the red scare as providing leverage for the civil rights movement to pressure the U.S. government to live up to its boast as "the leader of the free world." More directly, however, the red scare gave bigots in the South a rationalization for the beatings, whippings, and murder inflicted on civil rights workers, and it gave segregationists in Congress a justification for upholding racism and Jim Crow as if they were in the national interest.

Federal and state governments used the red scare to attack and undermine labor and civil rights activists. A Tennessee investigative committee and a U.S. Senate committee run by Mississippi senator James Eastland persecuted Horton and Highlander, and in 1959 the State of Tennessee took away its legal charter and closed the school. Vandals burned it to the ground. (Undeterred, Horton and friends reorganized the school and moved it from west Tennessee to the mountains of east Tennessee, where it remains today.) Since the 1920s, FBI director J. Edgar Hoover had sought to use police and government power to destroy the Communist Party, the independent labor left, and the black freedom movement. Raised in a segregated, white environment in Washington, D.C., Hoover neither understood nor appreciated the importance of equal rights or unions. Like most segregationists, he could not believe that black people themselves had thought up their own liberation; he believed it had to be a communist plot. Under his leadership, the FBI provided HUAC with constant information and leads of people to go after.

Employers used anticommunist hearings to destroy interracial unions fighting for contracts. In southern states, legislatures created "little HUACS" to ostracize anyone who spoke up for labor and civil rights. U. S. Senators James Eastland of Mississippi and John McClellan of Arkansas held hearings to drive out leftist and black labor leaders, as well as white liberals like Grace Lorch, who had protected Elizabeth Eckford from a white mob in Little Rock Central High during its school desegregation struggle. Eastland hearings and media-sensationalized anticommunist attacks forced her and her husband, Professor Lee Lorch, out of Arkansas and silenced numerous leftists and civil rights advocates within unions.

HUAC and its state affiliates especially targeted white allies of the civil rights movement. In 1954, the year of the *Brown v. Board of Education* desegregation ruling, labor journalists Anne and Carl Braden had helped African American Andrew Wade and his family to buy a home in a white neighborhood in Louisville. Whites bombed the home but the state claimed the Bradens bought the home in a conspiracy to instigate race riots and overthrow the state of Kentucky. Although the U.S. Supreme Court later overturned state sedition laws, Carl nonetheless spent eight months in prison. Blacklisted from their profession of journalism, the Bradens became codirectors of the Southern Conference Educational Fund, dedicated to organizing white support for King and the civil rights movement. SCLC's Fred Shuttlesworth courageously served as president of SCEF, the most red-baited of all southern movement groups.

Although strongly opposed to state communism, when pushed to do it King stood against the red scare, which he accurately saw as a threat to civil liberties. In 1958 Carl Braden and Frank Wilkinson refused to testify about the integration movement before HUAC in Atlanta, citing their First Amendment rights to freedom of speech, press, thought, and association. King petitioned for clemency on their behalf and, on the night before they began a yearlong prison sentence, held a celebratory dinner for them. In 1964 Anne Braden published a pamphlet that explained how the red scare stifled integration, *House Un-American Activities Committee, Bulwark of Segregation*. King signed on as a sponsor of the National Committee to Abolish the House Un-American Activities Committee.

Although he hesitated to be associated with people branded as radicals, and often spoke against communism from his religious and humanitarian point of view, King signed petitions for victims of the red scare like imprisoned CP member Henry Winston and stood for First Amendment rights during the 1950s and into the 1960s. The red scare caused people to lose jobs, homes, reputations, and even their lives. Along with state antiunion laws and the Taft-Hartley Act, the red scare pressured unions to focus on servicing union members and on legal and contractual issues, and to shy away from social movements.

Meanwhile, King forged powerful relationships with unions that had strong civil rights platforms, most of them associated with labor's left. By the end of his life, King had became virtually an honorary member of the Distributive Workers District 65 and Local 1199 hospital workers in New York City; the United Electrical, Radio and Machine Workers of America (UE); and the International Longshore and Warehouse Union (ILWU), based in San Francisco. All these unions except District 65 had been purged from the CIO for leftist associations. The United Packinghouse Workers Union (UPWA), and its president Ralph Helstein, introduced to King by Bayard Rustin, also became one of King's strongest and earliest union supporters. In October 1957 King made his first union speech at the UPWA's biennial wage and contract and national women's conference in Chicago. He virtually repeated the speech he gave at Highlander, calling the organized labor movement the civil rights movement's greatest potential ally, and said a union and civil rights coalition provided a "powerful instrument" to overthrow economic and racial oppression. The UPWA was the one union that had maneuvered through the anticommunist minefield and survived within the AFL-CIO to create a model of civil rights unionism.

It is easy to see why the packinghouse union became one of King's most committed allies. The owners of the factories that packaged meat for America's growing and increasingly industrialized food industry—"packers," as they were called—had used racism to break up union organizing. During the 1930s, Communist and leftist organizers in the packinghouse industry overcame employer intimidation and racial division by making black and white unity and anti-discrimination the union's guiding principle. The UPWA developed strong, predominantly black locals, and in the 1950s fought white mob violence in Chicago to help its black members obtain housing in white neighborhoods. The UPWA also succeeded in breaking down racist and sexist hiring and promotion practices at its home base in Chicago, where Addie Wyatt and other black women played leading roles.

The UPWA had provided critical financial support to the Montgomery bus boycott, and during King's appearance at the 1957 UPWA convention, President Ralph Helstein turned over to King $11,000 created as a "fund for democracy" that largely funded SCLC's first year. Without the UPWA's funds and organizational support, SCLC might have failed in its first year. While people with large treasuries at their disposal, such as the UAW's Walter Reuther, would subsequently write larger checks to the civil rights movement, the UPWA did something special: workers themselves raised funds donated by UPWA locals and members. And at a time when White Citizens Council and Ku Klux Klan activists took over some union locals in the South, the UPWA challenged whites to join with black workers and to elect them to union office. African American Russell Lasley, UPWA vice president and director of the union's antidiscrimination department, and President Helstein both attended the SCLC founding convention. Helstein also worked on a research committee for King; Myles Horton was the union's educational director for a time. When the union was threatened with charges of "Communist domination" within the AFL-CIO, King wrote a letter vouching for the union. When HUAC decided to investigate UPWA, King and SCLC issued a statement saying, "It is a dark day indeed when men cannot work to implement the ideal of brotherhood without being labeled communist."

King's experience with the UPWA raised his hopes for a strong labor-civil rights alliance. Unions represented about one-third of

American workers, often had large treasuries, a vigorous labor newspaper network, and lobbying arms in Congress. However, both the CIO and the AFL supported U.S. foreign policy that overthrew democratically elected governments and replaced them with dictatorships that repressed labor movements in the name of anticommunism, in Guatemala in 1954, and elsewhere. After the AFL and CIO merged in 1955–56, the new federation's American Institute for Free Labor Development (AIFLD) continued to support right-wing dictatorships in Latin America that killed thousands of leftist unionists, peasants, and indigenous people, all in the name of winning the Cold War between the United States and the Soviet Union. In 1966 Walter Reuther's brother Victor revealed to the press that the AFL-CIO's AIFLD worked as a front for the CIA in developing countries.

Mainstream labor unions walked in lockstep with the country's anticommunist foreign policy, but King had visited Ghana, Africa, and India in 1957–58, and spoke against Western capitalist exploitation of their resources and American military interventions in Latin America, Africa, and Asia. The AFL-CIO's myopic anticommunism would make it difficult for King and the black freedom movement to court AFL-CIO unions to build a labor-civil rights alliance.

Between 1957 and 1960, King tried to develop SCLC with mixed results. The organization sponsored some big events, such as a May 1957 prayer pilgrimage for integrated schools held in Washington, D.C. King continued to give marvelous speeches, and funded SCLC in large part through a life of perpetual preaching and writing that often put him on the road for three hundred days a year. Incessant travel and his ministry kept him too busy to do grassroots organizing.

In 1958, SCLC hired Ella Baker, the executive secretary of In Friendship, the New York City group providing financial support to the southern civil rights struggle. Baker was a community activist and had been the key organizer of NAACP branches that doubled their membership across the South in the 1940s. She focused on leadership development, saying that "strong people don't need strong leaders." Baker, senior to King and others in SCLC, and with much more organizing experience, quickly found herself uncomfortable with SCLC's preacher-leader model. SCLC ministers knew how to run a church from the top but she knew much more than they did about how to organize a movement from the bottom up. She recalled, "The role of women in the southern church was that of doing the things that the minister said he wanted to have done." That was not her mode of operation. "It was not a comforting sort of presence that I presented," said Baker. She felt the "magic man" idea of saviors and messiahs reinforced dependency and undermined organizing capacity among people at the grass roots. Meanwhile, SCLC in its first years did not find a way to repeat the mass nonviolent resistance of the Montgomery movement.

Myles Horton believed people had to learn to think and do for themselves, yet he also appreciated how King's oratory and ideas awakened people to their self-worth and helped them to push forward. The Citizenship Education Program became one of SCLC's best grassroots efforts. It began as a program at Highlander when Horton hired Septima Clark, a black schoolteacher blacklisted for her civil rights activity in South Carolina. Traveling to various communities and holding workshops at Highlander, she explored ways to teach people literacy and citizenship consciousness to counteract years of indoctrination that black southerners could not vote and function as citizens. In collaboration with Highlander, SCLC more or less adopted the program. In July 1961 King hired Andrew Young to supervise and expand the program, and also put Virginian Dorothy Cotton in charge of its field operations. Through nurturing citizenship and literacy skills in African Americans who were denied the vote, Cotton, Clark, Young, and others in citizenship education prepared thousands of working-class people to take charge of their lives across the South and to fight for their rights.

During the civil rights movement, debates often erupted over the effectiveness of organizing versus mobilizing, but activists, including those in SCLC, typically did some of both. And women were always involved in SCLC, as in other organizations.

* * *

ON FEBRUARY 1, 1960, King moved back to Atlanta to copastor Ebenezer with Daddy King, resigning from Dexter Avenue Baptist church and freeing himself to spend more time as SCLC's president. On the same day, four black students in Greensboro, North Carolina, staged the first sit-in, demanding to be served at a Woolworth lunch counter that excluded African Americans. A powerful core of organizers, including C. T. Vivian, John Lewis, Diane Nash, James Bevel, Bernard Lafayette, and others also emerged out of Lawson's Nashville study groups. They had extraordinary success in the spring of 1960 desegregating downtown Nashville and opening jobs to African Americans. Nonviolent resistance spread like wildfire across the South. By the end of the year, an estimated 70,000 black students had held sit-ins or other protests; some 3,600 were arrested. In Memphis, black student sit-ins, a strong NAACP, and court orders proved especially successful in desegregating many public places.

On April 15–17, a new moment emerged with the founding of the Student Nonviolent Coordinating Committee (SNCC). Ella Baker organized a conference and insisted that the students needed their own, independent organization rather than becoming part of SCLC or the NAACP. King and Lawson gave powerful speeches at the conference and supported the SNCC students, and Baker left SCLC to become SNCC's veteran adviser. In May 1961 black and white activists defied segregation by riding together on buses across the South. In Alabama, the police let local thugs firebomb buses and nearly kill freedom riders by beating them with tire irons and chains. Rev. Lawson and other freedom riders spent harrowing days in Mississippi's state penitentiary, Parchman Prison. Despite horrific violence, nonviolent sit-ins, freedom rides, and community-based desegregation and voter registration campaigns exploded across the South from 1960 to 1965, arguably the most dynamic phase of the black freedom struggle. SNCC members and students became the movement's shock troops, with Baker, Lawson, King, Shuttlesworth, and others in support.

King did not start the civil rights movement, nor was he always at the center of it, but he remained a powerful spokesperson frequently called upon to support local movements or to negotiate with the power structures that repeatedly tried to eliminate him. In April 1960 A. Philip Randolph led the Committee to Defend Martin Luther King that rallied thousands of trade union leaders and others in New York to defeat the State of Alabama's indictment of King on false charges of perjury and income tax evasion. Unions co-sponsored "A Night of Stars for Freedom" at Carnegie Hall that helped lead to his acquittal. On October 19, 1960, after King was arrested for sitting in with SNCC workers at an Atlanta department store, a judge vindictively sentenced King to a potentially life-threatening four months at hard labor on a chain gang in the notorious Reidsville Georgia State Prison. Massachusetts senator John F. Kennedy helped to get him out, galvanizing blacks who could vote to provide a margin of victory in electing Kennedy to the presidency of the United States in November.

Fearful of alienating segregationist southern Democrats, however, President Kennedy shied away from supporting the civil rights movement, but it kept forcing his hand. On May 21, 1961, a mob with guns and torches barricaded King and freedom riders in Ralph Abernathy's church in Montgomery. Those inside only escaped when a new U.S. attorney general, Robert Kennedy, the president's younger brother, rescued them with federal marshals. On October 16 King met with President Kennedy and called for racial reform as the nation approached one hundred years since emancipation in January 1863. President Kennedy resisted introducing a new civil rights law, but King and the movement would ultimately prevail.

In December 1961, King's advocacy of the labor–civil rights alliance came once again to the fore when he spoke at the annual convention of the AFL-CIO in the resort town of Bal Harbour, Florida. King was not among clear allies. George Meany, a white plumber from New York, claimed he had never walked on a picket line and supported the American business model, euphemistically called "free enterprise." On day one of the convention, Meany began his fourth two-year term to a standing ovation of three thousand overwhelmingly white male delegates, and made a vitriolic speech condemning communism and putting unions on the side of U.S. foreign policy. President Kennedy followed Meany, praising unions as a bulwark of American freedom. King's chance to speak came on Monday, after a holiday weekend at the beach for the convention's delegates.

King faced both Cold War and racial obstacles to building a civil rights–labor alliance with the AFL-CIO. Labor anticommunism did not fit King's worldview. In the Cold War and hot war context of the 1960s, civil rights advocates often appealed to the American power structure to support civil rights as a necessary part of the country's crusade for capitalist freedom in the world. In contrast, King took a more critical stance. He rejected a bipolar struggle between communism and capitalism and viewed the anticolonial independence movements in Africa, Asia, and Latin America in the context of the Social Gospel. He hoped that people could create a "third way" between capitalism and communism that combined economic justice with individual initiative and democratic rights. His support for third-world liberation would continue to put him in conflict with U.S. and AFL-CIO anticommunist foreign policy.

A. Philip Randolph—King's guide to the contested terrain of labor and civil rights—and George Meany were also in heated conflict over racial issues. As an anticommunist Socialist Party member and president of the Brotherhood of Sleeping Car Porters since the 1920s, Randolph had spent his life forging powerful links between labor and civil rights while avoiding identification with the communist left. He left the presidency of the National Negro Congress in 1940 because he thought communists had too much control. In 1941, by threatening a march of black workers on Washington, he won a presidential executive order mandating equal hiring within America's burgeoning military industries, albeit with few enforcement powers. Randolph continued to spearhead efforts to break down racial discrimination while going along with the expulsion of the left unions. These internal labor and civil rights politics created a minefield for a relative outsider like Dr. King.

NAACP labor secretary Herbert Hill, in his pamphlet "Racism Within Labor," had thoroughly documented how some craft unions barred blacks from skilled employment by denying them union apprenticeships and some even banned them from union membership. Many industrial-union contracts institutionalized departmental and occupational seniority that forced blacks to hold on to the least desirable and worst jobs, losing their seniority if they tried to move into another department. Hill wrote that automation of laboring jobs where blacks were concentrated combined with union racial barriers was creating "a permanently depressed economic group" of black workers. Randolph insisted that discriminating unions should be censured or even expelled. Instead, Meany responded by denouncing and censuring him, while King defended him.

On December 3, 1961, King came to the AFL-CIO convention exhausted, not only from his constant travel but also from his hair-raising confrontations with southern segregationists. In the midst of his harrowing and frenetic life, King at Bal Harbour found himself speaking to an audience of older white male union leaders. Many of them had gained ascendency in the 1930s, but now smoked cigars and discussed union issues near the seashore in upscale hotels. ("Nothing's too good for the working class," went a self-serving joke.) With King at the podium, Randolph and Meany remained locked in battle over whether union antidiscrimination resolutions would just be window dressing or bring about substantive change.

Unlike his more lively talks to civil rights unions like the UPWA, King gave a sober and careful speech. He recalled the exploitation of workers in pre-union days and pointed to the "unity of purpose" between organized labor and blacks, who "are almost entirely a working people." The civil rights movement, he said, had adopted many of the tools of the labor movement, including "sit-ins, civil disobedience, and protests."

In this and other speeches to unions, King repeatedly referred to the methods and demands common to unions and the civil rights movement. In the 1930s, workers had fundamentally changed the rules of American capitalism through nonviolent direct action in the form of strikes, factory sit-ins, boycotts, and picket lines. In 1936, workers had massively voted to reelect President Roosevelt, who produced his "second New Deal" laws mandating minimum wages, social security, and union protections. What the New Deal did not do was pass civil rights and antilynching laws, or extend labor protections to agricultural and domestic workers, where African Americans, women, poor whites, and Latinos remained concentrated. Nor did government administrators provide equal access for racial minorities to Federal Housing Administration loans and other forms of economic support to working-class families. Southern white administrators of the New Deal and subsequent government programs largely shut black people out. The U.S. Department of Agriculture and state and local agencies withheld loans and information that decimated the ranks of black farmers in the South.

King and his labor advisors knew all this, but in coming before the AFL-CIO sought to build an alliance based on what blacks and organized labor had in common. African Americans were mainly "a working people," King declared—"our needs are identical with labor's needs," including the need for good wages and working conditions, secure jobs, housing, old-age security, education, and respect. But he also warned that both labor and civil rights movements confronted a virulent right-wing and racist crusade. The twin-headed "labor-hater and the labor-baiter" typically spews "anti-Negro epithets from one mouth and anti-labor epithets from the other mouth." This description mirrored union experiences in many locales and industries, especially in the South.

The Southern States Industrial Council, the Chambers of Commerce, and businesspeople had long adopted the idea that the South's main advantage was low wages, enforced by destroying unions. However, low wages reduced consumption, stifled economic growth, and kept the South's people poor. King did not have to explain this, because everyone in the AFL-CIO knew it. The question was what to do about it. King sounded a theme of unity between labor and civil rights forces and cited the role of black voters in defeating a ban on the union shop in Louisiana as one example of how the civil rights movement could help labor.

In summing up, King asserted that "the two most dynamic and

cohesive liberal forces in the country are the labor movement and the Negro freedom movement," and that they could together open the South to progress. He affirmed the idea that "if the Negro wins, labor wins." Since his first labor-related talk at Highlander in 1957, King had held to the position that if black voters in the South could be enfranchised, a voting coalition of labor and civil rights forces could change the South. This was not a utopian fantasy. A good example was Memphis, Tennessee, where blacks had never lost the right to vote, and combined with unionized voters to help elect relatively moderate Democrats like U.S. senators Albert Gore (elected 1952) and Estes Kefauver (elected 1949) at the state level, and others at the local level.

In his AFL-CIO speech, King offered not only hope for the future but a dark and unfortunately prophetic challenge to unions. They seemed to be at the height of their power, but labor economists also forecast that automation, as King put it, "will grind jobs into dust as it grinds out unbelievable volumes of production." King also warned against the rise of what he called an "ultra-right" alliance between business, Republicans, and southern Democrats. Unless countered by a powerful labor–civil rights alliance, he argued, the ultraright would threaten "everything decent and fair in American life." In a chilling prediction of organized labor's future decline, he said failure to meet this challenge with a united interracial movement could "drive labor into impotency." King emphasized that the ultraright, not "scattered reds," posed the real threat to unions.

King challenged his audience to undertake "thoughtful examination of Randolph's criticism of labor's efforts to end discrimination within its own ranks." He pointed to "shameful conditions" of union discrimination and complained that a plan by AFL-CIO unions to raise two million dollars for the civil rights movement had never materialized. (In fact, the relatively tiny UPWA had done much more than the awesome AFL-CIO to help finance the southern movement). "Labor should accept the logic of its special position with respect to Negroes and the struggle for equality," asserted King, and should also recognize that "the standard expected of you is higher than the standard for the general community." These comments elicited grim silence from his audience. King finally roused the delegates from their seats with his vision of a different kind of future with his invocation of the words of the old Negro spiritual: "Free at last, free at last, thank God Almighty, we are free at last!"

King's AFL-CIO speech opened a discussion on civil rights the next day. UPWA's black leaders Russell Lasley and Charles Hays pointed out that there were "only a handful of Negro delegates present here," and called on the AFL-CIO "to close the gap" between fine resolutions and real action. The AFL-CIO convention passed a civil rights resolution and Meany praised King and had pinned a union button on his jacket. Various unions subsequently donated to SCLC; the Transport Workers Union of America published thousands of copies of his speech. But the federation did not raise the funds for civil rights that King hoped for and he never spoke at another AFL-CIO national convention. Less than a week after his AFL-CIO speech, King returned to a jail cell in Albany, Georgia, for demonstrating for civil and voting rights.

King subsequently took his message of civil rights and labor alliance to dozens of unions, and Meany and the AFL-CIO would prove crucial to passing the 1964 Civil Rights Act and the 1965 Voting Rights Act, powered by President Lyndon Johnson's ability to defeat filibusters and get key Republicans to support these laws. Yet despite successes in mobilizing the union–civil rights alliance, it would always be strained by a deep history of racial and gender discrimination that more often than not kept blacks and other minorities and women from higher-skilled jobs and union office holding. King had warmer relationships with civil rights unions on the left of the American labor spectrum than with the AFL-CIO. The interests of working-class whites, who had jobs and seniority to hold on to, remained at odds with civil rights demands to open those jobs to people of color and women. The zero-sum game of capitalism always seemed to ensure that if someone made gains, those gains came at the expense of someone else. Conflicts over jobs, housing, and school integration would split the progressive forces for change, as would American foreign policy and the Vietnam War.

In July and August 1962, King experienced repeated incarcerations as he continued to work with a mass movement to integrate jobs, businesses, schools, and public accommodations. Returning from Albany, Georgia, to the North on September 8, King gave a speech to some of his strongest allies at a convention of District 65 of the Retail, Wholesale, and Department Store Unions (RWDSU), held in upstate New York. African Americans, Puerto Ricans, and Jewish workers comprised most of the members of this union of department store and wholesale workers based in New York City. Its African American secretary-treasurer, Cleveland Robinson, over the years raised about $100,000 to support King's work, and would play a crucial role in the coming March on Washington. King repeatedly returned to give speeches, stand on picket lines, and express solidarity with workers in RWDSU and 1199 Hospital Workers Union, who represented some of the poorest workers in New York City.

Among these committed supporters, King went right to the heart of his Social Gospel critique of American capitalism. Naming war, economic injustice, and racial injustice as the world's three major evils, King repeated his mantra, "There is something wrong with a situation that will take the necessities from the masses to give luxuries to the classes." Sounding like someone from the Occupy movement in the twenty-first century, King decried the fact that "here in America, one-tenth of one percent of the population controls almost 50 percent of the wealth." He called segregation a "cancer" rooted in slavery. Although he didn't name his ancestors, he could have been thinking about them: "We worked right here two centuries without wages. We made cotton king. And we built our homes, and the homes of our masters, in the midst of injustice and humiliation . . . if the inexpressible cruelties of slavery couldn't stop us, certainly the opposition that we now face will not be able to stop us."

* * *

J. EDGAR HOOVER'S tracking of King's activities began during or right after the Montgomery boycott, and escalated after King's

AFL-CIO speech, when Hoover learned that Stanley Levison, whom he considered a closet communist, had written the first draft. The FBI began conveying warnings to the White House that Levison had "infiltrated" King's movement, even though it had no evidence that connected Levison to the CP for at least five years. On March 6, 1962, the FBI broke into Levison's home office, installed a microphone, and began wiretaps, conveying conversations between King and Levison to Attorney General Robert F. Kennedy and others. On May 11, 1962, the FBI added King's name to one of its "enemies" lists, making Levison and King targets of detention if the United States ever declared a national emergency.

Hoover and his agents worked with HUAC and other governmental agencies and selected news media outlets to "expose" King. Hoover believed, despite overwhelming evidence to the contrary, that "Communism is the agitator of every social crisis in America." And he cited the civil rights movement—the most American of movements, based on the ideals of the Constitution and Declaration of Independence—as "the most artificial of all such social crises, instigated by the Communists within America to add racial hatred to class hatred."

Hoover's anger at King grew during the Albany campaign in the summer and fall of 1962. Spelman College professor Howard Zinn commented that the FBI's white agents collaborated with local police and did nothing but take notes while police and white supremacists arrested, beat, and even killed civil rights workers. When in answer to a reporter King confirmed that Zinn's comments were true, and commented that all the agents he saw were white and worked closely with the local white police, Hoover was enraged—not by the behavior of his agents but by King's critique.

In response to demands to protect civil rights activists, Hoover insisted the FBI was merely an information-gathering agency—despite its history of destroying Al Capone and the Mafia in the 1930s with machine guns, as well as the FBI's relentless campaigns to destroy communists and assorted radicals. Hoover knew Levison had completely broken any presumed ties with the Communist Party in 1957, but he led presidents John Kennedy and Lyndon Johnson to believe Levison was a communist infiltrator into the civil rights movement. Astonishingly, the FBI also continued to intimate that the Baptist King was either a Marxist-Leninist or was following a Communist Party line.

On October 23, 1962, the FBI began a "Communist infiltration" (COMINFIL) investigation of SCLC, including wiretaps on various people related to King. A year later, between November 1 and 8, 1963, with the approval of Attorney General Robert Kennedy (who had worked with Senator Joseph McCarthy's anticommunist investigating committee in the 1950s), the FBI installed wiretaps on King's home phone and four phones at the SCLC office in Atlanta. It set up a secret office across the street to monitor the wiretaps, with clerks listening in twenty-four hours a day, seven days a week. Agents began to spend hundreds of hours at taxpayer expense monitoring King and his key associates, following King around the country in a labor-intensive operation that required breaking into homes and offices and churches and hotel rooms to place electronic devices. Agents sat in cars or rented rooms, often around the clock, listening to private conversations of dozens of people. Hoover's relentless efforts to spread disinformation on King to the government and the media and to HUAC all helped to foment a right-wing campaign to destroy King.

On September 28, 1962, when King spoke at the annual convention of the Southern Christian Leadership Conference in Birmingham, Alabama, he had mentioned approvingly how entertainers Sammy Davis, Jr., an African American, and May Britt, a blonde considered the beauty of Hollywood, had married. Enraged, White Power advocate Roy James bolted from his aisle seat, jumped onto the stage, and smashed King with a right cross to the face. King staggered, as James then slugged him in the side of the head, followed that with two kidney punches, and then hit King on the trunk again. Faced with this unexpected physical assault, King dropped his hands at his side and put up no resistance. Confused, James stopped his assault as King's aides

Wyatt T. Walker and Ralph Abernathy seized him. King spoke calmly to James, and then returned to his talk. King refused to press charges, but a judge sentenced his assailant to thirty days in jail and a $25 fine. Dorothy Cotton remembered King's presence of mind and self-control under assault as awesome.

As a result of his assault on King, James became a hero to the American Nazi Party. *The Rockwell Report* published an interview, "How I Bashed Nigger King," in which James claimed to be "administering justice to a vile communist race-mixing nigger agitator." Four months after the Birmingham assault, James jumped onto a speaker's podium in Chicago and punched King again. James and an entourage of Nazis threateningly approached King in a reception line after his talk, but then left. The party's leader, George Lincoln Rockwell, renamed the U.S. Nazi Party the National Socialist White People's Party, and turned his anti-Semitic movement into a broader defense of white privilege under the slogan, "The color of your skin is your uniform." Rockwell dismissed others on the ultraright because they engaged in talk instead of action. In 1963, *The Rockwell Report* published an article headlined, "Is Martin Luther King a Communist? The Shocking Record!"

Rockwell's stormtroopers specialized in startling public attacks on individuals. One of Rockwell's followers published a magazine called *Kill!* A group of Nazis assembled to confront civil rights marchers outside the White House on June 14, 1963, with signs saying, "Separation or Death!" and "They Don't Want Civil Rights; They Want Special Rights." As always, when black people demanded change, some whites claimed themselves as victims. Rockwell's thuggish followers initiated other assaults. They physically attacked people involved in the civil rights movement at various protest gatherings. But Rockwell had a special hatred for King. He complained that communists directed King's actions and called him "Martin Luther Coon," a phrase favored as a point of pride by many white supremacists in the South.

Some media commentators in the era of the supposed "liberal consensus" viewed right-wing bigots as merely a handful of ignorant crackpots. A disgruntled follower of Rockwell would assassinate the Nazi leader in 1967. The president of the American Jewish Congress at the time said Rockwell had "made no impact on American life." But King could not dismiss Rockwell or the radical right so easily. They were after his blood. In Chicago in the summer of 1966 Rockwell's followers fomented mobs of young white men with their shirtsleeves rolled up to the shoulder, pounding baseball bats on the ground, chanting "We want King!" King remembered this mob attack as his most threatening encounter with white supremacy. Rockwell's movement would pave the way in later years for skinheads, White Power, and Christian identity movements. The Southern Poverty Law Center continues to track hundreds such groups from its Montgomery, Alabama, headquarters.

In the 1960s, right-wing groups demonized King and the movement he represented. The Ku Klux Klan in Alabama and Mississippi bombed black churches, murdered civil rights activists, and made life hell for SNCC organizers in Mississippi. A segment of evangelical white Christians based in the Southwest also demonized the civil rights movement. The Christian Anti-Communist Crusade mass-distributed a vituperative pamphlet with a drawing of King wearing a mask, titled, "Unmasking the Deceiver, Martin Luther King, Jr." This eight-page flyer outlined the standard anticommunist lines: "King Associates With Communist School"; "King Lauded by Communist Press"; "King Works with Communists"; "Lawlessness and Violence Accompany King"; "King Aids Communist Party Objectives"; "Top Communists Speak for King." This pamphlet flooded the South and showed up in Memphis around the time of the March on Washington in 1963.

The leader of the Crusade, Rev. Billy James Hargis, graduated from Ozark Bible College in Bentonville, Arkansas, also home to Sam Walton and the emerging WalMart business empire. Hargis parlayed a rudimentary education into a frenzied life of preaching against the devil communism. He promoted a national evangelical movement through whirlwind tours attacking the United Nations, UAW president Walter Reuther, the Kennedys, King, and the federal government. His Christian identity movement spouted a patriotic and militantly nationalistic doctrine in which American power would spread across and transform the globe, with white Americans taking the place of the Jews as God's chosen people. Hargis swore he would turn the world into a Christian, freedom-loving, white empire. He claimed the country's founders advocated a "Christian Americanism" and unlimited property rights. The Crusade aimed to turn back all forms of modernism and liberalism, especially the integration and civil liberties rulings of the U.S. Supreme Court since 1954.

Hargis developed a formidable army of followers. In 1963 the Crusade took in three-quarters of a million dollars, paid seventy-eight employees, and distributed Hargis sermons to over 450 radio stations and a dozen or more television stations in forty states. The right wing across America took flight based on its own media empire. Twenty-four-hour radio telethons raised money and promoted thousands of books and pamphlets with titles such as "Communism and Labor Unions," and "Communism and Racial Tension." A monthly magazine, *Christian Crusade*, a summer school for young people, and fifty to sixty youth chapters called "Torchbearers" all worked on behalf of anticommunism and Christian America. Hargis constantly toured, giving speeches and interviews and holding mass rallies in which white nationalists shouted out their beliefs. Hargis called the civil rights movement a "crisis bred in the pits of Communist debauchery and conspiracy," and declared that "segregation is a law of God."

Harding College in eastern Arkansas created a National Education Program that propagated paranoia on private religious campuses and on U.S. military bases. It passionately promoted free enterprise, the Christian gospel, and anticommunism through "Freedom Forums" hostile to labor, civil rights, and the New Deal. Christian identity speakers built an impressive network among Protestant, white, working- and middle-class southerners. Christian anticommunists drew upon social elements in the Southwest that Sam Walton would also draw upon to create his Walmart empire: alienated, semirural, and suburban whites; antiunion businesspeople enamored of right-to-work laws and angry at New Deal protections for workers; and whites fearing that equal rights for blacks would somehow take away their own rights. The right-wing network produced "Project Alert," which claimed to have held 520 meetings including 50,000 people by the early 1960s, and organized groups to watch for subversives. It circulated a John Birch Society film called "Communism on the Map," showing the nation riddled with subversives and encircled by communist powers. Bob James in Memphis screened to dozens of organizations that would help to elect him to the Memphis City Council in 1966.

Moderate Republicans outside the South scratched their heads when looking at the southern-based radical right. Oregon's moderate Republican U.S. senator Mark Hatfield saw Hargis as a harbinger of strife and predicted that the Far Right would reshape his party. "Instead of participating in an exchange of ideas, one finds himself listening to a monologue of conditioned responses to emotional slogans," Hatfield complained. "This unholy marriage of religion and politics has produced a perverted Christianity based not on love but hate, not on charity but persecution." As he predicted, the "white backlash" would lead to more and more tragic incidents of violence, affecting King and everyone on the progressive side of labor and civil rights and political activity.

Beyond white backlash politics lay something even more threatening to King's hope for an alliance of labor and civil rights in the South. The idea for "right-to-work" laws emerged in the Texas-based Christian American Association, funded by southern oilmen and northern industrialists. The Association helped to institute a right-to-work law in Arkansas in 1944, prohibiting requirements that workers in unionized shops belong to the union, while fighting against black civil rights tooth and nail. This was the antilabor, antiblack alliance that King warned the AFL-CIO about. "Right to work," King explained, was a fraud: such a law guaranteed "no rights, and no work." Rather, "it is a law to rob us of our civil rights and job rights. Its purpose is to destroy labor unions and the freedom of collective bargaining by which unions have improved wages and working conditions of everyone. Wherever these laws have been passed, wages are lower, job opportunities are fewer and there are no civil rights." The so-called National Right to Work Committee and the American Legislative Exchange Council, backed by the Koch brothers, oil and extractive industrialists, would continue to lobby and extend right-to-work laws even into previous union strongholds such as Wisconsin and Michigan.

However menacing the machinations of the right-wing campaign, during the first phase of the black freedom movement King insisted progress was not only possible but inevitable. He believed segregation would fall when a majority of Americans turned against it, and that was just a matter of time. But what about the madness and insecurity of the Cold War, and of the possibility of nuclear destruction following President Kennedy's April 1961 failed Bay of Pigs invasion? What about the madness that white supremacy had inculcated for generations? James Baldwin, writing *The Fire Next Time* in 1963, ruefully noted that too many whites had accepted slavery and segregation while failing to examine themselves or their "white" identity. "It is not permissible that the authors of devastation should also [claim to] be innocent," Baldwin wrote.

* * *

IN 1963, THROUGH blood and tear gas and jail, King and the movement would bring the country to a new high point of hope. Drawing on lessons King and the movement had learned during over a year in Albany, Georgia, that had produced few victories, SCLC set out methodically to combine demonstrations with economic withdrawal in order to create a crisis in one of the most violent centers of white supremacy in the South. In Atlanta, Coretta and Martin King had their fourth child on March 28, 1963, but, as was often the case, King was not there for the birth. SCLC had begun its campaign of nonviolent resistance in the steel-making city of Birmingham, Alabama, known by a young freedom-movement militant named Angela Davis and its other black residents as

"Bombingham." The city had a large black working class, many of them unionized, yet they had little power. The KKK had bombed people's homes and even castrated a black man as he walked down the street, with no legal consequences. On April 23, William Moore, a white postal service worker from Baltimore nicknamed the "Freedom Walker," was shot to death as he tried to demonstrate support for the civil rights movement by walking down an Alabama highway with a sign supporting black civil rights.

Jailed for leading protests in this frightening setting, King wrote his powerful "Letter from Birmingham Jail." It was a classic explanation of nonviolent refusal, addressed to clergymen who called the movement's demonstrations ill timed and ill advised. King explained the four steps of nonviolent resistance—research, negotiation, self-purification in nonviolent principles, and then, when nothing else worked, direct action—to confront the source of oppression. King explained, "The purpose of our direct-action program is to create a situation so crisis-packed that it will inevitably open the door to negotiation." In his letter, written on the margins of newspapers and on toilet paper and smuggled out of the jail in pieces, King called on white clergy to join him in opposition to segregation and the violence unleashed on demonstrators by Police Commissioner Bull Connor, who claimed the movement was a communist plot. King also called on ministers to identify with the movement as a protest for justice that affected everyone and to likewise recognize the worldwide revolution against injustice taking place across the colonized, colored world of Asia, Africa, and South America.

King's succinct phrase "Injustice anywhere is a threat to justice everywhere" would be repeated by later generations, including the Black Lives Matter movement. From Birmingham City Jail, King held to the position that noncooperation with evil laws required breaking them and paying the price through redemptive suffering. King and a nonviolent army of high school student demonstrators filled the jails and pursued an economic boycott of downtown businesses. On May 7, cameras and newsreels picked up brutal images as Bull Connor unleashed fire hoses and attack dogs on teenagers.

Black workers in steel and related industries could not risk arrest and lose their jobs, but many of their children marched. As oral-history interviews demonstrate, informal black working-class networks supported efforts on the job, in the courts, and in direct action by younger people to bring down all the barriers of Jim Crow.

Tragically, however, many working-class and union whites went over to the KKK and even to the ferociously antiunion White Citizens' Councils and John Birch Society. Not only in Birmingham but across the union spectrum "divided we stand" often supplanted the labor–civil rights solidarity King promoted. This split in the working class forced black civil rights movements to operate without the support of white union members at the local level, even as national unions put up tens of thousands of dollars in bail money to get protesters out of jail. Only a near-riot among inner-city blacks caused an extremely reluctant President Kennedy to send in federal marshals and force white businesspeople to settle the conflict. But the 1963 movement in Birmingham did not lead to the kind of conciliation King hoped for as a fourth step in campaigns of nonviolent direct action. Instead, "white voters flocked to the Republican party, which promised solutions to all social problems in the free market," as historian David Montgomery wrote. "The dynamiting of homes and churches in Birmingham was replaced by the blasting of a highway route through the Red mountain so that white residents could move to new suburbs."

However, responding to movement pressures, on June 11, 1963, President Kennedy proposed a limited civil rights act to guarantee equal protection of the laws to all citizens under the protection of the Fourteenth Amendment. The next day, in Jackson, Mississippi, an assassin killed NAACP leader Medgar Evers in his driveway. Despite such repression, demonstrations and sit-ins accelerated and swept through some eight hundred southern cities and into the North. In Homewood, Pennsylvania, and other places local people picketed and put pressure on companies that did not hire black workers or refused to open up skilled jobs to them.

Meanwhile, King, Randolph, Rustin, and black working-class

and union organizers merged their demands. In 1961, the Negro American Labor Council had proposed a mass demonstration outside of AFL-CIO headquarters in Washington, D.C., to protest its failure to implement strong civil rights policies. Now black labor activists turned this protest of AFL-CIO policies into a much broader march to support both economic and civil rights. A flyer promoting the march warned, "TOKENISM IS DEAD. The Negro is the Last Employed and the First De-employed." And it also warned of the danger to white workers: "THROUGH AUTOMATION WHITE AND BLACK LABOR IS EQUALLY ENDANGERED."

But before Washington came Detroit.

On June 23, 1963, twelve days after the murder of Medgar Evers, labor and civil rights joined forces. The UAW had supported the Montgomery bus boycott, provided bail money to get freedom riders and Birmingham freedom fighters out of jail, and according to one estimate ultimately donated $100,000 to SCLC. King and Walter Reuther had formed a strong alliance, and led a massive march of 125,000 through the streets of a then-prosperous Detroit. The march produced powerful feelings of fellowship that shaped people for the rest of their lives. In Detroit, King spoke directly to the urban North, saying, "I have a dream this afternoon that one day, right here in Detroit, Negroes will be able to buy a house or rent a house anywhere that their money will carry them and they will be able to get a job."

King unabashedly called on marchers "to engage in that something called love," not by asking oppressed people to love their oppressor but rather by adopting the ideology and practice of nonviolent direct action. Speaking of agape love, King's expansive ideology aimed not just to help one group, be they workers or oppressed African Americans. Rather, he said, "I'm talking about a sort of understanding, creating redemptive goodwill" for all people. King exulted that someday everyone would be able to say together, in the words of a spiritual from slavery days, "Free at last! Free at last! Thank God Almighty, we are free at last." King used this now-famous invocation in a number of speeches, but in 1963 it came directly out of his hopes for a labor and civil rights majority coalition that would change the nation and end America's apartheid both at work and in the whole society.

The Kennedy administration had tried to persuade King and his associates not to organize a march on Washington, but when the president realized that the movement would go ahead no matter what he said, he tried to line it up with a demand for a moderate civil rights bill. King came to the nation's capital to confer with the president on July 22, 1963. While discussing the proposed March on Washington with King, the president took him into the White House rose garden. Perhaps, Kennedy feared that the FBI had tapped his office. In a confidential tone, the president insisted that King disassociate himself from Stanley Levison, whose knowledge and advice proved invaluable to King, especially in regard to writing and arranging his labor speeches. King was taken aback and made no promises.

President Kennedy also asked him to distance himself from Hunter Pitts O'Dell, who King was planning to promote to executive director of SCLC. As it turned out, King had already been forced to change his mind but had not made it public. Prior to King's meeting with Kennedy, the FBI had released files to southern newspapers to "expose" O'Dell as a communist. The negative publicity had the intended effect. In a letter to O'Dell even before he met with the president, King wrote, "The situation in our country is such . . . that any allusion to the left brings forth an emotional response which would seem to indicate that SCLC and the southern freedom movement are Communist inspired. In these critical times we cannot afford to risk such impressions." Along with King's letter was an SCLC statement against the "ethical relativism," "metaphysical materialism," and "crippling totalitarianism" of communism.

However, O'Dell had quit the Communist Party around 1958, and both King and the FBI knew it. In a letter to King, O'Dell explained his journey as a merchant mariner and member of the National Maritime Union (a Communist-led union) during the war, as a volunteer organizer in Operation Dixie, and then as a civil rights organizer in the 1950s. O'Dell wrote to King that his ancestors had been slaves on the Hunter Plantation in Louisiana, and he would like "to finish the job of emancipation" through full-time work for King. He denounced "the big lie technique" of Hoover, and said he left the CP because he thought the civil rights movement now was the best means to advance the cause of black freedom.

O'Dell brought invaluable organizing experience as a working-class intellectual and activist. Nonetheless, the NMU had expelled him when it turned anticommunist after the war, and HUAC questioned him in two separate hearings, where he denounced it as a tool of segregationists. O'Dell actually had views not too different from King's, seeing slavery and racism as part of American capitalism's search for profits based on dividing the working class. King believed neither Levison nor O'Dell belonged to the CP, and he also believed in civil liberties, but he could not go against the president. King broke his formal ties with both men. Letting go of O'Dell, he said, was a painful experience. He would still communicate with Levison through other people, and increasingly relied upon him after President Kennedy died. O'Dell remained an important supporter of King and went on to edit *Freedomways*, a theoretical journal of the freedom movement, to teach at Antioch School of Law in the District of Columbia, and to advise Jesse Jackson and others on strategy and politics.

On August 28, 1963, a month after Detroit, the "March on Washington for Jobs and Freedom" brought to fruition the vision of A. Philip Randolph back in 1941, when he had proposed such a march in order to open up jobs for blacks in defense industries. Historian William Jones documents how women and men since the 1940s had put together a labor-based campaign to create the mass interracial coalition of labor, civic, religious, and civil rights movement groups that ultimately brought together a quarter of a million participants in 1963. Malcolm X decried it as "the farce on Washington" because organizers made a strategic decision not to disrupt the nation's capital. Randolph persuaded SNCC leader John Lewis to temper his rhetoric and the criticisms of Kennedy's bill he had intended to make from the podium. Randolph laid out specific demands long sought by black workers and, Jones summarized, the rally "linked struggles for racial and economic justice more effectively than any other mobilization in the postwar era." Although the AFL-CIO did not endorse the march, King's allies in the UAW, 1199, Distributive Workers, and other unions brought tens of thousands of workers to the march carrying signs demanding both jobs and freedom.

The March on Washington provided a great and hopeful moment in American history. King's speech has been written about and viewed millions of times, and rightly so. It is important to remember that King began by reminding the nation that in 1863 the country had emancipated the slaves, but one hundred years later African Americans were still not free. Befitting the purposes of a march for "Jobs and Freedom," King began with the economic dimension, indicting a prosperous nation for leaving African Americans stranded "on a lonely island of poverty in the midst of a vast ocean of material prosperity," and saying the country had given a "bad check"—the promise of freedom—to the sons and daughters of former slaves. In a far shorter version of the speech than the one he had previewed in Detroit, with his soaring rhetoric at the end of the speech King opened the minds of millions of white Americans. King reinforced the idea that "all men are created equal" as integral to the American dream for men and women alike, and helped people to commit themselves to make freedom real.

The march culminated the civil rights–labor alliance, with thousands of trade unionists brought to the march by unions from industrial and urban centers across the country. In October, Distributive Workers District 65 and other unions put together a massive labor-based rally in New York City's Madison Square Garden to raise thousands of dollars for the civil rights movement. The labor–civil rights alliance established at the march in the next two years succeeded in pressuring Congress to pass the most important civil rights laws since Reconstruction.

The great blot on the history of the march is that only one woman, activist leader Daisy Bates of Little Rock, spoke, briefly, as part of a tribute to Rosa Parks and other women who had fought for equal rights. No women's names were on the call to the gathering, and they were almost entirely absent from the podium, despite the key role of women labor activists in initiating and organizing the march. "That's how chauvinistic the leadership was at that time," wrote Coretta Scott King. She ruefully recalled that the men organizing the event would not even allow her to march in the front line with King. Nor did she get to go with King afterward to meet and thank President Kennedy, whom she had spoken to on the phone in 1960 to get her husband out of jail.

Through mass media coverage, the March on Washington reached into the homes of millions of Americans, linking the promise of economic justice and equal rights for working people to the American creed of individual freedom. Even Charlton Heston, who later became an icon of the National Rifle Association, appeared at the march with many other Hollywood celebrities. But only three weeks later, on September 15, white supremacists linked to the KKK bombed the 16th Street Baptist Church, the gathering place for the Birmingham children's crusade. The murder of black teenagers Addie Mae Collins, Carol Denise McNair, Cynthia Diane Wesley, and Carole Robertson reminded everyone of continuing violent white resistance and the suffering borne by civil rights advocates. It weighed heavily on movement organizers and especially King, who had approved bringing teenagers out of school to stand up to police dogs and water hoses. Wrote Coretta Scott King, "What could be more evil than bombing children in church on a Sunday morning?"

In a eulogy at the church on September 18, 1963, Dr. King declared, "we must be concerned not merely about who murdered them, but about the system, the way of life, the philosophy which produced the murderers." Even in this dark moment, he called on people to believe that, among our "white brothers," even "the most misguided among them can learn to respect the dignity and the worth of all human personality." A month later, November 22, 1963, in Dallas, a city fraught with a poisonous climate fostered by right-wing hate for the president and his civil rights bill, an assassin shot and killed Kennedy. Watching the story unfold on television, King told Coretta, "This is exactly what's going to happen to me. I keep telling you, this is a sick society." Coretta attended Kennedy's funeral and thought, "If they could kill a president, what did that say about Martin's chances for survival in America?"

Before the country could even begin to grieve for the dead president, nightclub owner Jack Ruby stepped in front of police escorting alleged Kennedy killer Lee Harvey Oswald to jail and shot him to death. With witnesses claiming to see evidence of a second shooter in the Kennedy assassination, a deeply unsettled country would doubt who killed the president and why. Meanwhile, King's prophetic calls for peace, for economic justice, and for racial equality kept him on the "enemies list" of FBI director J. Edgar Hoover. King's season of suffering for economic justice and equal rights had only just begun.

King and a photo of Mohandas Gandhi in his Southern Christian
Leadership Conference office in Atlanta, 1966.

Chapter 3

"NORTHERN GHETTOS ARE THE PRISONS OF FORGOTTEN MEN"

Labor and Civil Rights at the Crossroads, 1964–1966

> *I have the audacity to believe that peoples every-*
> *where can have three meals a day for their bodies,*
> *education for their minds, and dignity, equality,*
> *and freedom for their spirits.*

—KING NOBEL PEACE PRIZE SPEECH,
OSLO, NORWAY, DECEMBER 10, 1964

ON JANUARY 3, 1964, *TIME* ONCE AGAIN PUT MARTIN Luther King on its cover, naming him "Man of the Year." The magazine lauded 1963 as a transformational year, as schools desegregated, some previously closed job opportunities and apprenticeships opened for some blacks, and the mass media finally began to feature African Americans. *Time* noted, "The most striking aspect of the revolt, however, is the change in Negroes themselves." More black people were more sure of themselves, and less afraid. King, who traveled 275,000 miles and gave over 350 speeches in 1963, had faced down death threats and inspired the nation while living in modest circumstances and sleeping about four hours each night, according to the article. It concluded, "After 1963, with the help of Martin Luther King, Jr., the Negro will never again be where he was."

This kind of admiration for King only convinced J. Edgar Hoover that King's subversion had to be exposed. On January 5–7 the FBI placed microphone surveillance on King's room at the Willard Hotel in Washington, D.C. At least fourteen more times between January 1964 and November 1965, the FBI placed "bugs" in rooms occupied by King and his entourage.

After President Kennedy's death, Hoover continued to feed poisonous lies to President Johnson and the media about King and his supposedly communist associates. In 1965 a congressional committee led by a powerful segregationist planned to investigate Hoover's claims that King was a secret communist. Fearing his "counterintelligence" would be exposed by hearings, Hoover stopped the wiretaps on King's home and office. But the FBI continued to wiretap Stanley Levison, attorney Clarence Jones, and others who worked with King. The FBI's continual campaign of harassment and intimidation against King ranks as one of the most sordid and unconstitutional uses of governmental power against one individual in American history.

In 1964 FBI harassment proved minor compared to the violence visited upon movement organizers. In March through June, King undertook desegregation marches through the old slave quarter in St. Augustine, Florida, with marchers suffering attacks by white vigilantes and police using whips and tire irons. Dorothy Cotton recalled with horror how racists poured acid into a swimming pool when protesters tried to "integrate" it. King's June 11 imprisonment there produced no intervention by the federal government. In July, as King published *Why We Can't Wait,* on the urgency of the civil rights movement, SCLC went into Mississippi to support SNCC's Freedom Summer voter registration campaign.

On June 21, 1964, nine white men, including the Neshoba County sheriff, kidnapped northern white volunteers Andrew Goodman and Michael Schwerner and black Mississippian James Chaney from a jail and beat them to death. Finally taking some action to enforce the law in the South, the FBI undertook an investigation and found their bodies buried in an earthen dam two months later. Mississippi refused to prosecute, and it would be years before the federal government could put anyone in jail for this brutal crime. In the last

week of July, King also lobbied on behalf of the Mississippi Freedom Democratic Party (MFDP) in its effort to replace the state's
white segregationists at the Democratic Party national convention.
That ended with Walter Reuther pressuring King to pressure the
MFDP to accept two seats at the convention, even as the all-white
Mississippi "regulars" walked out. Fannie Lou Hamer famously
rejected compromise, saying "We didn't come all this way for
no two seats." The labor–civil rights alliance between Reuther
and King did not look good to SNCC organizers, who saw it as
a sellout. SNCC remained alienated from the Democratic Party,
but some in the MFDP went on to elect blacks to office in Mississippi. Hamer organized the Mississippi Freedom Labor Union, but
mechanization continued to destroy efforts to raise wages for agricultural workers.

Despite such setbacks, the summer of 1964 showed promise for the
civil rights–labor coalition. Powerful combined lobbying by the
AFL-CIO and the civil rights movement helped Johnson to defeat
a long filibuster of southern Democrats and northern Republicans.
After President Johnson got some moderate Republicans to sign on
to the legislation, on July 2 Congress passed the Civil Rights Act.
It banned segregation in all public accommodations and made
employment discrimination based on race, national origin, or gender illegal. Through Title VII, women and workers of color could
now sue employers and unions alike for excluding them from union
apprenticeships, for perpetuating color-coded wage and departmental discrimination in factories, and for keeping them out of better
jobs. This change in the law had profound effects on the workplace.

The new law opened up decades of direct action and litigation by
workers of color and women. Black workers in places like Memphis
challenged "whites only" job classifications and entered skilled and
semiskilled jobs, as did black workers across the South in the rubber, textile, and other industries in record numbers. They experienced violent resistance from white workers and marauding racists.
On February 28, 1967, Klansmen would use a car bomb to murder
Wharlest Jackson, a military veteran and treasurer of his NAACP

branch, after he obtained a semiskilled job in the Armstrong Tire plant in Natchez, Mississippi. Despite such violence against black workers who tried to get better jobs, the civil rights "revolution" would have a major impact in reshaping the demographics of the workplace.

Just as some economic progress began, President Johnson, persuaded that military intervention around the world was necessary to stop countries "falling like dominoes" to presumed Soviet domination, increasingly intervened in the worsening military conflict in Vietnam. A constant escalation of bombing and troop deployments over the next few years would lead to nearly 500,000 American troops in Vietnam by 1967, to millions of deaths, and to a massive diversion of attention and money from civil rights and economic justice concerns.

The full scope of this tragic move was not apparent in November 1964, however. President Johnson overwhelmingly won reelection with 61 percent of the vote, defeating Republican Barry Goldwater, who opposed the Civil Rights Act and all federal efforts on behalf of the poor as an encroachment on individualism and free enterprise. Before 1964, segregationist southern Democrats had controlled Congress, but many civil rights and labor-backed Democrats as well as moderate Republicans now came into power. Together they enacted a whirlwind of progressive legislation, including increased social security benefits, and Medicare and Medicaid that guaranteed older and poorer people would not die for lack of health insurance.

In January 1965, in his State of the Union address, Johnson called for a "War on Poverty." Michael Harrington's book *The Other America* (1962) had publicized the desperate plight of millions of poor people in a supposedly affluent society. In a later speech at Howard University, Johnson proclaimed that "freedom is not enough." The president called not just for equal opportunity in the law, but for some measure of equal results. This remarkable shift in public policy and rhetoric could be traced to the rising power of civil rights and the labor movements at the grass roots and in the halls of Congress. King optimistically believed that "Goldwaterism" had been defeated and that the trajectory of history favored greater equality and human rights throughout the world. Ominously, however, white voters in four southern states, where most black people could not vote, switched from Democrat to Republican in the presidential election in opposition to civil rights gains. This realignment of white southern voters was just what President Johnson feared.

In the aftermath of the passage of the Civil Rights Act and the 1964 elections, an exhausted King, lying in an Atlanta hospital bed, learned that he had won the Nobel Peace Prize. On November 18, a countervailing pressure came from FBI director Hoover. Incensed that a black man whom he despised would get world recognition, Hoover publicly denounced King as "the most notorious liar in America." Nobody knew what he meant. On December 2, King went to Washington to try to talk with Hoover and defuse his personal animus. Instead, Hoover lectured King on the merits of the FBI and avoided any discussion of the issues between them. But he had already launched a surreptitious program to destroy King's personal life and national reputation.

On December 10, 1964, King accepted the Nobel Peace Prize in Oslo, Norway. He called the award "a profound recognition that nonviolence is the answer to the crucial political and moral problems of our time: the need to overcome oppression and violence without resorting to violence and oppression." Nonviolence provided a viable "method which rejects, revenge, aggression and retaliation" based on a foundation of love. King now broadened his public agenda from civil rights to human rights, to peace, and to end poverty. He donated his $54,000 award to American civil rights groups. The Nobel award raised his spirits immensely. He and his family and some staff all went to the ceremony (Coretta and her husband flew separately, as a safety measure to protect their four children if something happened to one of them). The prize was a joy, but it also raised a challenge: King now had the mantle of a peace and human rights world leader, and he would have to live up to it.

* * *

ON HIS WAY home from Oslo, large crowds in New York City showered praise and a ticker-tape parade on King. King and his staff had already planned a voting rights campaign. When President Johnson invited him to stop at the White House on his way back to Atlanta, King pressed him to introduce new legislation to guarantee voting rights. The Civil Rights Act had already cost him the votes of many white southerners, and Johnson did not want to alienate white southern Democrats in Congress whose votes he needed to pass his antipoverty programs.

The day after King got home to Atlanta, he went out on the picket line with some seven hundred black women, wearing a sign around his neck that read, "Scripto employees are on strike for a living wage." His companion, preacher-organizer Ralph David Abernathy, wore a sign proclaiming, "We Wont be Slaves No More." Scripto's sprawling pen-and-pencil factory was located only two blocks from Ebenezer Church. Most of its women production-line workers lived in the neighborhood and many of them went to King's church. The Scripto strike tested his idea that labor and civil rights forces could work together to obtain a greater share of economic justice for workers. The strike and related events and situations also demonstrated the complications of a labor–civil rights coalition.

Scripto and its white president, James Carmichael, had led Atlanta's civic and political life for years, and claimed Scripto was a boon to black workers. In 1964, this factory employed black women who would otherwise be consigned to jobs as domestic, laundry, and service workers under worse conditions and with poorer wages. However, the company always remained entangled with the South's racial and economic injustices. It had been the site of the notorious lynching of a Jewish plant manager named Leo Frank, and it had always profited from the low wages of blacks. In the 1930s the Scripto company violated the New Deal National Recovery Administration's minimum wage code, paying black women workers between six cents and thirteen cents an hour, arguing that it was doing a favor to women who might otherwise have to do lower-paid domestic work.

Through speed-up and overwork, the company received multiple awards for high levels of production by its black women workers during World War II, but then those workers organized a union. In October 1946 they went on a strike that lasted into the Christmas season, but in the face of a determined antiunion employer they lost the strike and their union. Eighteen years later, black women replayed that struggle. They now made $1.25 an hour, a total of about $2,600 a year before deductions, when the commonly estimated national poverty level for a family wage earner was $3,000. At far better wages, the company employed 117 skilled and semi-skilled male workers, all of them white except for six black men. It insisted that undereducated black women could not do these better-paid skilled and semiskilled jobs.

As the freedom movement exploded across the South, in late 1962 a black Baptist minister named James Hampton had arrived as an organizer for the International Chemical Workers Union (ICWU), building support among black churches. A year later, boosted by supporters in the church and community, a majority of the women turned in cards calling for a union. Scripto appealed that election to the National Labor Relations Board (NLRB) and the company's President Carmichael gave a speech to a captive audience of workers, calling "a vote for the union a slap in the face of one of the truest friends the Negro ever had in Georgia." The company objected to the NLRB that the union had unfairly enlisted support from the civil rights movement.

Indeed, civil rights unionism had flared up everywhere in the wake of the 1963 Birmingham desegregation campaign. At Scripto, black women like M. L. Spearman and Emma Love saw no reason to hold back. Rosella Jackson had lied about her age to get a job at Scripto because it paid better than her previous laundry work. On September 27, 1963, a week after the KKK's infamous Birmingham church bombing, these women voted for a union. A total of 519 Scripto workers voted for the union, with 428 against.

The NLRB required the company to respond, but Scripto stalled and made a charade of collective bargaining. Under the state's right-to-work law, the company's skilled workers knew they could benefit from any gains made by the union without having to pay dues or cooperate with black women workers. That was the point: the "right to work" kept workers divided.

In the fall of 1964 the women lost patience. Jerry Levine, a Brooklyn native and the union's new organizer in Atlanta, told the women they had no strike fund and would lose a Christmas bonus if they struck. Levine pleaded with them to hold off, but, like the Memphis sanitation strikers in 1968, they followed their own leadership. On Thanksgiving Day 1964 they voted to strike, hand-lettered strike signs, and walked off the job the next day. Large numbers turned out for rallies, and women walked the picket line for weeks to come.

Scripto resisted a check-off system that would allow the union to collect dues from worker paychecks—the same issue that would stall the Memphis sanitation strike in 1968. Scripto fired 155 of the strikers and operated the plant with a skeleton crew of nonunion workers ("scabs"). It offered a two-cent wage increase to black women classified as unskilled, and a four-cent increase for white male workers and six black men classified as skilled. Black women workers saw this wage differential as an insulting form of discrimination. One of them told the Atlanta *Daily World*, a black-owned newspaper, that the strike represented "a struggle for human dignity."

SNCC chairman John Lewis, located in Atlanta, wrote to the General Services Administration asking them to review the Scripto Company's two federal contracts. The only reason the company could outbid others for federal contracts, he wrote, "is because of the low wages they pay their colored employees." Lewis also wrote to the union, "Scripto has been allowed to perpetrate virtual economic slavery and poor working conditions for such a long time." King wrote the company a letter threatening a national boycott of its products if Scripto did not settle with the workers. As soon as King got involved, national media such as the *New York Times*, the

Washington Post, and the *Wall Street Journal* covered the strike. On December 17, after King had returned from Oslo, he told a reporter, "We have decided that now is the time to identify our movement very closely with organized labor."

SCLC's director of branches Rev. C. T. Vivian enlisted himself as a strong ally of the women workers. SCLC and the union distributed half a million leaflets calling for people to boycott Scripto products. Under Taft-Hartley, unions could not engage in a secondary boycott in support of other workers, but as a nonbargaining agent SCLC had no such limitations. Vivian walked on picket lines throughout the six-week strike. He told the workers, "Labor cannot have what it wants in America until the Negroes have what they want in America. Let us see here in Atlanta that this is not just a protest but a movement." Daddy King also supported the strikers.

In a 1997 interview, Rev. Vivian told me that he had worked in a factory in his hometown of Peoria, Illinois, and learned about unions through a pamphlet handed out by the United Packinghouse Workers Union. Vivian said unions would only succeed in the South if they frankly confronted the racism of white union members, as the UPWA did. "We depended on labor to deliver for us and it didn't happen," he recalled, and yet unions still provided "one of the only allies that black people really had, and one of the only ones that needed us as much as we needed them." Vivian saw the Scripto strike as a means to promote civil rights unionism, which Vivian would go on to promote in Chicago.

King had spoken at union conventions, met top union leaders, and raised thousands of dollars from unions, and he now walked a union picket line. The week before Christmas, at Ebenezer Church, King spoke to 250 strikers and community supporters. "Along with the struggle to desegregate we must engage in the struggle for better jobs," he said, and "the same system that exploits the Negro exploits the poor white man." However, the plant's white men and six black men in skilled employment refused to strike. Scripto claimed black women did not know how to do these jobs. King told the cheering crowd, "Negroes can learn to do anything a white man can learn. It was our hands that built up this southland and made cotton King. . . . It's all right to talk about milk and honey 'over there' but we need food down here." He finished his talk with a call for a world boycott of Scripto products.

Fortunately, as happened later in the Memphis sanitation strike, the Atlanta AFL-CIO's white union leaders gave financial and moral support to the strikers. But, also as in Memphis, many white union members proved uninterested or hostile. A possible black church split also emerged when workers claimed that one of the city's leading black ministers, William Holmes Borders, who had a close personal relationship with Scripto's James Carmichael, had brought strikebreakers into the plant.

Despite such schisms, on the picket line and in church gatherings workers shared labor and civil rights songs such as "We Shall Not Be Moved" and "We Shall Overcome." But by Christmas Eve, the workers lacked food and presents for their children. They had grown weary of the constant cold and miserable rain on the picket line. Scripto, however, knew it was getting a bad name. A new manager for the company, a northerner, decided to end the strike, and violated NLRB rules to do it. He ignored the union representatives and instead began meeting privately with Dr. King, excluding organizer Jerry Levine.

King had invested himself in this struggle. Suffering from depression and anxiety during the strike, King left his home one night and went off by himself. No one knew where he was. His mother feared something had happened to him and asked a black police officer who had been King's childhood friend to find him. The man located King outside the Scripto plant, waiting for workers to come out at shift change so he could speak to them. Associated Press reporter Kathryn Johnson later recalled King picketing the plant on a cold night and then inviting her into his home, where Coretta and Martin hosted her for coffee until 1:00 a.m. She thought King's "ability to put into words the longings, the hopes and dreams of his people" helped the strikers win.

She also remembered that someone had burned a cross on the King family's front lawn. When a story on the Scripto strike came on the television, her mother spotted Kathryn walking alongside

King. Johnson wrote that her mother warned her, "Honey, be careful. I'm afraid someone's going to try to kill him." Johnson reflected that "at this time, King was either admired or hated."

King's distress and exhaustion were partly thanks to the FBI. On January 5, 1965, the Kings discovered an unusual package in the mail. William Sullivan, Hoover's agent in charge of ruining King, had sent a tape recording of King and friends partying at the Willard Hotel in Washington, D.C., with an anonymous note suggesting King should kill himself or be exposed for supposed extramarital affairs. The Kings listened to it together, and Coretta said the tape proved nothing. King and his staff also listened to it and realized the FBI was recording his every act. FBI pressure became a source of tremendous anxiety. King concluded, "They are out to break me."

Meanwhile, Atlanta union lawyer Joe Jacobs had taken over Scripto negotiations, and on January 9, 1964, the strike ended. Both skilled and unskilled workers received a four-cents-an-hour wage increase each year for the next three years, and the company rehired strikers it had fired. Workers who refused to pay union dues or strike now got the same wage increases as the women who had won the strike by paying dues and holding out in the cold for six weeks. The company pledged to open up skilled jobs to more black workers, while SCLC promised to publicize Scripto's good work and call off its boycott.

Some white business leaders in Atlanta were incensed. Though some of them accepted that King had become world-famous, they did not expect him to challenge one of the city's major employers and the city's long-time public servant James Carmichael. An event to recognize King for his Nobel Prize was now in doubt. The KKK denounced King, and white merchant Lester Maddox put ads in the newspaper airing his openly racist views: "And thanks to Scripto for not surrendering your plant to the Communist inspired racial agitators. . . . All Americans are going to lose unless the Communists and racial agitators are stopped and stopped soon." Subsequently elected as Georgia's governor, Maddox became infamous for brandishing axe handles and threatening to beat civil rights demonstrators. He referred acidly to King as the "Great Black Father."

Dorothy Cotton wrote that many white leaders did not want to ever honor a black man. Yet the city's business and civic leaders held a successful banquet honoring King. And for a moment, the civil rights unionism of black women in Atlanta triumphed. As did the civil rights unionists of the 1940s, black workers voted in NLRB elections even when their voting rights remained restricted in southern society. Speaking to the National Maritime Union in 1962, King had called the secret ballot "our secret weapon" to stamp out segregation. Workers at Scripto had won their rights (and started a scholarship for Atlanta students in King's name after his death), but they ultimately lost out to the demands of global, corporate capitalism when the company moved away and a Japanese company took it over. On King's birthday in 1996, the National Park Service purchased the old Scripto property, ruined by decades of the company's environmental pollution in a neighborhood bereft of industrial jobs. The property became part of the King Center for Nonviolent Social Change, honoring King's legacy.

* * *

IN JANUARY 1965 both SNCC and SCLC, although using different organizing strategies, sought to complete the first phase of the civil rights revolution by demanding federal implementation of the right to vote granted by the Fifteenth Amendment after the Civil War. The Supreme Court had already overturned the poll tax, which charged people a continually accumulating fee to vote, and the "white primary," which excluded black people from the primary of the whites-only Democratic Party, then defined as a private entity. African Americans voted in some places in the South, but in Alabama and Mississippi and most of the region, racist registrars and violent police prevented blacks from voting.

In the first week of February, at a time when President Johnson began relentless bombing of North Vietnam and U.S. troop expansion, King ended up in jail in Selma for protesting voter suppression.

Malcolm X gave a speech in Selma criticizing civil rights leadership as not militant enough, but privately told Coretta Scott King that he fully supported her husband's voting-rights campaign. "If the white people realize what the alternative is," he told her, "perhaps they will be more willing to listen to Dr. King." Many people observed Malcolm X moving increasingly toward political action and coalition-building, while King moved increasingly toward a stronger critique of the American system. Activists hoped for an alliance between them. King pointed out more than once, however, that the two men radically differed on the role of self-defense versus nonviolence in social movements.

The Selma campaign brought out other contradictions in the movement. SNCC members campaigned through grassroots organizing. They were "a lot like members of the early Christian church, going out with virtually nothing but the clothes on our backs to bring the Gospel of Freedom to the people," SNCC chairman John Lewis recalled. They relied on local people to house them and to take leadership for themselves. Many SNCC members did not welcome King's preacher-led mobilizing strategy in Selma. But whatever method activists used, white southerners responded violently. As in Mississippi during Freedom Summer, activists in Alabama suffered a reign of terror. Economic justice seemed far out of reach without first getting civil and voting rights, but getting those rights cost many lives and left a legacy of post-traumatic stress for many victims of white supremacist violence.

"For blacks, Selma was rock bottom," wrote Coretta King, "a place where words such as *democracy, representative government,* and *citizenship* had no meaning." On February 18, in her hometown of Marion, Alabama, state troopers attacked marchers and police murdered young military veteran Jimmie Lee Jackson when he tried to protect his mother from a violent police officer. Jackson's aunt had been one of Coretta's best friends in high school. It was a fraught time. On February 20, assassins shot Malcolm X to death in Harlem, eliminating one of the era's great advocates for African-American solidarity and for racial and economic justice in the world.

SCLC's James Bevel proposed a march from Selma to Montgomery to protest Jimmie Lee Jackson's murder. King and SCLC supported it and SNCC did not. John Lewis went to the front of the line anyway as marchers tried to cross the Edmund Pettus Bridge. On March 7, before the march could even begin, police and state troopers viciously clubbed him on the head and attacked the marchers with whips and on horseback, in beatings publicized through the mass media all over the world. King led another march but turned marchers around at the bridge, waiting for a federal court judge to rule on behalf of their right to march without police interference. In the meantime, local whites clubbed white Unitarian minister James Reeb of Boston to death in downtown Selma, setting off a national outcry, including a protest from President Johnson, in a way Jimmie Lee Jackson's death had not. With court approval and state trooper protection, the epochal march from Selma to Montgomery took place March 22–25. In a huge rally at the end of the march in Montgomery, King cited the ways society's economic elites had used racial division to separate poor whites and blacks, who could be allies and had everything to gain by joining together to build a "society of plenty where greed and poverty would be done away." The American Dream would culminate, he said, in a "March on Poverty" that would leave no one behind. "We must come to see that the end we seek is a society at peace with itself, a society that can live with its conscience. And that will be a day not of the white man, not of the black man. That will be the day of man as man!"

After the march, KKK members shot to death Viola Liuzzo and wounded her nineteen-year-old African-America rider Leroy Moten. FBI informer Gary Thomas Rowe sat in the car of Klan nightriders and may have even pulled the trigger himself. A white woman born in Georgia who rebelled against racism, the working-class wife of an Italian-American Teamster union organizer in Detroit, Liuzzo had driven alone to Selma, determined to support the movement. King and top government officials attended Liuzzo's funeral in Detroit, and Teamster president Jimmy Hoffa later shook hands with King and donated $25,000 to the movement. But white violence only escalated after the Selma-to-Montgomery march. In "Bloody Lowndes County," a police "volunteer" killed white seminarian and SNCC worker Jonathan Daniels with a shotgun blast. The killers of Jimmie Lee Jackson, Daniels, Reeb, and Liuzzo all went free. The UAW sent nearly three thousand dollars collected at plant gates on behalf of Jackson's family and the movement. Twenty people (that we know of) died in civil rights protests in 1965; fourteen in 1964; thirteen in 1963. "Securing the right to vote was a blood covenant, a right won and sealed by the deaths of men and women, whites and blacks, whose blood spilled onto Alabama soil," wrote Coretta Scott King.

* * *

THE SELMA-TO-MONTGOMERY MARCH marked the high tide of what Bayard Rustin and King called the politics of "convergence" between unions and the civil rights movement. King had written to UAW president Walter Reuther suggesting that SCLC activists should be trained as union organizers in the antiunion South. King and Reuther regularly corresponded and tried to make alliances. In June 1964 George Meany thanked King for helping to mobilize black voters to defeat a right-to-work referendum in Oklahoma; King said "so-called right-to-work will rob us of our civil rights and job rights." King and Teamster president Jimmy Hoffa discussed alliances but could not cement them. But King regularly traveled to New York City to speak at union rallies and conventions, to give statements, and especially to collaborate with District 65 and 1199 unions. With their diverse memberships, King felt at home in these two unions and considered himself part of their union family. The labor–civil rights coalition seemed strong.

Yet union racial politics remained contradictory and complicated. As soon as King became well known, from 1957 onward, black workers in various places asked him to take up their cause against both employer and white worker union racism. In his hometown of Atlanta during the summer of 1963, leading up to the Scripto strike, black workers at Atlantic Steel sent King detailed complaints of racism in their United Steelworkers Local 2401. King sent written complaints on their behalf to both the federal government and the union hierarchy, prompting a letter of shock and outrage by United Steelworkers international president David McDonald. At Atlantic Steel, about 900 black workers, out of a total of 2,500 in the plant, remained shut out of skilled and semiskilled jobs. They were forced to use separate water fountains, bathrooms, locker rooms, and cafeterias. In this and other situations, black workers found the original appeal of interracial CIO industrial unions sadly lacking. They usually remained the strongest union supporters, but black workers criticized and increasingly challenged unions and battled for equal rights at the point of production.

King thus found himself appealing to international unions for funds and support while challenging these same unions to live up to their civil rights advocacy. In March 1964, at almost the same time that King thanked Transit Worker Union president Michael Quill for hosting him in a speech and donating to SCLC, black workers in that same union at Chicago's O'Hare Airport wrote to King protesting that the local TWU union was thoroughly racist and he should not cooperate with the union. And when King supported union organizing drives, he almost always ran into difficulties from employers or competing unions.

Nonetheless, many unions supported the Selma campaign, and the heroic dedication of organizers and community activists led to passage of the Voting Rights Act, signed into law by President Johnson on August 6, 1965. It abolished Jim Crow voter restrictions and Section 5 subjected states of the former Confederacy to Justice Department or federal court review whenever they adopted new voter laws. After 1965, African American and Latino voter registration shot up in the South—until 2013, when the U.S. Supreme Court nullified Section 5. Republican legislatures began imposing restrictions to shrink black and Latino voting once again, and mass incarceration disfranchised many of them.

Despite the triumph of the Voting Rights Act in the summer of 1965, countervailing forces, including the direction of American foreign policy, began to undermine the civil rights movement. In

April 1965, Johnson had sent Marines into the Dominican Republic to restore a dictatorial regime overturned by voters, as the United States solidified support for military regimes in Latin America. In July the president announced sending 50,000 more troops to Vietnam, for a total of 125,000. On August 12, at a mass rally in Birmingham, King called for negotiations to end the war, but pressure from the administration forced him to retract his proposal. The "convergence" between labor and civil rights interests that seemed so promising in the voting rights struggle began to turn into divergence as the AFL-CIO unions followed in lockstep with Johnson's anticommunist militarism and interventionism.

The politics of divergence also accelerated on August 11, only five days after President Johnson signed the Voting Rights Act. A conflagration in the Watts neighborhood of Los Angeles, the nation's third largest city, demonstrated how little dismal economic conditions outside of the South had been touched by the civil rights movement. Police violence and rumors triggered a virtual civil war between unemployed and underemployed young black men and white police and National Guard troops, who had most of the guns and all of the tanks. Six days of looting and burning of storefronts and homes led to the deaths of thirty-four people (all but one of them black) and $40 million in property damage.

King had thought the 1964 presidential election sidelined "Goldwaterism"—a call for low taxes, opposition to government programs for civil rights and economic justice, coupled with support for military spending increases and militant anticommunism. But the white reaction to the Los Angeles riots proved King's optimism wrong. Many white voters turned to the right, while the mayor, police chief, and many white residents blamed King, communists, and ghetto residents for the breakdown in "law and order." Almost alone among whites, UAW Western Region 6 representative Paul Schrade refused to blame ghetto residents. Speaking to a Governor's Commission, he said half a million residents of central LA lived near or below poverty level and had half the income and twice the unemployment of whites. Although 50,000 people worked in auto and aerospace and parts plants in the LA area, few blacks or Latinos had those jobs, and they would soon disappear for whites as well.

When King and Bayard Rustin made an emergency trip to Los Angeles, the severity of poverty and tensions between inner-city residents and the police brought them up abruptly against the limits of the civil rights movement. Young African Americans derided King, and white city officials practically ran him out of town. LA was only the tip of the iceberg. Schrade counted up to 43 percent of the nation's population as economically distressed, with 38 million in deep poverty. Whites made up a majority of the poor, but African Americans and Latinos remained disproportionately poor. Police brutality had touched off riots in New York and elsewhere in the summer of 1964, and now it looked as though riots would happen every summer. King, Randolph, Rustin, and others had been pointing out the link between poverty and racial problems for years, but Watts now placed resolving urban racial-economic injustices at the top of their list of priorities.

Black poor people had moved to the cities during the "Great Migration" from the 1920s through the 1950s, but most of them ended up trapped in old housing and bad schools, subject to police brutality, lacking good jobs, and in neighborhoods that became increasingly impoverished as whites fled. Now inner-city upheavals forced unions and civil rights organizations to reorient their racial-economic justice agendas. The UAW ultimately invested about one million dollars in a Reuther-initiated Citizen's Crusade Against Poverty. It proved to be a drop in the bucket of need, and like President Johnson's War on Poverty raised unanswered questions about whether poor people themselves would take the leadership. King would say the War on Poverty turned out to be "not even a skirmish," as Johnson increasingly diverted federal funds to war.

Behind the freedom struggle of black people loomed a larger problem. Black scholar Manning Marable aptly called it "the crisis of the black working class." The access of black workers, male and female, to industrial employment had increased dramatically in the 1940s, giving rise to a generally higher standard of living and longevity. Unionization powered much of this improvement, narrowing the wealth gap between African Americans and Latinos and Euro-Americans. But the Korean War in the early 1950s marked the last period of relatively low unemployment (4.4 percent) for black males. Black male income had averaged 37 percent of white males' income in 1939, 54 percent in 1947, and 62 percent in 1951, but by 1962 it had dropped back to 55 percent, about where it had been in 1945. In the early and mid-1960s, racial-economic inequality only increased.

White-collar employment in professional, technical, and clerical jobs provided the most rapid employment growth between 1959 and 1964, but those jobs remained largely reserved for white men and women. Most black women remained concentrated in domestic, laundry, restaurant, and other service work, although some of them now made gains in the lowest-paid white-collar work. Black men remained overwhelmingly concentrated in unskilled labor, a declining portion of the overall labor force. A growing divide emerged between employed black women and unemployed black men.

In the South, manufacturing employment had increased by 80 percent between 1940 and 1960, but employers after 1946 largely defeated unionization. They kept wages in the South lower than the rest of the country, attracting companies fleeing unionized work forces in the North. Industrial employers also "whitened" their work force, which also undermined unions. Whites proved less willing to organize unions than blacks, the strongest pro-union element. And increasingly black workers lost their place in the rural economy, with nowhere to go for better jobs. The percentage of cotton harvested by machines went from 5 percent in 1950 to 50 percent by 1960 and 95 percent by 1970, forcing farm laborers to flee to urban centers like Memphis or Atlanta to become the working or unemployed poor, or remain behind in unremitting rural poverty.

In the mid-1960s, even as the United States expanded voting rights and greater racial equality in the law, low wages and unemployment afflicted blacks at about three times the rate of whites. Many black families disintegrated. In the 1940s, factory employment and unionization had driven up black income relative to whites in the South, but in the South of the 1950s black income relative to whites went down by ten percentage points. The economist Charles Killingsworth wrote, "In the past decade changing technology and changing regional and industrial growth patterns have made opportunity far less equal for Negroes than it was a quarter century ago." Clarence Coe, a United Rubber Workers Union member at the Firestone factory in Memphis, kept his job, protected by union seniority. But younger and sometimes better-educated black workers by the 1960s could find no such employment security. Industrial growth in the South exceeded that in the North, yet new jobs were increasingly nonunion, suburban, and given to whites. Conditions like these drove forward the civil rights movement, the Black Power movement, and the ghetto rebellions. By undermining unions and paying black workers less, corporate leaders stole wealth from the black community; said Coe, "Those people have got some of my money in their pocket." By the time of the Watts riot, black economic fortunes, on average, had declined for ten years.

Something else in the mid-1960s drove discussions of civil rights and economic justice: Goldwaterism had fired up the "New Right." In the South, many whites switched from Democrat to Republican in the 1964 election. After that, the Republican Party began its march to southern dominance based on the politics of what the media called "white backlash."

Outside the South equally powerful racial polarization emerged. California voters in a 1964 referendum overturned a state open-housing law. Many whites opposed school desegregation and feared competition for jobs and housing by African Americans and Latinos. In Detroit, white homeowners increasingly voted their fears, while unions and workers lost the battle against mechanization, job loss, and deunionization. Within the UAW, black workers demanded a seat at the union table but whites still overwhelmingly dominated union offices and skilled and supervisory jobs. Walter Reuther provided strong support for King and the civil rights movement but kept power within his union based on a white male anticommunist element hostile to black power within the union. Only about 4 percent of black workers in the auto industry held skilled jobs, even while they made up about a quarter of the work force in Detroit auto factories. Based in part on internal contradictions, the "heyday of liberalism" under UAW banners of labor solidarity began to wane and a movement of black workers and radicals began to challenge Reuther and labor liberals.

After Watts, what King saw was a shift to the right by a variety of conservative, libertarian, segregationist, procorporate, and antiunion forces—the very thing he had warned the AFL-CIO about in 1961. On September 18, 1965, Andrew Young represented King's views at the District 65 union convention in New York City. "The explosion in Watts reminded us all that the northern ghettoes are the prisons of forgotten men," said Young. Citing a black unemployment rate of 34 percent (and much higher for young black men), Watts demonstrated the need for "a shift in the focus of struggle," one that "will not abate until the root causes are treated." Speaking before some of King's strongest labor friends, Young said unions had failed to provide enough support for civil rights in the South or for economic justice in the North.

On October 7, 1965, King urged the Illinois AFL-CIO to address the root cause of urban rebellions. He said civil rights "has profound moral appeal," while "labor is stagnating and receding as a social force." Further, he said, "Labor has been on the defensive for years," as its "moral appeal flickers instead of shining as it did in the thirties." The "destructive hurricane" of automation was "sweeping away jobs and work standards," leaving behind nearly forty million poor people. Black workers had "moved from a decent standard of living to an essentially impoverished condition . . . identical with or worse than the depression thirties." King predicted that "where there are millions of poor, organized labor cannot really be secure."

"Nothing will be done until the issues are raised so dramatically that our nation will act. This was the lesson of both Selma and Birmingham," said King. "It is not a constitutional right that men have jobs, but it is a human right." How could anyone resolve the problem?

White workers with union wages feared the loss of their jobs and home values. No one wanted to give up their tenuous hold on the middle class. The only solution, King and others on the labor left concluded, was to do something for all workers. In October 1966, a booklet called "A Freedom Budget for All Americans," with an introduction by King, was published by the A. Philip Randolph Institute, recently established with funding and support from the AFL-CIO, the Packinghouse Union, and others, with Bayard Rustin as its director. One hundred thousand copies were distributed. The "Freedom Budget" proposed a second New Deal to promote job growth at living wages through public spending on social goods. A "freedom budget," the Randolph Institute said, "would not subtract from the income of anyone," particularly whites, the largest demographic group among the poor. Rustin said social movements had so far failed to adequately coalesce around a class-based agenda to address the causes of both urban rebellions and the growing displacement of working-class people of all colors. A number of economists believed that economic growth would easily allow the government to pay for new programs to restore full employment, decent incomes to those who could not be employed, decent housing, educational opportunities, and medical care for all. Funding to rebuild the nation's infrastructure, housing, and schools would also create new jobs. The "Freedom Budget" was King's answer to the zero-sum game of American capitalism.

King would use this platform in his fight for economic justice but with one exception: the Institute argued that it could create economic justice without disturbing American foreign policy and its escalating military spending. The AFL-CIO fully backed the war in Vietnam, but King saw military spending as a diversion of resources needed for economic development. On January 6, 1966, SNCC officially condemned that war as neocolonial aggression, and that view mirrored King's. He saw the war as a moral evil and, on April 11, SCLC called on President Johnson to consider U.S. withdrawal.

Johnson disparagingly dismissed critics as "nervous Nellies" and said worse things about them in private.

King and Bayard Rustin at this point did not agree on the way forward. In a February 1965 article in *Commentary* magazine, Rustin had argued that the movement should go "from Protest to Politics" through a labor and civil rights electoral coalition. King accepted the political coalition idea but still believed nonviolent resistance remained the most potent weapon of struggle. On November 13, 1965, King published an article in the *Atlantic Monthly*, "Beyond the Los Angeles Riots," which proposed to take campaigns of nonviolent direct action into the centers of the black working-class crisis in the North. As he had with the Birmingham campaign, he picked the hardest nut to crack: Chicago. Rustin warned him, "You don't know what Chicago is like. You're going to get wiped out."

* * *

ON JANUARY 26, 1966, Martin and Coretta King moved their children into 1550 South Hamlin Avenue, in a Chicago slum neighborhood. "Its towering housing projects loomed like upright concentration camps, placing abject black poverty within sight of white opulence," wrote Coretta. King came to Chicago hoping to use the Birmingham and Selma models in which a local campaign could dramatize issues and thereby change the national framework. "If we can break the backbone of discrimination in Chicago, we can do it in all the cities in the country," King said. He still dreamed of a convergence of religious, labor, academic, and civil rights forces mobilizing to address urban problems through the Chicago Freedom Movement, using SCLC staff to join with preexisting organizations in the community. Chicago clearly demonstrated the intertwined crisis of the unemployed and the black working class. Some 700,000 African Americans lived in slums on the West and the South Side, while manufacturing jobs eroded, and 20 percent of Chicago's black families lived below poverty. King sought to develop a mass movement that could dramatize the problems of segregated jobs, housing, and schools. He and his allies also tried to organize the youthful street gangs of Chicago into a political force to demand social and economic justice.

Over six months and more of intense campaigns, the Chicago movement brought the problems of the urban north to the attention of the nation. Chicago revealed howling mobs of white supremacists threatening King and marchers who demanded the end of segregated housing; real estate, insurance companies, and absentee landlords invested in segregation; craft unions that refused to open their doors to racial and ethnic minorities and women; the horrors of slum housing; the lack of infrastructure and transportation to get people to schools and jobs; the failure of the schools to educate, and the failure of legislatures to provide adequate funding; white bigotry, police brutality—and much more.

The Chicago Freedom Movement, with participation by black and white leaders in the packinghouse and others in unions, sought to address fair employment, job training, increased minimum wages, and other working-class issues. But the movement ran into a stone wall of resistance from craft unions vested in whites-only occupations. King and the CFM highlighted a range of economic issues through a classic civil rights campaign of mass rallies, marches, and escalating demonstrations. Some argued, however, that only in-depth community organizing could attack the intertwined issues in northern urban terrain. The CFM ultimately focused on demands to end housing segregation, with the hope that the Chicago movement could force national legislation, as other local campaigns had done.

The Chicago Freedom Movement targeted redlining by banks that would not give loans to African Americans, real estate company policies of screening blacks and Latinos out of white neighborhoods, and profiteering by flipping neighborhoods from white to black. Some organizers thought an open-housing strategy did not lend itself to a campaign for jobs in the ghetto: it could seem more like a campaign to get out of the ghetto that pitted inner-city blacks and Latinos against white working-class people of limited means and fearful of losing their home equity. Yet demands to open up housing had long been a major goal of the civil rights movement in

Chicago. King and the Chicago Freedom Movement also initiated Operation Breadbasket, led by Jesse Jackson, which would successfully use the pressure of consumer economic boycott to demand and obtain jobs for African Americans from employers.

To complicate matters, however, on June 6 events in Mississippi interrupted King's feverish efforts to build a mass community movement in Chicago. A white military veteran shot down civil rights activist James Meredith (he survived) as he attempted to walk from Memphis to Jackson in a March Against Fear. A white postal worker named William Moore had earlier been killed in Alabama when he tried to walk across the South for civil rights. King, Stokely Carmichael, James Lawson, and others now continued Meredith's walk. On June 21, when he should have been in Chicago, King found himself in the small town of Philadelphia, in Neshoba County, Mississippi, where deputy sheriff Cecil Price had helped to murder SNCC's Goodman, Schwerner, and Chaney two years before. Some three hundred jeering whites surrounded King and Sheriff Price stood right behind King as he prayed, "We are here to save America. We are here to save you. Why don't you whites understand this?" Angry whites threw cherry bombs while King tried to speak, and a mob with switchblades and rocks attacked marchers, who would later suffer from police attacks nearly as bad as marchers had endured in Selma. Mass-media sensationalism focused on Carmichael's "Black Power" slogan to create a story of internal conflict that blocked out news that the actual movement, including both King and Carmichael, had shifted dramatically toward a "dual agenda" of racial and economic challenges to the deep institutionalized racism within the American capitalist system.

In between his trips to and from Mississippi, King in Chicago led the largest civil rights rally of 1966. On July 10, 30,000 people gathered at Soldier Field, and many marched through downtown to post their demands on the door of City Hall. Two hot summer nights later, riots erupted on the West Side in response to conflicts with the police. They lasted for three days, leaving two dead, four hundred arrested, and $2 million in property damage. A few days later, riots also broke out in Cleveland, Ohio. From July 30 to August 25 the movement's open-housing demonstrations in Chicago suburbs of Gage Park and Cicero brought out ugly crowds of young white men wielding baseball bats, shouting "We want King!" Someone threw a rock and hit him in the head. George Lincoln Rockwell and his Nazi Party followers inflamed the crowds, openly sporting the Nazi insignia. King said the campaign for open housing created some of the most frightful scenes of white hatred he ever encountered, south or north.

White terror in both Chicago and Mississippi highlighted a problem with King's efforts to build a civil rights–labor coalition for economic justice. In the Deep South white workers sometimes joined their class enemies in the White Citizen's Councils, the KKK, and the John Birch Society, while in Chicago, open-housing demands faced a wall of fear from second-generation white ethnics. White craft-and-construction-trade unionists also put up a militant wall of opposition to minorities and women getting into the workforce. King and CFM leaders ultimately negotiated with Mayor Richard Daley and top city leaders, obtained some concessions, and hoped to win national legislation for open housing. But the mass media reported the Chicago campaign as a failure. King would later write, "We found ourselves confronted by the hard realities of a social system in many ways more resistant to change than the rural South." Deindustrialization and other forces driving racial-economic conflict in the 1960s continued to spin out of control in Chicago, Detroit, and other urban centers in subsequent decades.

Instead of sensationalizing debates over the Black Power slogan, the media would have done better by focusing on the overriding problem that King tried to address: the lack of well-paying jobs. Generations of African American, Euro-American, and Latino workers had relied upon the steel industry and packinghouse and other manufacturing jobs to make their way to home ownership, higher education, and a better life. But between 1957 and 1966, Chicago workers lost tens of thousands of jobs. Packinghouse workers nationwide lost 38,000 jobs as mechanization of the meatpacking industry mixed with union busting undermined King's ally, the United Packinghouse Workers Union, and forced it to merge with the craft-oriented amalgamated meat cutters and butcher workers' union in 1968. King's aide C. T. Vivian tried to open the door to more craft, construction, and public service jobs in Chicago, and worked with informal and union networks of black workers, including black bus drivers who led strikes in July and August 1968. They met fierce, militant opposition from unionized white workers in crafts and construction trades. Some criticized the Chicago Freedom Movement and King for not digging more deeply into the problems confronting black labor that continued to fuel racial injustice, but the problems they faced were immense.

Chicago illustrated the intertwined, hard-to-solve problems of economic and racial injustice and white worker opposition to black advances in the second phase of the freedom movement. Thomas Jackson writes that King saw race and class issues as intertwined parts of a "malignant kinship" that required changing the whole system of America's racial capitalism. But how to do it?

Gandhi called his nonviolence campaigns "my experiments with truth," and James Lawson said King viewed the Chicago campaign that way: as a learning experience that revealed the power of those seeking change, and the power of those lined up against it. SCLC organizers discovered what they were up against in trying to create a social movement that could address the problem of poverty and open up jobs, housing, transportation, education, and other social goods to people in the inner cities. In Chicago and beyond, historian Clayborne Carson wrote, King "was returning to his deepest convictions as a social gospel minister after a decade-long detour into civil rights leadership," and "the most prophetic period of his life still lay ahead."

* * *

In August 1966, at the tenth SCLC convention, held in August 1966, some nine hundred delegates focused their attention on economic justice. They reiterated SCLC's support for repeal of 14(b) of the Taft-Hartley Act that encouraged right-to-work laws, and they demanded a $2 minimum wage and a guaranteed family income. Delegates heard King and A. Philip Randolph endorse the "Freedom Budget" for $100 billion over ten years to wipe out poverty, and heard RWDSU's black union leader Cleveland Robinson and Bayard Rustin speak on behalf of a "labor–civil rights alliance" as the way forward. Expectations remained high for a new round of federal action to deal with institutionalized racism and poverty. The labor–civil rights coalition seemed intact.

In November 1966, however, a new kind of disaster hit: the Republican Party swept congressional elections, overshadowing the labor–civil rights coalition that had played such a powerful role in enacting legislation in 1964 and 1965. The Democrats lost more seats in the House in 1966 than Republicans had lost in the 1964 elections. Many of the seats won by liberals in 1964 now went back to conservatives. Whites in districts near urban riots voted their fears. The election shattered hopes of major reform by both unions and the civil rights movement. In Memphis, as one example, the 1966 election replaced a relatively moderate Democratic congressman, George Grider, with a reactionary Republican named Dan Kuykendall and set the stage for a shift to the right in the city's political establishment.

In the November 1966 issue of the AFL-CIO's *American Federationist,* in an article titled "Civil Rights at the Crossroads," Rustin argued that the "first phase" of the movement had produced a democratic revolution. But now that had to be followed primarily with electoral politics rather than campaigns of nonviolent resistance. He wrote that working-class whites "have only barely made it themselves," and feared to lose their modestly priced homes and tenuous hold on jobs. However, the 1966 election returns now threw doubt on his optimistic view that a labor–civil rights coalition would win out through politics. In addition, the AFL-CIO and its member unions remained tightly wedded through the Democratic Party to the escalating war in Vietnam.

Most people in the New Left and antiwar movement saw unions

and the Democrats as part of the problem. The Black Panther Party, formed in Oakland, California, in the summer of 1966, formulated a ten-point program that demanded housing, health care, jobs, withdrawal of African Americans drafted for the Vietnam War, an end to police brutality and mass incarceration. These were King's demands as well, but expressed in a more inflammatory tone and calling for a movement of armed self-defense. By 1967, vast numbers of people were fighting for social change but their means differed, and they all confronted a stone wall of war spending, escalating police violence, racism, and deep social ills.

King said it was now "the most difficult phase of the civil rights struggle." Following the election of the full-blown racist Lester Maddox as governor of Georgia in the 1966 election, King feared, "We could end up with a full scale race war in this country. It is very frightening."

Coretta and Martin Luther King with Stokely Carmichael and others in the 1966 March Against Fear in Mississippi.

Chapter 4

"IN GOD'S ECONOMY"

Organizing the Poor People's Campaign, 1967–1968

> *I'm not only concerned about the black poor. I'm*
> *concerned about the white poor. I'm concerned*
> *about the Puerto Rican poor, the Indian poor.*
> *I'm concerned about the Mexican-American poor.*
> *We are going to grapple with the problem of poor*
> *people. And we are going to do it in spite of the*
> *philosophical debate, black and white together.*

—KING IN BIRMINGHAM, ALABAMA,
ST. THOMAS AME CHURCH, FEBRUARY 15, 1968

WHILE TRYING TO WRITE A BOOK ASSESSING THE
state of the country and the movement, Martin Luther King
saw the January 1967 edition of *Ramparts* magazine, which provided horrible pictures of Vietnamese children burned by napalm
made in America by Dow Chemical and delivered by the U.S. military. During the Chicago campaign, Vietnamese Buddhist monk
Thich Nhat Hanh had met with King to explain why monks
were burning themselves to death to protest the repressive South
Vietnamese regime supported by the United States. King had spoken against the war previously, but advisers urged him to downplay
the issue. By January 1967 he saw the moral issues as overriding any
sense of tactical politics. As a nonviolence leader, he had to speak
out more forcefully regardless of the consequences.

On February 25 King spoke out against the war and on March
25 he led an antiwar march through the streets of Chicago with

the author and well-known pediatrician Dr. Benjamin Spock. Coretta King had spoken out against war and nuclear weapons in Washington, D.C., in 1961, in Geneva, Switzerland, in 1962, at Madison Square Garden in New York City in 1965, and she continued to support the peace campaigns of Women Strike for Peace and the Women's International League for Peace and Freedom. The power of the antiwar movement kept building, and now Dr. King irrevocably committed himself to oppose the war as strongly as possible.

In a much-anticipated speech delivered on April 4, 1967, at Riverside Church in New York City, King tied the nation's faltering War on Poverty to a searing moral indictment of America's escalating war. Military action with a disproportionate number of working-class black draftees, King said, taught inner-city residents that violence in pursuit of one's goals was all right. Vietnam was a "working-class war," in which white and black workers primarily paid the price for American military adventurism. At the same time, as King put it, the war consumed society's resources like a "demonic suction tube," at the expense of economic development at home. The War on Poverty, he said, was "shot down on the battlefields of Vietnam," while "flame throwers in Vietnam fan the flames in our cities. The Vietnamese, he said, must see the U.S. forces as "strange liberators," as they destroyed their families and burned down their villages. King's "Beyond Vietnam" speech provided one of history's sharpest and most prophetic moral critiques of American foreign policy.

King not only indicted the war as a moral horror, but as "a symptom of a far deeper malady within the American spirit." Prophetically, he commented that when "profit motives and property rights are considered more important than people, the giant triplets of racism, materialism, and militarism are incapable of being conquered." All of the issues, as he said, remained entangled in such a way that the nation could not solve one of those issues without addressing all of them. He called for "a true revolution of values" and economic restructuring. King had previously called on people to follow the path of agape love to make a wounded community whole; he could hardly avoid applying the same idea to the Vietnam War. He said America should seek peace not "as a distant goal" achieved through military strength, but as a practice of resolving conflicts through peaceful means. "In Christ there is neither Communist nor capitalist," he said, because the universe ultimately "hinges on moral foundations."

On April 15, 1967, King spoke against the war again in New York City to a huge crowd of 200,000, and Coretta spoke to some 60,000 on the same day at a mass march in San Francisco. The antiwar movement grew by leaps and bounds, but the labor–civil rights alliance now looked tattered and worn. On May 2 King expressed his concerns before a gathering of Teamsters Union Local 815 shop stewards in New York City in a speech titled "Civil Rights at the Crossroads." When most people thought of Teamsters they thought of Jimmy Hoffa, the union's president indicted by the federal authorities for corruption (who would disappear in 1975, probably the victim of mob violence). The Teamsters Union, however, had 450,000 black members: it was one of the largest black union memberships in the country. In his speech King emphasized a bitter truth: few whites, unionized or not, recognized or welcomed the new phase of the movement that began after the passage of the 1965 Voting Rights Act. Civil rights legislation had cost the nation little, but King's demand to end widespread economic disparities would cost billions of dollars in taxes. He recounted how the federal government had heavily subsidized white advancement at various stages—through land grants, the GI Bill, and Federal Housing Administration loans, for example. Yet many whites resisted subsidizing poor people of color to bring them into the mainstream, and reacted violently to further demands.

"To put it in plain language," King told the Teamsters, "many Americans would like to have a nation which is a democracy for white Americans but simultaneously a dictatorship over black Americans." The civil rights movement, he said, was at a crossroads.

* * *

IN 1967, THE mass media celebrated "the summer of love," a time for predominantly white "hippies" to reject middle-class conformity through "flower power." But it was also "Vietnam Summer," a door-to-door educational and community-based campaign to stop the war. As one example of what people did, in Lansing, Michigan, I and other activists produced an antiwar newspaper to reach out to auto factory workers and others. Yet no matter what we did, the war raged on. Hundreds of soldiers came home in body bags. That summer, inner-city riots or uprisings swept through the country. On July 12, 1967, the police beating of a cab driver set off an upheaval over pent-up inner-city grievances in Newark, New Jersey. In five days of riots and police violence, twenty-six people died, among them a white police officer and fireman. A few days later, on July 23, the summer's worst riot erupted in Detroit. Despite a reasonably progressive Democratic mayor and the presence of Walter Reuther's UAW, six days of looting, shooting, and burning consumed Detroit, as 7,300 National Guard troops and 4,000 police occupied the city.

"I'm gonna shoot anything that moves and is black," a young white guardsman told a reporter. Guard troops returning from Vietnam killed civilians with machine guns and M-1 rifles, while white police officers tortured and then murdered three black men at the Algiers Motel, and received no punishment. Both calculated and indiscriminate violence by the forces of law and order along with fires and street fighting produced forty-three deaths, thirty-three blacks, ten whites. *Newsweek* magazine published photos of black men oozing blood onto sidewalks. The march on Detroit had sent hopes soaring in the summer of 1963, but after the summer of 1967 the city went into a deadly economic decline as whites fled for the suburbs. Army experts and others predicted guerrilla warfare in America, "a new Vietnam developing in our ghettoes." People at the grass roots asked, "whose Detroit" was it? Less than a year later, black auto workers formed the Dodge Revolutionary Union Movement (DRUM) and then the League of Revolutionary Black

Workers, and carried out actions targeting the white-run union bureaucracy of the UAW as well as the corporations.

At least thirty cities erupted in riots in the summer of 1967, leading to the deaths of an estimated sixty-nine people, most of them African Americans killed by police and National Guard troops. The bloodshed prompted King to telegram President Johnson: "There cannot be social peace when a people have awakened to their rights and dignity, and to the wretchedness of their lives simultaneously." Yet the president had cut antipoverty funds in half to pay for the war.

In that same summer King wrote in his book *Where Do We Go From Here: Chaos or Community?*: "Before you can come up with a cure, you first have to know the disease." He blamed a bloody war abroad and economic and racial injustice at home, and elaborated on the issues he had been speaking about day in and day out. "Riots are indefensible as weapons of struggle," he wrote, but the failure of whites to understand the history of slavery and racism and to adequately respond to poverty and unemployment had created a "Negro community in the North [that] has a short fuse and a long train of abuses." While the nation had accepted phase one of the freedom struggle for civil and political rights, "when Negroes looked for the second phase, the realization of equality, they found that many of their white allies had quietly disappeared. A coalition of conscience had converged at Selma, and then movements for change "like a giant X began to diverge." King wrote, "Cries of Black Power and riots are not the causes of white resistance, they are consequences of it." He called for a "true revolution of values" that would allow Americans to make common cause with the poor people of Latin America and the rest of the world.

King realized that embittered inner-city youth felt that his promises of equality had come to naught for them. He felt responsible, and felt embittered himself. He thought only a national economic justice agenda could stem the tide of riots and death in the streets. At the SCLC convention in August 1967, King called for a program "that will drive the nation to a guaranteed annual income," and jobs at livable wages. "We must create full employment or we must create incomes. People must be made consumers by one method or the other." He went against conservative narratives that every individual can make it alone in a market economy. Misfortune, racism, mechanization, or other historical circumstances had left many people without a purchase on the American Dream. "We've got to begin to ask questions about the whole society. We are called upon to help the discouraged beggars in life's marketplace. But one day we must come to see that an edifice which produces beggars needs restructuring." In King's view, reform was not enough. Speaking to his allies at the SCLC conference, he declared that, as Jesus had told Nicodemus, "America, you must be born again!"

In the middle of conflicting, swirling eddies of social movement politics and a government dead set on pursuing war at the expense of everything else, King's last months became his most prophetic and perhaps his most heroic as he faced criticism from all sides. In response to his antiwar speech on April 4, the *New York Times* decried his statements as reckless and unfounded, while the *Washington Post* practically called him a traitor, writing that he had "diminished his usefulness to his cause, to his country and to his people." The *Wall Street Journal* and practically every other corporate newspaper condemned him. *Time* said King as a black leader had no business opposing the war. The mass media that once oversimplified King as a "civil rights leader" now derided him for taking his citizenship rights seriously on other issues. King said that when "you have the national press against you," it was almost impossible to make your case.

Now when King spoke before crowds of young people in the cities, he often heard taunts and boos. In May, when he visited Louisville, Kentucky, a group of hostile white youths surrounded his car; while he told them he loved them like his own children, a rock came through his window. In September, at the National Convention for a New Politics conference in Chicago, attended by 3,500 people, young black men shouting "Black Power" derided King in the parking lot, and in the conference he could barely finish his speech, as many attendees walked out in apparent boredom. King called out economic injustice, saying "Capitalism was built on the exploitation of black slaves and continues to thrive on the exploitation of the poor." After he left, a minority black nationalist caucus took over much of the proceedings.

King's call for a civil rights–labor coalition no longer resonated with the New Left, if it ever did. Urban revolts and discord continued. So did the politics of white backlash, which King said was nothing new: "White America has been backlashing on the fundamental God-given and human rights of Negro Americans for more than three hundred years," he wrote in *Where Do We Go from Here.* The AFL-CIO still supported the war to the hilt; Black Power, antiwar, and student movements of the New Left had become disgusted with alliances with liberals; what union critics in Michigan called "pork chop unionism" benefited employed, unionized workers but not poor people and welfare recipients. No one could find a way out of the zero-sum game of capitalism in which some workers seemingly gained something at the expense of others. And now the war had created a huge gulf of violent disagreements over foreign policy that made it difficult to address pressing issues of economic justice. By coming out strongly against the war, King had in effect cut his ties with the AFL-CIO and the Johnson administration.

King returned to clear allies on November 11, 1967, meeting with about five hundred trade unionists at the University of Chicago for the National Labor Leadership Assembly for Peace. This was a coalition of fifty national unions and union locals, most with strong civil rights records, some of them survivors of the purge of the left from the CIO in 1949. Their gathering challenged years of anticommunist, militarist foreign policy supported by mainstream unions. King called his talk "Domestic Impact of the War in America," and complained that millions of people from all walks of life had protested the war. "But one voice was missing—the loud, clear voice of labor. The absence of that one voice was all the more tragic because it may be the decisive one for tipping the balance toward peace."

He told unionists that not just white backlash, but the violence and division of the war, had turned the nation rightward. King said the war "has made the Great Society a myth and replaced it with a troubled and confused society. The war has strengthened domestic reaction. It has given the extreme right, the anti-labor, anti-Negro, and anti-humanistic forces a weapon of spurious patriotism to galvanize its supporters into reaching for power, right up to the White House." He thought the fact that Ronald Reagan, a Hollywood actor in grade B movies, was now the governor of California due to the 1966 elections exemplified the "irrationalities" and "psychosis" induced by the war. "The war has smothered and nearly extinguished the beginnings of progress toward racial justice" and divided young people from the older generation.

King and his staff had already begun to formulate ideas for a new kind of coalition beyond the labor–civil rights nexus, a multiracial freedom movement demanding "a radical redistribution" of wealth and power in America. It would hope to end America's pursuit of militarism and war in favor of jobs or income for the unemployed poor and working poor. It would draw on a new constituency and a new agency for change. He told a reporter, "We are dealing in a sense with class issues, the gulf between the haves and have-nots." He called it the Poor People's Campaign.

* * *

KING SPENT OCTOBER 1–3, 1967, in jail because of old and fraudulent charges against him from the brutal 1963 confrontation with Bull Connor and his police in Birmingham, Alabama. Suffering from a virus, he had trouble sleeping, but jail gave him time to think about how nonviolent resistance in Birmingham and Selma had focused the nation's attention on the evils of segregation and voter suppression and led to new civil- and voting-rights laws. The freedom movement had learned in Chicago that in large, northern urban areas white politicians could ignore, absorb, or coopt mass marches. But King still believed that nonviolent demonstrations could provide group power for otherwise powerless people. At the urging of Marion Wright Edelman, Senator Robert Kennedy had toured the poorest areas of Appalachia and the Deep South, and what he saw brought tears to his eyes. Kennedy asked Edelman to tell King to bring the poor people to Washington, and that's what King decided to do. He had started every campaign by finding a way to dramatize conditions and tell a story. Bringing the poor to the nation's capital would make visible millions of people in "the other America," victims of slavery, racism, and the outsourcing and loss of jobs due to mechanization.

We rightly remember King as a man of love and peace. But, like Gandhi, he had learned that "love in action" required both nonviolent resistance—refusal to go along—and nonviolent coercion. Upon his release from jail, King told a Birmingham rally that the movement needed an alternative to riots, "a method that will disrupt our cities if necessary, create the crisis that will force the nation to look at the situation, dramatize it, and yet at the same time not destroy life or property." King wanted to apply the Birmingham model of "massive civil disobedience" to create "nationwide city-paralyzing demonstrations" to demand jobs or income for the poor. In a press conference, he talked of closing down branches of government through nonviolent sit-ins, blockading traffic, and encamping poor people on federal property. Nonviolent strategy required first trying to negotiate with those in power, but if that failed, finding a way to bring issues to the surface. Creating a crisis through direct action provided the first step toward resolving deep social issues.

King called for a Poor People's Campaign to demand that government spend money for social reconstruction instead of war. He feared that if the movement did not do something, another summer of inner-city riots with no programmatic focus would ensue, creating more white backlash and more deaths and misery in the ghettoes. Instead of more riots, he envisioned a "long, hot summer" of demonstrations, arrests, and nonviolent confrontations leading to a solution. Much of the news media had already turned against King because of his antiwar stand. Now the *New York Times* called King's Poor People's Campaign proposal a "formula for discord." African-American journalist Carl Rowan used information fed to him by the FBI to write an article in *Reader's Digest* claiming that communists had influenced King.

King persisted. He was nothing if not consistent. Going back to his days in graduate school, he had spoken of his strong concern for the poor based on his Social Gospel theology. He had championed "we, the dispossessed" in Montgomery. He had constantly spoken and written about and organized around issues confronting poor and working-class people. He had indicted the Vietnam War as a crime that used poor people as cannon fodder and destroyed resources that should have gone to ending their poverty. Stokely Carmichael, Bayard Rustin, A. Philip Randolph, and others also wrote and spoke out against systemic racism and unemployment, but no mainstream leader criticized capitalism or American foreign policy as sharply as King did in the last months of his life.

King had told his congregation at Ebenezer in September 1966, "There are few things more sinful than economic injustice." Now, in October 1967, he talked of bringing some of America's thirty-five to forty million poor people to Washington in mule carts and sitting down in the street until the government took action. As King traveled and spoke to thousands of people from all walks of life in his last months, the idea of creating a poor people's movement consumed him. Coretta Scott King wrote that her husband imagined what a movement could be, and then set out to build it, whether he had the full resources to do it or not. In that same way, he set out to create the Poor People's Campaign; it was a faith act. But building that campaign would prove far more difficult than he had imagined.

At SCLC's staff and officer retreat in Frogmore, South Carolina, November 27–December 1, 1967, King said, "Something is wrong with capitalism as it now stands in the United States." He had told a group of ministers behind closed doors during the autumn of 1967, "We are not interested in being integrated into this value structure"; rather, "a radical redistribution of power must take place." But SCLC staff members felt at sea. They had spent their lives in the civil rights movement and the black church, appealing to people from all walks of life. Now King wanted them to organize a multiracial constituency around class issues. James Bevel, Jesse Jackson, and others wanted to prioritize opposing the war, which King himself had argued was the biggest obstacle to improving conditions in America. King now argued that opposing the war could not unite the broadest segment of the population, but a campaign to end poverty could. At Frogmore he called for a fundamental critique of American capitalism and for the movement to go from "an inadequate protest phase to a stage of massive, active, nonviolent resistance to the modern system. . . . Our economy must become more person-centered than property-centered and profit-centered." Rather than integrating into existing values, as the early civil rights movement seemed to demand, the movement needed to change those values. King's top aide, Andrew Young, later summarized King's critique of capitalism: "Even if you're a winner in a rat race, you're still a rat."

On January 7, 1968, King set forth a moral framework in a sermon at Ebenezer Church, telling his congregation, "Two thirds of the peoples of the world go to bed hungry at night. These are the least of God's children." In India, in Nigeria, and in the Mississippi Delta, King said, "I have met people by the hundred who have never had any money in their hands in their lives. They live on plantations, and they go up to the plantation store, and they get their flour and their meal, and the humble things that they get," only to end up further in debt. He preached that, "in God's economy, the man who has been to no house is as significant as the man who's been to Morehouse" and that "the man who lives in the slum, and in the alley, is as significant as Henry Ford, or John Rockefeller." King told them to never forget the poor.

King could have been talking to himself as well as his congregation. He drove an old car and turned his Nobel Prize money, lecture fees, and book royalties over to the movement. He only bought a modest house when Coretta insisted on it. Even so, he knew he had privileges that the mass of African Americans did not enjoy. King challenged himself and the black middle class to "see" the poor. As more educated and slightly more affluent blacks strode toward economic and political advances as the result of civil- and voting-rights laws, poor black people and workers in places like the Mississippi Delta or the inner city of Chicago still had little access to employment, training, education, transportation, decent housing, or leverage on the white power structure. Native Americans, Latinos, Puerto Ricans, and poor whites also suffered devastating poverty, though it was based on different histories. King reminded audiences of their moral obligations to support poor people in struggles for dignity and a better life, while seeking to take middle-class people further politically than most of them felt prepared to go.

On January 16, 1968, the day after his thirty-ninth birthday, during SCLC's staff conference, King formally announced the Poor People's Campaign. He said sixty staff members would recruit and train some three thousand demonstrators from fifteen poverty-stricken rural areas and from northern cities such as Baltimore, Philadelphia, Newark, New York, Boston, Cleveland, Chicago, and Detroit. Three caravans of poor people would converge on the capital and be joined by many thousands more in mass rallies until Congress and the president either created jobs or a modest, livable income for those who had neither.

King in his "Freedom Budget" and "Bill of Rights for the Disadvantaged" had called for $30 billion a year for ten years to eradicate poverty, and to provide jobs by building 500,000 units of new low-cost housing per year. Instead of giving the poor food stamps and welfare, Band-Aids on the problem of poverty, King proposed a guaranteed annual income (or "reverse income tax") so the poor themselves could pay for education, housing, and the other endowments anyone needed to get into the economic mainstream.

These were not wild ideas. Esteemed economists like John Kenneth Galbraith and three presidential commissions had documented how mechanization created structural unemployment among vulnerable populations that could not be alleviated by economic growth alone. *Newsweek* and the Ford Foundation had also supported the idea of a base level of income for all. Norway, where King had traveled to receive his Nobel Prize, and other western European countries had already restructured capitalism, using redistributive tax laws aimed at the rich to fund universal health care, provide free higher education, and guarantee jobs or income. King also recalled how the public-service and infrastructure jobs created by President Roosevelt had helped to alleviate the Great Depression. King said "jobs or income" would make poor people into consumers and keep the national economy growing, instead of forcing poor people into lives of welfare, crime, drugs, and prison— problems that cost government billions of dollars to deal with. Opinion polls and various studies suggested it was possible.

King's goals of federal spending to end poverty might seem utopian, but it might well have been possible to eliminate poverty in 1968. Rapid economic expansion, a high level of unionization, and high taxes on the rich following World War II had created a much more egalitarian society. Some economists believed the "growth dividend" based on expansion of the economy could pay for programs to end poverty. The United States was the richest country in the world, and King said it had the money to end poverty if it had the will to do it. Since his time, the U.S. has spent trillions of dollars on war, bank bailouts, and tax cuts for wealthy people that could have been invested in schools, housing, health care, and job creation. King said the money was available to end poverty and the country needed to revise its priorities about how it was spent.

When reporters asked King how the military budget figured into his campaign, he said that instead of "squandering a great deal of unnecessary money fighting an unnecessary and unjust war in Vietnam," the government should "constructively use money for life and development." As if to emphasize his concerns, on January 21 North Vietnamese troops attacked a U.S. military base at Khe Sanh, and at the end of the month the National Liberation Front of Vietnam launched its Tet offensive. These bloody escalations shocked Americans into realizing that an end to the war was nowhere in sight. Dr. Benjamin Spock and King urged draft-age men to become conscientious objectors and turn in their draft cards. Spock and others were indicted for counseling draftees to resist.

The obstacles to organizing the Poor People's Campaign proved daunting. King's speaking schedule constantly overwhelmed him, as did maintaining the shaky finances and organizational structure of SCLC. Neither he nor his staff had the resources and networks needed to organize a massive, multiracial poor people's movement, and many people advised him against even trying. They recalled the events of 1932, when unemployed World War I veterans had camped out in the nation's capital demanding early payments of their military pensions, only to be routed (and two of them killed) by the military with bayonets, tear gas, and clubs. Some of King's advisers feared blood flowing in the streets again. They also knew that bringing poor people into a movement required more than an organization of black preachers in SCLC. King needed a multiracial cadre of organizers and access to people deeply based in communities of the poor, but he had neither. If the campaign failed to attract followers or degenerated into violence, King's credibility as a nonviolence leader would be finished. Yet King pledged to go forward.

Building a poor people's movement almost from scratch, however, was a daunting if not impossible task. Following the SCLC staff conference on January 15–17, 1968, in Atlanta, King traveled nonstop and had no time to oversee or direct his staff, scattered in various locales. Myles Horton of Highlander Folk School, longtime veteran of labor and civil rights struggles, explained King's weakness: "He was more effective as a symbol than a programmer. One of his problems was that he was becoming something of a one-man institution. With his charisma and fame separating him from some of the untested but dynamic forces within the black community."

Among those dynamic forces were some 10,000 welfare mothers who had joined the National Welfare Rights Organization (NWRO), under the leadership of chairperson Johnnie Tillmon and organizer George Wiley. On February 3, in Chicago, King and his entourage of Ralph Abernathy, Andrew Young, Bernard Lafayette, and Al Sampson, a staff member whom King himself had ordained as a minister, met with Tillmon, Wiley, and thirty NWRO leaders at a YMCA. They sharply questioned his failure to actively support Senator Robert Kennedy's efforts to beat back legislation by southern Democrats to freeze welfare funds and force recipients to work for the pittance they received without providing a way for them to take care of their children while at work. President Johnson had signed the bill into law in January, despite militant NWRO confrontations with federal authorities all over the country. They asked King how he could possibly claim to speak for the poor when he did not even know about their struggles or about the various laws concerning welfare mothers.

In fact, King had spoken out in Chicago on January 5, criticizing welfare cuts and provisions that would "force mothers to go out and to work and to get jobs and they already have jobs." King told the media that mothers with eight and ten children who wash and iron and work very hard every day could not be replaced. "If this is not work then I don't know what work is," he had said. Foster homes removed children from mothers who did not take proper care of them, but forced them to go to work for low wages with no childcare. King had also decried a welfare system that forced men to leave their families in order for their wives to get financial support.

Nonetheless, Tillmon remarked: "You know, Dr. King, if you don't know about these questions, you should say you don't know, and then we could go on with the meeting." King replied, "You're right, Mrs. Tillmon. We don't know anything about welfare. We are here to learn." In subsequent organizing, King began to incorporate the issue of welfare into his talks. "Poverty is the Negro woman getting up early in the morning, having to leave her home because her husband can't make an adequate income, and she has to go over to the white lady's kitchen and cook breakfast for the white lady," he would tell an antipoverty rally in Waycross, Georgia, in March.

Women in the welfare rights movement became a powerful force in the late 1960s and proved strong allies for the Poor People's Campaign. After the Chicago meeting, Geraldine Smith of the NWRO helped organize King's speeches across Mississippi, and Carol Williams of the Southern Consumer Cooperative set up much of the tour in Alabama. Women ultimately became the majority of the registrants to go to Washington, and the NWRO would lead the Washington movement off with a Mother's Day March on May 12.

Just as they made up the backbone of many of the communities involved in southern freedom and northern community struggles, women held up many of the families among the working class and poor. As Andrew Young freely admitted, "In SCLC we were working with college students, with independent business people. The civil rights movement, up until 1968 anyway, was really a middle-class movement." By contrast, he said, Cesar Chavez and the United Farmworkers Union and the NWRO already had built poor people's movements. More than SCLC, SNCC had specialized in organizing with and among working-class people, as had the labor movement. Nonetheless, Myles Horton thought that SCLC's preacher-led activism might evolve toward a more grassroots, community-based movement with more women in the leadership. He later said of King, "Martin was constantly learning and growing."

What he lacked in grassroots cadre and organizational resources, King tried to make up for with his own superhuman efforts. In February, he undertook a whirlwind of speaking and organizing, giving as many as five talks a day in a grueling schedule that might have destroyed most people. The "President of the Negroes," as Coretta called him, traveled much as a candidate would in a presidential campaign, but spoke like a prophet who moved his audiences into spiritual realms of anger, inspiration, joy, and commitment. His preaching drew upon his own family's history as slaves and poor people and upon themes he had developed in a social movement for over thirteen years.

On February 7, 1968, at Vermont Avenue Baptist Church in Washington, D.C., King cried out, "There is something wrong with our nation. Something desperately wrong." The poor in the slums, young people turning into prostitutes and drug addicts, "are the ones who've been overlooked, and who've been left on the outskirts of hope." Instead of fearing, criminalizing, and condemning them, King said, the nation should help them. But the conditions of this "underclass" of people had only worsened over the last twenty years.

President Johnson's War on Poverty had helped to ultimately reduce the number of poor people from 23 percent of the population in 1962 to 11 percent in 1973, but King saw it as only a start toward eliminating poverty.

On February 15, in Birmingham, Alabama, speaking to leaders preparing the Mississippi leg of the Poor People's Campaign, King said solving the problem of poverty would require social-change movements to demand "a radical redistribution of economic power." But, he warned, "It is easier to guarantee the right to vote than it is to guarantee an annual income or to create jobs." The next day, King returned to Montgomery, where the black poor and middle class had joined together for 381 days in the bus boycott. He had seemed like a "militant moderate" then, but now he returned as a fiery advocate for the poor, sometimes using the dialect of unlettered people in the Deep South. Moving on to Selma, he told a mass meeting that "the Negro haves, and I say partial haves, must join hands with the Negro have-nots." King reminded them that, as in their past unified struggle for the right to vote, "you know when we do things together they can't chop us off . . . let me assure you that we all go up together, or we all go down together."

Like King himself, most people in black church audiences came from families whose ancestors had lived through slavery and sharecropping, and most of them now lived only one or two paychecks away from poverty. "Middle class" in the black community in most cases meant people with steady working-class jobs, mixed with more educated teachers, preachers, businesspeople, and professionals. Nearly all black churches contained a lesser or greater number of the poor and working poor, and the black church still offered the most promising route to organizing the black middle class together with the poor and workers. King especially called on black ministers who were paid by their congregations and had a degree of independence from white employers that most blacks did not.

King also thought a campaign to end poverty could resolve a racial impasse in the New Left. SNCC activists in the spring of 1967 had voted for whites to leave the organization, based on the idea that whites and blacks should organize separately. Since then, interracial coalition building in the New Left had nearly ceased. King had reluctantly accepted the popular Black Power slogan, but he found it wanting. During the campaign he commented, "When you stand in action, and you begin to move together, you don't go arguing over whether white people should be in the movement." Referring to the expulsion of whites from predominantly black movements, he said, "That argument should never have come up anyway. We don't enlist races in the movement, we enlist consciences. And anybody who wants to be free, and make somebody else free, that's what we want."

As King traveled the land making stump speeches for the Poor People's Campaign, the right-wing hate campaign against him escalated. When he went to Miami to speak to ministers organized by SCLC and paid for through a Ford Foundation grant to involve them in the struggle to end poverty, neither King nor the delegates could go out of the hotel because the police were so concerned with threats against King's life. King had stressed his vocal cords so heavily that he could hardly speak during his address to the conference on February 23 titled, "To Minister to the Valley."

King said that the ministers, rather than he, would have to be the ones to change the nation. He recognized that he was a symbol of the movement, "but a symbol isn't worth anything without the support and backing of individuals whose names may never be in the headlines." He urged the assembled ministers to go to the "valleys filled with men and women who know the ache and anguish of poverty." He called on them to follow the Social Gospel and the example of Jesus, "the greatest revolutionary that history has ever known." This nonviolent crusader, he said, was more potent for poor people than Karl Marx. Like the character Dives in the Bible, who went to hell for failing to "see" and heed the needs of Lazarus, the middle class could also go to hell for forgetting to see and address the problems of the poor. King called on preachers to practice "dangerous altruism" by joining in action with the poor. "Christianity is not a euphoria or unalloyed comfort and untroubled ease," King said. "What is it? It means taking up the cross. Taking it with all of its tension-packed agony and bearing that cross until it leaves the very marks of Jesus Christ on you body, and on your soul."

* * *

SNCC CRITICS HAD always charged that SCLC and King, though expert in providing emotional buildup, leadership, and media coverage for a campaign of mobilization, did not do grassroots organizing. The Poor People's Campaign highlighted this problem. Mobilization campaigns relied on churches, unions, and preexisting community networks, and they had produced powerful results for SCLC. But hardly anyone, much less the SCLC's preachers and staff, knew how to develop multiracial leadership among poor people who had few resources and massive difficulties in just trying to survive day-to-day. King complained to Andrew Young, "There are no masses in this mass movement."

On March 14, Highlander tried to help SCLC bring together a multiracial coalition in a meeting in Atlanta. The Minority Group Conference of nearly a hundred people from various ethnicities, wrote historian Gordon Mantler, suggested the "great potential to build a class-based alliance for the first time." Chicanos demanded enforcement of the Treaty of Guadaloupe Hidalgo, giving them access to the land; Native Americans from Puget Sound pushed to reestablish their treaty-based fishing rights in ancestral waters; Puerto Ricans called for the island's independence; poor whites from Appalachia asked for jobs and health and nutrition programs. They chose a Committee of 100 to represent them in the PPC. King addressed the gathering late at night. Forty years later, farm labor organizer Baldemar Velasquez still remembered what he said: "His comment was when you impede the rich man's ability to make money, anything is negotiable."

Myles Horton and Carl Braden were there, both of them white southerners well versed in organizing working-class communities, and they thought the movement had turned a corner. Horton wrote to King, "I believe we caught a glimpse of the future. We had there in Atlanta authentic spokesmen for poor Mexican-Americans, American Indians, blacks, and whites, the making of a bottom-up coalition." The meeting on May 14 infused the campaign with energy and it picked up steam as King planned his "people to people" tour into the Deep South. But it also met with disturbing crosscurrents.

King that evening had just returned to Atlanta from Grosse Point, Michigan, where he faced the increasingly personal right-wing campaign against him. On March 14, at a high school gym filled with 2,700 people, Donald Lobsinger's right-wing group called Breakthrough had shouted him down. Protest signs read, "King: a red road runner," and "USA Forever - Traitors Must Die!" As King tried to speak on his theme, "The Other America," Lobsinger strode down the center aisle shouting, "King, you're a traitor!" King had experienced the shock politics of the extreme right before. As Lobsinger climbed the stairs to the podium, King extended his hand and suggested dialogue, but to no avail; the chanting continued and King shut down the question-and-answer part of the evening.

Remembering this moment nearly twenty years later, Lobsinger expressed no regrets. He decried "Martin Luther King and his communist associations and his communist background," and asserted, "Martin Luther King was no patriot! He was an enemy of the United States!" He remained furious at anyone who had opposed the Vietnam War or spoken up for black rights in the aftermath of the 1967 Detroit conflagration. Lobsinger's group in 1968 had not only threatened King, but bombarded Jude Huetteman, a white librarian who organized the meeting, with hate calls threatening her and her children. The school closed in the afternoon due to bomb threats. She drove King to the airport after this encounter, and in an article recalling those events wrote that both she and King felt shaken. Because of his leadership in the freedom movement and his opposition to the war, a crosscurrent of hate was building against King.

In the midst of King's fight for economic justice and an end to the Vietnam War, a new struggle moved to the forefront of his agenda. It began with, and would end with, tragedy.

MACE
WON'T
STOP
TRUTH!

After a police attack against them on February 23, 1968,
striking members of AFSCME Local 1733 unfurled the
iconic "I Am A Man" slogan.

Chapter 5

"ALL LABOR
HAS DIGNITY"

Uprising of the Working Poor, 1968

> *Now our struggle is for genuine equality, which*
> *means economic equality. . . . We can all get more*
> *together than we can apart . . . and this is the way*
> *we gain power.*

—KING, MEMPHIS, MARCH 18, 1968

> *We just got together, and we decided to stand up*
> *and be men, and that's what we did.*

—TAYLOR ROGERS, SANITATION STRIKER

LOCATED ON A BLUFF ABOVE THE MISSISSIPPI RIVER, AT the nexus of eastern Arkansas, western Tennessee, and northern Mississippi, Memphis often drips with humidity and heat reaching one hundred degrees. Slaves had worked producing cotton in the surrounding Mississippi Delta and unloading it on the docks of Memphis, the largest slave-trading and shipping point between St. Louis and New Orleans. They called Memphis "home of the blues" not only because W. C. Handy and generations of black musicians came through there, but because life there was often harsh and short. In 1968, King Cotton was no longer king, but black workers still did most of the hard, heavy, hot work.

In the wintertime, people working outside faced cold, driving rain. On February 1, Echol Cole, thirty-six, and Robert Walker, thirty, had been drenched while carrying garbage, without gloves, uniforms, or a place to shower provided by the city or the county. On the way to the Shelby County dump they jumped inside the compactor of one of the sanitation division's old "wiener barrel" trucks. The truck was caked with putrefying garbage but riding inside it was better than riding on the outside of the truck in the rain.

At 4:20 p.m., crew chief and driver Willie Crain heard the hydraulic ram go into action. He pulled over to the curb and jumped out of the cab, hoping to turn off the compactor. It was too late. One of the men nearly escaped from the compactor, but it snagged his raincoat and dragged him back. A white homeowner told a reporter, "He was standing there on the end of the truck, and suddenly it looked like the big thing just swallowed him." The unit crushed the two men to death like so much garbage, leaving one man's twitching legs hanging out from the rear of the compactor.

T. O. Jones, a union organizer, rushed to the scene. He knew both of the men, and furiously called their deaths "a disgrace and a sin." Jones had taken grievances to the commissioner of the Department of Public Works, asking to take this particular truck out of commission. Instead, the DPW extended its life by putting in a second motor to run the compactor after the first one wore out. Workers jump-started it in the morning and poured in fuel periodically to keep it running. Jones called it an accident just waiting to happen. Two men had previously been killed when another faulty garbage packer caused a truck to roll over them in 1964.

Walker and Cole had not been able to afford the city's self-financed life insurance policy and, as unclassified, hourly employees, had no coverage by the state's workmen's compensation. A funeral home had to hold the men's bodies while their families struggled to find a way to pay for their caskets. The city paid for one month of the men's salaries and $500, and burial expenses of $900 for each worker used most of that up, leaving their families destitute.

It goes without saying that the two dead men were black. Jones was black. Thirteen hundred men doing unskilled labor in the sanitation division of Public Works were black. James Robinson, a refugee from the bottomed-out sharecropping economy of Earle, Arkansas, where planter violence had crushed the Southern Tenant Farmers Union in the 1930s, was black. In an interview, he told me the accident happened because the city, as it always had, economized on the backs of low-wage black laborers. "We didn't have no job, we just had somewhere to get up and go every mornin'."

White supervisors arbitrarily sent black sanitation workers home if they came in a moment late, and would fire them for talking back. Whites expected obsequious behavior from black workers, and the city's outmoded labor relations resembled those of a plantation more than a modern urban center. Most white Memphians had what blacks called "the plantation mentality." Union organizer Jesse Epps said that when whites boasted they had a "good relationship" with blacks, they meant "on a servant to master basis. You know, they say, 'I like John. He's a good boy.'"

Black sanitation workers did every dirty job imaginable. Robinson told me, "We had to pick up trash out of the back yard. You had to tote it on your head in a tub. The tub's full of water, rain, garbage, maggots, everything else running out. Back then you had to supply your own clothes, own gloves, they didn't give you anything but the tubs. If you'd get a hole in it the water'd run all out the tub down on ya. Boss would sit around drinkin' coffee, come around once or twice a day to check on the truck."

Black workers had no regular work breaks, no bathroom in which to wash up or relieve themselves, and nowhere to eat their lunch, for which they were typically given fifteen minutes. Robinson recalled how a supervisor made him and his crew get out from under a shade tree and eat their lunch at the side of their truck because a white woman complained about them lounging near her property. "Truck had maggots and things all fallin' out of it," Robinson told me; "you gotta get out from under the shade tree and sit under the truck to get some shade." Sometimes when it rained workers even ate lunch in the garbage compactor.

Depending on the weather, they might work from dawn till after dusk, without any wages at all for overtime. When it rained hard enough, the DPW dismissed its laborers for the day with only two hours' worth of pay. In a city where sixty inches of rain fell every year, this policy meant many days of lost wages for black workers. White supervisors got paid rain or shine. A few whites operated heavy equipment and belonged to a craft union of engineers, but only a few blacks, like Willie Crain, worked as drivers, crew chiefs, or foremen. Blacks could not move up, and their backbreaking work earned them low wages, few benefits, and no job security. As unclassified day laborers, they could also be fired without cause.

In the 1960s, successive city governments had refused to raise already inadequate wages to keep up with the rising cost of living. "At the time of the strike I'd been there fifteen years and I made one dollar and sixty-five cents an hour," recalled Robinson. But what the workers hated the most was their lack of dignity as workers. Sanitation worker Taylor Rogers told me, "We didn't have no say about nothing. Whatever they said, that's what you had to do: right, wrong, indifferent. Anything that you did that the supervisor didn't like, he'd fire you, whatever. You didn't have no recourse, no way of gettin' back at him. We just got tired of all that."

* * *

BEFORE EMANCIPATION, AFRICAN Americans had done much of the skilled work in Memphis. At the end of the Civil War, in 1866, whites drove black workers off the docks and burned down black churches, homes, and schools. White craft unions subsequently drove most blacks out of the skilled trades. In 1896 whites ran the courageous black journalist and antilynching crusader Ida B. Wells-Barnett out of town. In 1905 whites erected a monument downtown to Nathan Bedford Forrest, the city's preeminent slave trader, leader of a Confederate massacre against black and white Union Army troops during the war, and a founder of the Ku Klux Klan afterward, thus keeping alive a romanticized version of the Confederate "lost cause." From the 1910s until his death in 1954, a white businessman from Mississippi named Edward H. Crump ran the city as if it were a plantation. A poll tax ($1.50 each time you voted,

Police escort strike breakers during the
Memphis sanitation strike, March 1968.

and accumulating when you didn't pay it) allowed Crump's political machine to manipulate the vote by paying people's poll taxes and telling them how to vote. Under Crump's reign, civil liberties barely existed, and Memphis was a hard nut to crack for civil rights and union organizers.

But by the end of World War II, tens of thousands of black and white workers had joined the CIO. Union wages allowed workers to pay their own poll taxes and vote for union-endorsed candidates. The NAACP drew on the ranks of organized black workers to establish one of the largest branches in the South. The votes of unionists and African Americans at times elected relatively moderate public officials, compared to the rest of the South, even more so after the death of Crump in 1954. Black union members produced children who challenged Jim Crow in 1960–62 and desegregated most public places without the full-blown crises seen in Birmingham and other cities. In 1959, at a Memphis voter registration rally, King had optimistically predicted that "something is going to take place that never happened before." By contrast to the rural areas surrounding it, Memphis appeared racially moderate if not progressive.

In the election of 1964, however, the electoral tide began to turn. Many white voters shifted from Democrat to Republican, a majority going against President Johnson for Barry Goldwater, who carried four southern states. In 1966 Memphis white voters also replaced a relatively moderate Democratic congressman, George Grider, with the anti–civil rights, antiunion, anticommunist Republican Dan Kuykendall. Memphis voters created at-large districts that made it possible for blacks to elect three African Americans to the city council in 1967, but in a runoff election for mayor the majority white electorate also placed Henry Loeb in office. A former mayor, he ran on the slogan, "Be Proud Again. Elect Loeb Again." African Americans regarded him as a segregationist and almost none of them voted for him. The Memphis-Shelby County AFL-CIO endorsed Loeb in a nonpartisan election, and would live to regret it. Loeb's father had busted unions of black women in the shops of his laundry- and dry-cleaning business. A fiscal conservative, Loeb hewed to the Republican model of low wages, low taxes, low expenditures, and no unions.

Yet despite Loeb's election, or perhaps because of it, King's prediction that something new would happen in Memphis did come true, initiated not by students, lawyers, or ministers, but by the dogged efforts of T. O. Jones. As Rev. Ezekial Bell recalled years later, "If there were any heroes in the strike situation, it was T. O. Jones. Not the preachers who came to the front and made the orations, and raised the money, and so rallied the community. I think it was T. O. Jones. He is a man who certainly deserves everything that can be said kindly about Memphis."

A native Memphian, Jones had worked in a unionized West Coast naval shipyard, but lost his job to mechanization and a recession in 1957. When he returned to Memphis, the only work he could find was in the sanitation division of the Public Works Department. In the summer of 1963, assisted by black business and civil rights activists, Jones and thirty-two other sanitation workers pulled a wildcat strike. The city fired them all. By January 1964 some had gotten their jobs back and the sanitation workers had formed the Independent Workers Association. Bill Ross, a white Mississippian from the printing trades and director of the Memphis Trades and Labor Council, kept Jones and his family from starving by paying him to clean the council's union hall. Ross also went to Washington, D.C., to meet with the national office of the American Federation of State, County, and Municipal Employees (AFSCME). The fastest-growing union in the country, AFSCME hired Jones as a full-time organizer and chartered AFSCME Local 1733, named to honor the thirty-three men who had been previously fired. In August 1966, after failing to get any concessions out of the city, Jones organized the workers to go on strike, but the city stopped them with a court injunction threatening jail to anyone who promoted strike activity.

On January 31, the Public Works Department sent Ed Gillis and twenty-one other black sewer and street workers home without pay during a rainstorm while white supervisors and drivers remained on the job and collected wages. Gillis and his cohort never got paid for their lost time, and had no grievance procedure or written rules. A few days later, Echol Cole and Robert Walker got ground up in a garbage packer.

On Sunday night, February 11, between five hundred and eight hundred black men packed into the Memphis Labor Temple to pour out their grievances. They could not afford union dues, so fewer than a hundred of them belonged to the union, but they demanded union action. Said Jones, "The men wanted something and wanted it signed, they wanted it spelled out and they wanted the public to know they had protection on their jobs." While the meeting continued, Jones took their demands to the head of the Public Works Department, to no avail. Jones declared himself ready to violate the antistrike injunction still in effect and to go to jail. He returned to the AFL-CIO Labor Temple. Without taking a formal vote, the men yelled their approval to quit work.

On Monday morning, February 12—Abraham Lincoln's birthday—in a scene reminiscent of the Montgomery bus boycott, homeowners looked out of their windows but saw no workers riding on the back of garbage trucks. Had anyone planned it, the workers would have struck in the summer, when uncollected garbage really smells, instead of in the dead of winter. They could have also consulted with their international union, but they knew it would have objected. Holding a strike in the South, with strong laws against public-employee unions, seemed like suicide. "The men weren't thinking of strategy; they were thinking of justice and injustice," said Jones. Taylor Rogers told me, "We just got to the point that we had to do something . . . we wanted somebody to represent us, so that we could have some say about our hours and working conditions."

As striking workers gathered at the AFL-CIO union hall, Labor Council director Ross called AFSCME organizer P. J. Ciampa, a working-class Italian, at the national office in Washington, D.C. Ciampa said he knew nothing about it and needed a strike in the South "like I need a hole in my head." He asked Ross to get the men to go back to work. "I told him buddy, I'm the only white soul here with 1,300 angry black men. You come and tell them yourself," Ross recalled.

Ciampa and organizer William Lucy left the next day for Memphis. Lucy, a young African American from the North and a rising star in AFSCME, expected a quick settlement and left his rental car in a parking lot in Detroit. It remained there for the next six weeks, as Lucy, Ciampa, and others from AFSCME dedicated themselves to the struggle for black labor rights in Memphis. On Tuesday, February 13, the workers held their first strike meeting at the Firestone union hall, and then marched to city hall. Once there, Mayor Loeb told "his men" they were breaking the law and to go back to work or lose their jobs. The men heckled him. When Loeb defended Public Works director Charles Blackburn as a "straight shooter," one man shouted out "Yeah, but he shoots the wrong way." T. O. Jones later said, "The people just booed him right down." Loeb stalked out of the meeting, furious.

Jesse Epps, an African American raised in Mississippi who joined the AFSCME crew of organizers, observed, "There was an insurrection among the slaves." Bill Lucy was amazed. He said these workers had "the least to gain and the most to lose." These were not the young people who put their bodies on the line in the civil rights movement, but mostly older, churchgoing men with families who had a precarious hold on life through a job. But in coming weeks they would face down guns and tanks and the chemical Mace, marching day in and day out, producing one of the most powerful and extended labor-civil rights struggles of the civil rights era. They had no idea of the possible outcome, said Lucy, but "simply put life and limb on the line." Little did anyone imagine how their strike would challenge white supremacy and the exploitation of the working poor, with staggering consequences for the nation.

Mayor Loeb would talk incessantly to union representatives but refuse to bargain. His employer father taught him the way to handle a strike was to keep talking until union members wore out and gave up. Loeb had the "plantation mentality" or, as Lucy put it, "the sense of the bluebloods and all this who gather at the mansion for the social affairs of the season and sort of living in a world of fantasy" reminiscent of slavery days. Loeb could be gracious in his own way, but he was inflexible. According to state law, public employees had no right to strike, so Loeb reasoned that by bargaining with the union he would be breaking the law. His refusal to make any compromises with the union would throw the city into turmoil.

AFSCME national president Jerry Wurf, a militant socialist and equal-rights advocate from New York City, immediately came to Memphis, thinking that since he and Loeb were both Jewish they would be able to reason their way to a compromise. But Loeb, who had switched to the Episcopal Church when he married the queen of the Cotton Carnival, seemed to have no grounding in either a Jewish or Protestant social-justice framework. Wurf got nowhere in face-to-face meetings with Loeb, but vowed that AFSCME would stay in the struggle until Memphis black workers achieved union rights.

Stalled negotiations forced the workers to take matters into their own hands. On February 22, hundreds of workers marched several miles from the Firestone union hall to interrupt an ongoing city council meeting, demanding that it step in to adjudicate the strike. The workers sat in for hours, with mass singing led by beautician Tarlese Matthews, one of a number of activist black women who played crucial roles in strike support. The trapped council members told them to come back the next day and they would settle the strike. Instead, when the men returned, the council turned off the microphones, turned out the lights, and turned the matter back over to the intransigent mayor. With vocal support from Rev. James Lawson, workers and their ministerial and community allies left city hall to express their outrage in a march. The NAACP had already endorsed the strike on its fourth day, as a civil rights struggle as well as a strike. Now that reality became crystal clear.

The Memphis police, following a seemingly premeditated plan, used long clubs to beat ministers and workers alike, sprayed Mace in their faces, and chased hundreds of people through the streets. They picked out Ciampa, already beaten and blinded by Mace, for further harm, but black workers pulled him away. The Rev. Lawson had been chatting with a police officer about how he should join a union when the officer turned and hit him full in the face with Mace. Beaten and gassed, straggling marchers reassembled at Clayborn Temple and poured out their outrage. When Rev. Samuel Kyles heard the news of the beatings, he was at the ministers' meeting with King in Miami. He and his wife Gwen cancelled their planned wedding anniversary vacation to the Bahamas and returned home.

On February 24 Kyles joined nearly half of the city's three hundred or so black ministers gathered at Clayborn again to form the Community on the Move for Equality (COME)—a network to support the strike. They elected Lawson, King's close ally and one of the most fearless and well-schooled advocates of nonviolence in the nation, to lead it. For the next six weeks, workers met every day at the Firestone union hall or at Clayborn Temple, marching to the downtown and attending mass meetings at a different church every night. Rev. Henry Starks, president of the black Memphis Ministerial Alliance, became a powerhouse in the strike as he and other ministers led picket lines and marches and organized church meetings. A few white Catholic, Protestant, and Jewish religious leaders joined in support. Black community activist Cornelia Crenshaw and other women raised funds, food, and clothing for the workers, who had no strike fund. Outside donations, AFSCME support, and church fund-raising kept them going. As with the civil rights movement, the strike in Memphis would not have succeeded without the support of black women in the community. As the city began bringing in scabs to take the jobs of strikers, Bessie Rogers and other women found ingenious ways to feed their families in order to keep their striking husbands from going back to work.

The workers responded to the February 23 police attack by emblazoning the slogan "I Am A Man" on their picket signs. Rev. Lawson declared in a press conference that Mayor Loeb "treats the workers as though they are not men, [and] that's a racist point of view. . . . For at the heart of racism is the idea that a man is not a man, that a person is not a person." Sanitation worker James Robinson put it more bluntly to me many years later, saying, "I am a man [meant] that they weren't gonna take that shit no more." Women used the slogan too. Ortha B. Strong Jones, a hospital worker, said it meant having a union with "backbone" to protect the workers. The slogan was not about reinforcing male domination, but about overturning inequalities that for generations had placed huge burdens on black men and women alike. The black community recognized it as a rallying cry for equality. One striker explained the goal of the strike on his picket sign with one word, "Dignity."

In the wake of the police attacks, the city arrested T. O. Jones for "night riding," a charge usually used against KKK terrorists. Enforcing the injunction against union leaders proved to be a strategic mistake by the city. Black ministers could not be charged under the injunction or under labor laws for leading a secondary boycott as union leaders could. Union leaders avoided the expenses and dislocation involved with jail, while black ministers took an increasingly leading role in fighting for worker rights. As King had long advocated, black ministers and churches had become a potent organizing force on behalf of the black working poor.

The ultraconservative Scripps-Howard morning paper, the *Commercial Appeal*, and the afternoon *Press-Scimitar* both helped to turn the strike into a racial conflict. Following the February 23 beatings, with a headline, "Beyond the Bounds of Tolerance," a *Commercial Appeal* cartoon caricatured T. O. Jones as a large black man sitting on a garbage can labeled "city hall sit-in." Garbage reeked all around him; the words "Threat of Anarchy" loomed in the background. On February 24 the newspaper applauded the police for their "extreme constraint" and their "self control" in "protecting" themselves from the workers and repeated the false charge by police director Frank Holloman—who had spent twenty-five years in his previous career working directly under J. Edgar Hoover in the FBI—that Jones had precipitated the police attack on the marchers by trying "to inflame the crowd into turning over a squad car."

At mass rallies protesters ejected reporters from both newspapers, and COME began a boycott of the white-owned and white-written commercial media, which had long twisted or ignored facts, used racist cartoons and language, and now failed to explain the worker grievances or the fact that other unions already bargained with the city and had dues check-off. "You can give [them] the facts and they just won't release the facts," T. O. Jones recalled. "The kindest word that I can use for them is, is not only hostile to unions, but hostile to what's right," Jesse Epps said. "And I'm being kind when I say that. Very kind."

Black Memphians boycotted the white media and turned to the *Tri-State Defender* weekly and black radio stations WLOK and WDIA. Women spearheaded a boycott by shoppers of white-owned businesses downtown. As in the Montgomery bus boycott and in Birmingham in 1963, economic withdrawal proved a powerful weapon. The boycott by women, who did most of the shopping, dried up downtown businesses, some of which never recovered. Black Memphians hoped that the white religious leaders, in a town with more churches than gas stations, would help to open dialogue with Loeb. However, not only the newspapers, but also most of the white businesspeople and religious leaders closed ranks behind the mayor. Unlike ministers in the black community, even slightly liberal white ministers and rabbis had to fight for their lives within their own institutions.

Yet the strike also radicalized a layer of white leaders and students as events revealed the depth of injustice and racism in the society around them. An assortment of black and white activist Jewish, Catholic, and Protestant women awakened to the plight of the urban poor during the strike. These church women organized relief efforts and after the strike went on to establish citywide networks to supplement the diets and improve the health conditions of the urban poor. The events of the strike brought more southern white women into the movement for civil rights and human rights in 1968 and years to come.

Out of a strike by black men came a labor, civic, and black community alliance that rivaled the power of any previous movement in the South. Bill Lucy called the guiding force "the spirit of

Memphis." With a few white lawyers and religious, academic, and student supporters, the strike brought out an important element of help from a surprising quarter. More than in any other southern civil rights struggle, white trade unionists gave crucial support. The United Rubber Workers Union Local 186 had spawned a group of black labor activists, and now the local's white president, George "Rip" Clark, opened the Firestone union as the strike's organizing center. Vigilantes blew out the hall's roof with a bomb. Yet Clark denounced "the right-wing people in our plant, that are supposed to be union members" and told them that they "will not prevent this union from supporting this, or any other group of workers, in their efforts to have a union."

Black trade unionists like Le Roy and Alzada Clark, Clarence Coe, George Holloway, Leroy Boyd, and many others had struggled for years in Memphis and joined in picketing, fund-raising, and mass meetings. Boyd had migrated to Memphis from Blackhawk, Mississippi, and had been among the black workers who went to Jackson, Mississippi, to protest the state's 1951 execution of Willie McGee for having an affair with a white woman. Boyd stayed in the fight for unions and marched with his children in the Memphis strike. When strike supporters went to the gates of the Firestone factory, the largest in Memphis, Local 186 workers put money in containers and donated a total of $835, the largest collection ever taken there. The white Labor Council and Butcher Workers' union president, Tommy Powell, whose union amalgamated with the United Packinghouse Workers Union, attended marches and rallies and initiated a petition drive to recall Loeb. The Tennessee state AFL-CIO blocked bills in the legislature to penalize strikers, and union-backed Senator James White proposed a state mediation board and forced Mayor Loeb to accept binding arbitration by a third party. Trade unionists knew that if the Loeb administration destroyed Local 1733, it would destroy Memphis public-employee organizing and set back all unions. Epps said that "Memphis was the dam or it was the gate. And to lose it was not losing it for State-County but losing it for the whole AFL-CIO in the South."

The strike was both a labor and a civil rights struggle. However, some white unionists weren't sure which it was; as in every community in America, in Memphis race had always divided workers. On March 4, the Memphis AFL-CIO mobilized some five hundred unionists, most of them white, to march with the sanitation workers. But they kept to themselves and behind the scenes debates whirled over whether to emphasize the strike as a workers' struggle, with hopes of drawing in more white unionists, or as a civil rights struggle, in order to solidify the black community behind it. UAW Local 988 had a history of militant racism, and many white workers and retirees did not want to pay the increased taxes that wage increases for sanitation workers would require. The building trades council, once one of Crump's former mainstays, took no official position. But when AFSCME president Jerry Wurf spoke to its members, they treated him like an outside agitator and told him he should write a letter of apology for the strike to the people of Memphis and publish it in the *Commercial Appeal*.

As in the Scripto strike, rank-and-file white workers were divided about supporting the Memphis strike. Approximately 110 union locals belonged to the Memphis AFL-CIO Labor Council, but the responses of their members varied. The AFL-CIO's regional political organizer Dan Powell knew black workers could win only by emphasizing their strike as a racial issue in order to mobilize the African American community behind them. Yet most white unionists who supported the strike did so only as an economic issue. "We had people telling us, 'I'll help you all I can, but if the NAACP becomes involved, you can forget about me,'" said Bill Lucy.

The civil rights community, led by the fiery Maxine Smith of the NAACP, also had its splits over labor issues. Black ministers had not supported black workers some years earlier when they struck at a black-owned life insurance company. Many African Americans resented the white building-trades unions that had blocked black worker advancement for many years. But police brutality and Loeb's hard-headed unwillingness to make any compromises with a union, and his failure to understand the racial issues, galvanized black ministers, black lawyers and professionals, and businesspeople like the Tri-State Bank owner and Memphis NAACP president Jesse Turner. Unions and the civil rights movement seemed to be moving toward that labor–civil rights "convergence" that King and Bayard Rustin had always spoken of. On March 12 Rev. Ralph Jackson declared, "Never in the recent history of our times has the Negro community been so united on an issue."

Most of those in the white commercial media continued to fan the flames of racial polarization. They rallied the white community behind the position taken by Loeb that this was an illegal strike and failed to interview workers or tell their side of the story. A month into the strike, strikebreakers were hauling garbage in white neighborhoods; strikers' families were losing their homes and cars. Even among black ministers, recalled Epps, "A number wanted to go back." But it was too late. "They said to themselves and to their congregations, 'This is no longer 1,300 men fighting, but it's this whole Negro community fighting. And if we lose we're all lost.'" Lawson and others raised the stakes, calling not only for union rights, but also for good jobs, better housing, an end to police brutality. Jerry Wurf and his staff at AFSCME knew they could not back down, because a loss to an intransigent employer in Memphis would imperil public-employee organizing everywhere else. Wurf, a strong civil rights advocate, also became enraged at the racism he encountered in Memphis and vowed to put every resource the union had into winning the strike. AFSCME held true to that pledge.

Many feared the strike was dragging on too long, had gotten too little outside press coverage, and could be lost. COME leaders drew national civil rights figures into Memphis in hopes of getting national press attention, including Roy Wilkins, national president of the NAACP. On March 14 Bayard Rustin spoke in Memphis and compared the strike to the Montgomery bus boycott. He called the Memphis strike "one of the great struggles for the emancipation of the black man today" and said it provided "the symbol of the movement to get rid of poverty. The record shows that in Memphis this fight is going to be won because the black people in this community and the trade unions stand together."

*　*　*

MEANWHILE, KING HAD been charging about the country drumming up support for the Poor People's Campaign. But King confronted indifference or hostility from many quarters. Mainstream unions and the AFL-CIO had barely responded. Speaking in New York City on March 10 to Local 1199 hospital workers union, King praised that union's interracial solidarity and idealism but complained that most unions had advanced the interests of the white and unionized working class while largely ignoring the interests of people of color and the poor. This depressing reality, King said, threatened to cancel out the larger message of social justice that gave birth to the labor movement in the first place.

On March 17 Lawson reached King by phone, asking him for the second time to come to Memphis. Earlier, King had told him that doctors told him to rest. He had gone to Mexico to sit in the sun and try to recuperate from the depression and exhaustion that continued to stalk him. He was now on the West Coast and typically going in too many directions at once. King's staff practically begged him not to go to Memphis, but he welcomed the struggle of the working poor, and after a speaking engagement in Los Angeles on March 17, King went. He decided to hold his next staff meeting in Memphis and to launch a planned "people to people" speaking tour for the Poor People's Campaign through the Mississippi Delta from Memphis.

King's spirits soared when he came to the Bluff City on March 18, thirty-five days into the strike. In anticipation of King's speech, thousands of people had already filled Mason Temple by 7 p.m., with many of them crowded into the doorways and aisles during a four-hour rally. When King walked through a side door a little after 9 p.m., the packed crowd of perhaps five thousand people or more greeted him with a standing ovation, clenched fists, and upturned thumbs. No shouts of Black Power or cries of "sellout" assailed King. The Memphis crowd punctuated his statements with shouts of "That's right," "Yeah," and interrupted his speech dozens of times with strong, swelling applause.

Memphis seemed to invoke once again the spirit of the early 1960s black freedom struggle, evincing unity, determination, and mass participation. "Martin was visibly shaken by all this," said Lawson, "for this kind of support was unprecedented in the Movement. No one had ever been able to get these numbers out before." No indoor setting in the black South—not in Montgomery, Birmingham, or Atlanta—equaled the size of Mason Temple, owned by the Memphis-based Church of God in Christ, the largest Pentecostal group in the United States.

Lawson called King a megaphone for the movement: he could bring national attention to local struggles just by giving a speech. Some in the movement resented King for this, but King well understood that much of the struggle for social change hinged on how, when, and whether the media covered events. In Memphis, King demonstrated why the movement still needed him so badly. Speaking with almost no notes, he put the situation into a context that could help people to see the strike as something more than a local issue, and gave them spiritual strength for the fight ahead. And he too gained strength. As he told the crowd, "It's been a long time since I've been in a situation like this and this lets me know that we are ready for action." For the first time in a long while, King saw people united across religious lines and beyond class lines. Said King, "You are demonstrating something here that needs to be demonstrated all over our country. You are demonstrating that we can stick together and you are demonstrating that we are all tied in a single garment of destiny, and that if one black person suffers, if one black person is down, we are all down."

In Memphis, King found the spirit of hope and unity that he had been preaching and teaching about for years. "The Negro 'haves' must join hands with the Negro 'have-nots'. . . they must journey into that other country of their brother's denial and hurt and exploitation. And this is what you have done." King told the massive crowd, "You are doing many things here in this struggle," and he outlined them. First of all, "You are demanding that this city will respect the dignity of labor." He said, "All labor has dignity" and that people should understand that the person who picks up the garbage is as essential to the health of society as the physician. He spoke of how the nation had cruelly devalued the labor of the working poor: "You are reminding, not only Memphis, but you are reminding the nation that it is a crime for people to live in this rich nation and receive starvation wages! And I need not remind you that this is our plight as a people all over America." He continued, "Do you know that most of the poor people in our country are working every day. And they are making wages so low that they cannot begin to function in the mainstream of the economic life of our nation. These are the facts which must be seen, and it is criminal to have people working on a full-time basis and a full-time job getting part-time income." Dives in the Bible, King reminded his audience, went to hell not because he was rich but because he refused to see the needs of the poor. "You are here to demand that Memphis will see the poor." To cheers and thunderous applause, King connected racism in Memphis to the insensitivity of the country as a whole. "If America does not use her vast resources of wealth to end poverty and make it possible for all of God's children to have the basic necessities of life, she too is going to hell."

In his inimitable way, King combined scriptural teachings and the black Social Gospel with a direct, political attack on the American power structure, speaking of God's coming "indictment on America" for ignoring its poor. "And that same voice says in Memphis to the mayor, to the power structure, 'If you do it unto the least of these of my children you do it unto me.'" King did not leave it to God, however, but reminded people of the power they themselves possessed by drawing on what the movement had achieved. In Montgomery, Alabama, for 381 days, "We substituted tired feet for tired souls," and stood up for the very best traditions of American freedom in the Constitution and Declaration of Independence. In Birmingham, black people "had a fire that no water could put out," and "we literally subpoenaed the conscience of a large segment of the nation."

According to King, the struggle for black equality had logically brought the movement to Memphis. While civil- and voting-rights acts had brought to an end one phase of the struggle, "now our struggle is for genuine equality which means economic equality. For we know that it isn't enough to integrate lunch counters. What does it profit a man to be able to eat at an integrated lunch counter if he doesn't earn enough money to buy a hamburger and a cup of coffee?" Poverty deprived African Americans of many of the things they had fought for in the civil rights movement. "We are tired of being at the bottom," tired of "wall-to-wall rats and roaches" instead of wall-to-wall carpeting, tired of "smothering in an airtight cage of poverty in the midst of an affluent society. We are tired of walking the streets in [a] search for jobs that do not exist."

Taking a male breadwinner's perspective, King protested that "our wives and our daughters have to go out and work in the white lady's kitchen leaving us unable to be with our children and give them the time and attention that they need. We are tired." Indeed, in Memphis and everywhere else, many, perhaps most, black women worked in factories, in service jobs, as teachers and as domestic workers in the homes of whites. Many of them were the main or only breadwinners for their families, and numerous black women, people like Alzada Clark and Ida Leachman, played active roles in the Memphis labor movement as both union members and organizers. Being tired remained endemic to the poor men and women in his audience. King declared, "We are saying now is the time," a time to "make real the promises of democracy." That promise should make an adequate income a part of citizenship. "Now is the time."

In the Poor People's Campaign thus far, King had focused on the poorest of the poor, those with no jobs at all. In Memphis he clearly linked poverty to the plight of the working poor, whose poverty resulted not from their lack of initiative or hard work but from low wages and a lack of power. In posing things this way, King spoke much as a labor leader would. "Let it be known everywhere that along with wages and all of the other securities that you are struggling for, you are also struggling for the right to organize and be recognized."

Placing the idea of Black Power in a different framework, he referred to Walter Reuther, who said power was the ability to make a corporation say yes when it wanted to say no. King said, "Power is the ability to achieve purpose, power is the ability to affect change, and we need power." Echoing antislavery leader Frederick Douglass from long ago, he asserted, "Never forget that freedom is not something that is voluntarily given by the oppressor. It is something that must be demanded by the oppressed." King exhorted the strikers, "if we are going to get adequate wages, we are going to have to struggle for it."

King had been building up a head of steam, responding to the cries and shouts of support from this packed audience of fired-up Memphians. Like any good organizer, he saw the potential in the moment to raise people's sights for an even more powerful mobilization. He paused, turning over an idea in his mind. "You know what?" he asked the crowd. "You may have to escalate the struggle a bit." If the city continued to fight unionization, he said, "You ought to get together and just have a general work stoppage in the city of Memphis!"

With this unexpected suggestion, pandemonium broke loose. King knew he was on the right track, and followed up: "And you let that day come, and not a Negro in this city will go to any job downtown. When no Negro in domestic service will go to anybody's house or anybody's kitchen. When black students will not go to anybody's school and black teachers" will refuse to teach. Everyone knew black workers did most of the hardest work in Memphis and together they could shut the city down. This rather stunning proposal placed King in his usual dilemma: people of course would want him to come back. And hastily King conferred with Lawson and AFSCME organizers, and announced that he would return to lead a mass march on March 24.

In just this way King had joined so many local struggles and found himself in so many jails. This was the dialectical process, in which the movement provided the context, the power, and the hope, and King raised the stakes. King's genius, Bill Lucy noted, was his acute ability "to understand and interpret the issues and what was taking place." Lucy said that with only "the most minimal of briefings" King recognized "people who worked forty hours a week and still lived in poverty, and he was able to arrange his presentation to demonstrate to the crowd that he understood this, and to give them a sense that their struggle was a legitimate struggle, that they had every right to carry on."

Because of his years of speaking before unions as well as almost every other audience imaginable, King had a sense of timing and of what needed to be said in a community movement, and a tactical intelligence about how to push that movement forward. In Memphis, he was speaking like a labor leader and a preacher, and from the heart. He knew just how to use the power of the spoken word. As many would comment, King had the ability to make you *feel what he was saying.*

As thousands of jubilant strikers and their supporters left Mason Temple after hours of singing, speeches, and prophecy, the "spirit of Memphis," as Lucy called it, became a tangible reality that could not now be easily quenched. King's presence not only invigorated the movement, but also awoke the national media. "We were forty-seven days into the strike and nobody knew it except us and the city of Memphis," said Lucy. Now national media covered the story and donations from unions and civic organizations began pouring into the COME-administered strike fund, eventually totaling over $300,000.

The "spirit of Memphis" was powerful, but the local press, predictably, garbled the message. According to the *Commercial Appeal*, King had once again cynically used a local movement for his own ends. At the rally, he "saw how many Negroes were aroused and quickly decided to attach himself to the local issue." His self-seeking pledge to return to Memphis to lead a march, "which is usually good for a spot on the evening television broadcasts," purely served his efforts to build himself up as a preeminent national leader with "ready made followers" in Memphis.

In just this way, writers in the Memphis commercial media erected a wall of misunderstanding of the strike, of King, and of the issues related to racism, poverty, and injustice. They failed to report on basic information such as the fact that several hundred union members worked in various city departments and that city teachers and bus drivers already had their union dues deducted from their paychecks. Newspapers, radio, and television failed to interview strike leaders, workers, or ministers, or to put the strike into any context that would make support of union rights understandable.

King said on March 18, "We can all get more together than we can apart," but that was not the King most white people in Memphis believed to be real. In the wake of his visit, racial hate and the racial divide would only widen, because of how whites and the media interpreted him.

*   *   *

"I'VE NEVER SEEN a community as together as Memphis," King told his New York adviser Stanley Levison, in a conversation wiretapped by the FBI. Memphis relieved King from the brooding depression, anxiety, and exhaustion that weighed him down. King in Memphis drew on a hallowed labor movement tactic, the general strike, and seemingly stepped into the role of labor leader as well as human rights leader. He could say things union leaders could not say without violating the injunction against them and getting arrested. His proposal of a general strike merging black workers and the community inaugurated something entirely new in the direct-action tactics of 1960s' freedom movements. Civil rights struggles had paralyzed places like Birmingham, but nowhere had the freedom movement shut down the economy of a city. Even in labor history, rarely had workers and their allies shut a city down through a general strike. This moment in Memphis looked like the civil rights–labor alliance that King and Rustin and A. Philip Randolph had long called for. King's appeal placed the sanitation strike into the context of a movement for both black unity and for labor rights.

He planned to start the Poor People's Campaign caravan going to Washington from Memphis, highlighting the fact that poverty resulted not just from a lack of jobs but from jobs that did not pay enough nor provide human dignity and union rights. Memphis could not have provided a more appropriate setting. Blacks made up more than 40 percent of the city's 500,000 people, but almost 60 percent of them lived in poverty, at four times the white poverty rate. Unemployment shattered many black families, as did diabetes, sickle-cell anemia, high blood pressure, high infant mortality rates, and cancer. But of those who did have jobs, over 80 percent of employed black men worked in laboring jobs, and 80 percent of employed black women worked in the homes of whites. Perhaps more importantly, Memphis had a movement to change these things.

Memphis also had the music. Historically, it was the crossroads of country and urban blues, gospel, and other genres of music planted deep in the soul of people who had lived through slavery, segregation, sharecropping, and rural and urban poverty. Although commercial black music was not often directly political, it had soul power. It had black and white radio stations and disk jockeys, and recording studios called Sun Records and Stax. Memphis music had an uplifting, sometimes smooth and sometimes raucous sound that made people want to move. It had not only Elvis Presley, Johnny Cash, and other previously poor white singers who transgressed the color line, but even more—scores of celebrated black musicians, from B.B. King to Al Green, Carla Thomas, Rufus Thomas, Isaac Hayes, Otis Redding and the Bar-Kays, and many others. No one who came to Memphis could be immune to the power of the "home of the blues." Black churches were bursting with inspiring music. It made Memphis bearable and, for some, desirable. And this musical community, both religious and secular, pitched in to the struggle during and after the strike. This too was part of the "spirit of Memphis."

In a period of depression and anxiety for King, Memphis uplifted his spirit and gave him hope. If he didn't have hope, he had told his staff in January, "I couldn't make it." As King moved down into the valley of the Mississippi Delta on his last speaking tour, he continued struggling to make the plight of the poor the main concern of his country. Many would call it his most desperate, but also his most heroic, hour.

King was shouted down by anticommunists in his talk on "The Other America" in Grosse Pointe, Michigan, on March 14, 1968.

Chapter 6

"DANGEROUS UNSELFISHNESS"

*Let us develop a kind of dangerous unselfishness
. . . I may not get there with you. But I want you
to know that we as a people will get to the
promised land!*

—KING IN MEMPHIS, APRIL 3, 1968

WHEN KING LEFT MEMPHIS ON MARCH 18, HE FELT euphoric. The movement he had struggled to build, uniting elements of labor, religion, the black community, students, and whites in and out of unions, seemed to be on track. Memphis made the Poor People's Campaign a true movement of the working poor. On March 19, a reenergized King toured Batesville, Marks, Clarksdale, Greenwood, Grenada, Laurel, and Hattiesburg (where he met his audience at midnight). In these Mississippi Delta towns, he confronted the desperate poverty of the unemployed poor. In Marks, he told an interviewer, "I found myself weeping before I knew it. I met boys and girls by the hundreds who didn't have any shoes to wear, who didn't have any food to eat in terms of three square meals a day, and I met their parents, many of whom don't even have jobs." Conservatives complained that the poor were on welfare, but King found that in Marks the really poor had no income at all. "I literally cried when I heard men and women saying that they were unable to get any food to feed their children."

In Marks, a town of 2,500, poor people had been cast off from the cotton economy. Landlords mechanized away their jobs. Poor people lived in shacks without plumbing, lighting, or ventilation in one of the most humid and hot places in the world. Some subsisted on berries, fish, and rabbits. Yet, remarkably, this is where King envisioned a core constituency for a poor people's solidarity movement. As Stokely Carmichael had observed when he worked with King in the March Against Fear in 1966, King was at ease, even happy among the poor people of the Delta. In Mississippi King found a core of poor people who would go to Washington in May and afterward put one of the largest contingents of black elected leaders into office in the United States.

As he viewed the horrible conditions of the black poor in Mississippi, King spoke as strongly about racism as any black nationalist. "The thing wrong with America," he told a rally in Laurel, "is white racism. White folks are not right. . . . It's time for America to have an intensified study on what's wrong with white folk . . . anybody that will go around bombing houses and churches, there's something wrong with him." King said the land was beautiful but "white folk want it all for themselves." Speaking in the idiom of the black poor he added, "They don't want to share nothing."

Slavery and the overthrow of Reconstruction provided his frame of reference. Emancipation, King said, produced "freedom and famine." It released slaves from bondage, but "America did not give the black man any land to make that freedom real." Africans did not come to America as immigrants looking for freedom; rather, they were ripped from their freedom in Africa to work without wages in America.

King recalled a conversation with a white man on a plane who said blacks should lift themselves up by their own bootstraps like immigrants. The "bootstrap philosophy" of American capitalism, as portrayed by fiction writer Ayn Rand and some economists, held that anyone could advance him- or herself through individual initiative. King recalled telling the man, "It's a cruel jest to say to a bootless man that he ought to lift himself by his own bootstraps." Few black people received the kinds of government support—the New Deal's low-interest home loans, the homesteads and land grant colleges and subsidies, and federal land acquisitions and military protections that gave birth to railroad and oil magnates in the West—that had boosted some immigrants and the white middle and upper classes. African Americans had accumulated little capital, while black labor exploitation had helped to produce some of the richest people in the world. In Sunflower County, Senator James Eastland, one of the wealthiest plantation owners in Mississippi, received hundreds of thousands of dollars in subsidies not to plant crops. Meanwhile, agricultural working people like Fannie Lou Hamer ended up desperately poor and black farmers lost their lands.

In contrast to the immigrant "self-made man" stereotype, King spoke of a man kept in prison for many years and then released when it is discovered he is not guilty. "And then you just go up to him and say, 'Now you are free.' And don't give him any bus fare to go to town. Don't give him any money to get some clothes to put on his back. Don't give him any money to get on his feet in life again. Every code of jurisprudence would rise up against this. And yet, this is exactly what America did to the black man."

In Quitman County, perhaps the poorest county in America, King pointed out that whites had tried so hard to keep blacks down that they had stifled economic development and education for themselves. Just as black poverty could never be eliminated without ending racial injustice, white poverty would continue as long as poor people allowed themselves to be turned against each other on the basis of race. King said the freedom movement sought "economic justice for the poor" regardless of race. Yet the only white ally King saw in Mississippi was a seemingly inebriated man named Mr. Mobley who walked up to him and slipped a hundred-dollar bill into his hand, and then left.

King in his "people to people" tour for the Poor People's Campaign warned that the second phase of the freedom movement would be harder than the first—hard to imagine after what people went through in the first phase. "It is much more difficult to eradicate slums than it is to integrate a bus," or to create jobs and incomes for all the nation's people, he said.

King ended his southern tour on March 22, in Albany, Georgia, a place where he had repeatedly gone to jail for demanding civil and voting rights. King declared the Poor People's Campaign would gather the sick, the hungry, the poor in a shantytown in the nation's capital that would let "the whole world know how America is treating its poor citizens." African Americans would be joined by Puerto Ricans, Mexicans, Indians, and Appalachian whites. It would be a "great camp meeting," with freedom schools teaching people's history, with better food than poor people normally get, and with music. As SCLC staff member Jimmy Collier sang to King's audiences, "I'm gonna walk the streets of Washington one of these days." King told audiences, "If you can't fly, run. If you can't run, walk. If you can't walk, crawl, but by all means, keep moving."

King too had to keep moving, as his time to serve the people ran out.

* * *

IN THE EARLY hours of March 24, King waited in the Atlanta airport for his flight to Memphis, where he planned to lead a mass march, perhaps even a general strike, on behalf of the sanitation workers. He waited in vain. A huge snowstorm blew in, shutting down the airports. James Lawson in a phone call with King joked that God must have called a general strike: the storm completely closed down Memphis. King rescheduled to come to Memphis on March 28. Before his return to Memphis, King spent four days recruiting and speaking in upstate New York and the New York City area. He intended to go to Memphis on the night of March 27, but he was too exhausted. "Martin must have been so fatigued he was almost in a daze," Andrew Young recalled. King told a reporter he had been getting two hours of sleep a night for the last ten days. He put off his flight to Memphis until morning, but then stayed up arguing late into the night with SCLC board member Marian Logan. She argued that his Poor People's Campaign would lead to riots and repression and swing more white voters to the right in the 1968 elections. He too was worried about this, but insisted that

After a police attack and a riot on March 28, 1968, the
Tennessee National Guard occupied Memphis,
but members of AFSCME Local 1733 continued to march.

she support the campaign. He drank and smoked and argued, and hardly slept. She feared King was "losing hold."

King typically tried to be in two places at once. He planned to make a quick trip to Memphis, lead a march, then leave that same day for meetings in Washington, D.C. He got up early, but his plane was late. Everything started to go wrong. Exhausted, frustrated, agitated, King did not arrive at the Memphis airport until 10:30 a.m., when AFSCME organizer Jesse Epps picked him up in a white Lincoln Continental borrowed from a black funeral home.

Since 8 a.m., strikers, their families, and community supporters had gathered outside Clayborn Temple. In a festive mood, they intended to show Mayor Henry Loeb the power of a united community. Hundreds of workers carried placards reading, "I Am A Man." Parents brought children with them. No one expected trouble. But by 10 a.m. police helicopters buzzed annoyingly overhead. Disheveled men trickled in from the area surrounding Beale Street's pawnshops, bars, and liquor stores. The boycott of downtown businesses had emptied it of shoppers and hurt the work of petty hustlers and thieves, and they resented it.

"There was an element in the crowd that we couldn't get rid of . . . nobody could do anything with them," recalled black city councilman Fred Davis. The "white presence wasn't exactly overwhelming" in the ranks of the marchers either, said one participant. That made the crowd more vulnerable to police attack, as people grew increasingly restless.

Nearby but out of sight, three hundred Memphis policemen and fifty Shelby County sheriff's deputies, almost all of them white and many of them natives of the plantation economy, sat or stood somewhere in the boiling sun. They too were on edge. Many of them had been working seven days a week since the strike began. They carried .38-caliber pistols, shotguns, Mace, and billy clubs, and deputies had their own personal weapons. On the South Side, police attacked black Hamilton High School students as they gathered to go to the march. An ambulance took fourteen-year-old Jo Ann Talbert away on a stretcher; it took twenty-three stitches to close her head wound. As 22,000 students boycotted school and many of them went downtown to join the march, rumors spread that police had killed a black female student.

At Clayborn Temple, a contingent of sanitation workers remained well organized and on message with their signs, "I Am A Man." But young people made their own incendiary signs, or tore the signs prepared for the march from their sticks and brandished the sticks as clubs. Charles Cabbage and other members of the youth group the Invaders stood at the edge of the crowd giving excited and angry speeches to young people. According to their strategy, nonviolent protesters only achieved their demands when the powers that be feared violence if they did not respond. The Invaders wanted to challenge King's disciplined, nonviolent methods and ramp up tensions through undisciplined street actions. Once the march started, the Invaders would disappear.

Everyone wanted to know, where was Martin Luther King?

At around 11 a.m., after some people had been waiting for three hours, King and Epps arrived in their Lincoln at Linden and Hernando streets. People swarmed around the car and King could barely get out. Once he got out of the car, "pandemonium broke out," recalled Lawson, as an unruly sea of people tried to get up close to King. Lawson and King started the march, with sanitation workers behind them, but younger people broke through to get right behind them. Photos show King looking happy at times, apprehensive at other times; film footage records King pressed on all sides and carried along by the crowd, his eyes glazed, his head bent to the side, almost asleep on his feet. As the march picked up speed, reporter Kay Pittman Black heard King exclaim that someone should "make the crowds stop pushing. We're going to be trampled." Organizers estimated 10,000 to 15,000 people in the march, funneled down narrow old streets and moving toward city hall. NAACP leader Jesse Turner saw trouble ahead; he considered aborting the march, but decided that could in itself precipitate a riot.

As the crowd moved down Hernando to Beale Street, marchers sang "We Shall Overcome" and chanted "Down with Loeb." But before King and Lawson got to Main Street, they heard windows breaking and shouts of "Burn it down, baby!" Behind them, excited young people and older men with hardened looks climbed through store windows and began to loot. Some men had looted liquor stores even before the march started. King in the past had been the victim of mob attacks, but never had seemed to be leading a mob. Lawson halted the march.

Up ahead at Main Street and Gayoso, police with gas masks, brandishing guns and clubs, formed a line to block the marchers from going toward city hall. Lawson told King he should leave. King protested, "Jim, they'll say I ran away," but Rev. Henry Starks and a cordon of men put their arms through his and took King down McCall, a side street. King's aide Bernard Lee flagged down two black women in a white Pontiac, and a white police officer escorted them out of the area. The officer later claimed disparagingly to a reporter that King's "only concern was to run and to protect himself."

Meanwhile, police and sheriff's deputies waded into the crowd, using clubs, Mace, and tear gas, as a police report later put it, to "restore order." Children lost their parents, older people who could not run ducked into doorways. T. O. Jones ran for cover, knowing he would be a special target, but lost his two sons in the swirling crowd. Police burst into the Big M restaurant and ordered people eating to leave; when they didn't readily comply, they beat them and dragged them out. One of the diners, named Kenneth Cox, and a Firestone worker got in Cox's car and tried to leave, but the police smashed in the windows and Maced and clubbed them both. It took eight stitches to close Cox's wound. He was one of hundreds beaten bloody by the police, who freely cursed and called people "nigger" while attacking marchers and bystanders indiscriminately.

Officers wearing gas masks and helmets and holding pump shotguns surrounded refugees from the march huddled together at Clayborn Temple, where Lawson had led people. In the adjacent headquarters of the African Methodist Episcopal Minimum Salary, an organization that aimed to raise salary levels for AME ministers, Lawson was on the phone to the chief of police, pleading with him to stop the mayhem. Tear gas wafted in, forcing Lawson to drop the phone and climb out a window. Reporter Black wrote that "inside the A.M.E. building was a horror show." People were bathing each other's faces with water, some lay comatose on the floor, and Clayborn Temple's white pastor Malcolm Blackburn found a man who he feared had a broken back, lying on the trunk of a car in the alley. Police shot tear gas into Clayborn Temple and beat people as they came streaming out.

In a scene all too familiar in many American cities, looting spread like wildfire from downtown to nearby business districts, as people ran off with televisions, alcohol, musical instruments, and guns. At the John Gaston Hospital, frequented by the city's black and poor population, doctors treated hundreds of people streaming in with lacerations, broken bones and teeth, concussions, buckshot wounds, and suffering from the effects of tear gas. Private ambulances refused to go into the area of police violence and looting, and all city buses stopped running.

White police officer Leslie Dean Jones, at the low-income Fowler Homes project ten blocks south of Beale Street, spotted Larry Payne, a black sixteen-year-old who the officer thought had looted a television set. Jones cornered Payne in a basement doorway and pulled the trigger of his 12-gauge shotgun. The black-owned *Tri-State Defender* published a picture of Payne lying against the basement stairwell, his eyes and mouth wide open, both hands above his head. A dozen eyewitnesses confirmed they had seen Payne with his hands up, pleading for his life. The Police Department produced a rusty butcher knife that they said belonged to Payne, but they could not lift any fingerprints from it. Five months after Payne's death, the department made the bizarre claim that the knife and other evidence in the case could not be examined because they had thrown it all away into the Mississippi River. No one could explain why. Officer Jones was not laid off, nor did a grand jury ever indict him.

Instead of King's nonviolent "dress rehearsal" for the Poor People's Campaign in Washington, the Memphis march left behind a wasteland, according to the press, with "Main Street and historic

Beale Street littered with bricks, blood and broken glass." One pathetic photo showed a picket sign with a photo of King's face lying with glass all over it in a smashed store window. Governor Buford Ellington declared a state of emergency and mobilized the National Guard. Stores in the South Side went up in flames as tanks and trucks rolled in. For the next several days Memphis was occupied territory in a military state of siege.

Who was to blame? The news media featured photos of officers who got hurt by flying glass and rocks or injured while fighting with people in the crowd. Fire and police director Frank Holloman, J. Edgar Hoover's former FBI assistant, claimed that black people had taken up "general guerrilla warfare," and said, "Yes, we have a war in the city of Memphis." He told reporters, "I think you should realize what the police department did. They used restraint."

This was Memphis, touted by its leaders as a city of racial moderation. But the violence that day, blamed by the white media on the black community, could more accurately be called a police riot conducted with impunity. Black Memphians suspected that the white media would cover up or rationalize the police violence, and Dr. King would get all the blame. And they were right.

James Lawson, for his part, appealed: "We are now saying to the city, will you please listen? Will you please recognize that in the heart of our city there is massive cruelty and poverty and indignity, and that only if you remove it can we have order."

* * *

IN MARCH 1968 the FBI responded to the escalating Black Power, New Left, and antiwar movements by stepping up its surveillance and illegal interventions against organizations and individuals. By the time King came to Memphis, the FBI was employing his accountant James Harrison as an informant; monitoring calls to and from King's close associates; and sending out regular reports slandering King and others in the movement to the president, members of Congress, the military, the police, and friendly news outlets. On March 4 Hoover had directed FBI field offices to do everything they could to "prevent the rise of a black messiah," and the FBI was sending out fake letters and disinformation to disrupt the Poor People's Campaign. The FBI had put King on its counterintelligence (COINTELPRO) "agitator index." Going back to the McCarran Internal Security Act of 1950, the United States actually had funded and designated detention centers and a list of people to be rounded up and put in them during a national emergency—and King was on that list.

Throughout March 1968 a steady drumbeat of hatred confronted King. Most southern news media ridiculed the report of the presidentially appointed commission headed by Ohio Governor Otto Kerner, mandated to investigate the causes of inner-city riots. Issued in early March, the commission's report supported King's conclusion that white prejudice, police violence, and institutional racism caused inner-city rebellions. Meanwhile, the political right continued to blame ghetto residents and King. George Wallace, running for president, blamed hippies, New Leftists, and African Americans for America's turmoil and pledged to run over any protester who lay down in front of his car. When the name of King came up in the media in 1968, it often sat next to a headline on "Communist aggression" during the Tet offensive and the siege of the American military base at Khe Sanh in Vietnam. Many newspapers made it appear that King and a host of subversive allies at home and abroad had the United States under siege. King had joined Jack O'Dell to give a speech honoring Dr. Du Bois at a *Freedomways* dinner held in New York on February 23, the same day as the first police riot in Memphis. In response, the FBI sent out an anticommunist alert to the media. The Birmingham *News* followed up on March 7, 1968, with a big front-page headline: "King, Red ex-aide team up again."

Conflict in the streets of Memphis on March 28 confirmed what most white southerners already thought, and what the FBI had long been preaching. Assistant FBI director William Sullivan, as part of the FBI's campaign to stop the Poor People's Campaign (code-named "POCAM") was in hourly contact with his agents in Memphis. His note to them highlighted the idea that although King "preaches non-violence, violence occurs just about everywhere he goes." On March 28 and 29, the FBI's "Racial Intelligence" section sent out "blind memos" to its press contacts around the country promoting this view. The *Commercial Appeal* wrote, "Dr. King's pose as a leader of a non-violent movement has been shattered." Another article was headlined "Chicken a La King," and an editorial cartoon pictured King shrugging his shoulders and saying, "Who, me?" with Beale Street in tatters behind him. The Jackson, Mississippi, *Clarion-Ledger*'s columnist Tom Ethridge revealed that "secret FBI records definitely tie Martin Luther King with Communism." The anticommunist drumbeat that had followed King most of his adult life now got louder. David Lawrence of *U.S. News and World Report* quoted HUAC, reporting that antiwar demonstrations in April that King planned to participate in "are part of a worldwide movement by the Communists."

The clamor must have reminded King of the days before President Kennedy's assassination, when the John Birch Society had agitated in Dallas that Kennedy was part of a communist plot. Indeed, if the southern mass media hated any public figure more than King, it was Robert F. Kennedy. Segregationists viewed him as an insidious interloper representing the northern liberal elite; on March 20, the Montgomery *Journal* on March 22 ran a cartoon that pictured Kennedy with horns on his head and decried a subversive "Kennedy-King Alliance."

Opponents of King and Kennedy merged their hatred for the two men. They were right that they had a lot in common: both wanted to bring the poor to Washington, and both would soon be dead at the hands of assassins.

* * *

AFTER THE HORRORS in Memphis, people close to King reported that he was devastated, anxious, and deeply depressed. But in public he carried on with a calm demeanor and discourse. When reporters in Memphis asked him about accusations that he "ran" when "the going got rough," King told them he left the march because "I have always said that I will not lead a violent demonstration." But he also reminded them of the conditions of poverty and police violence reflected in the events on March 28. He warned that no one could guarantee peaceful demonstrations unless American society did something about the dire conditions that set off violence in its inner cities. In reality, the breaking of store windows in a confined area of Beale Street only barely amounted to "riot"; police inflicted or set off most of the violence to people that occurred.

Remarkably, after leaving Memphis, King continued on his national campaign. Speaking to a packed crowd at the Washington, D.C., Cathedral on Sunday, March 31, he called on America to wake up to the "human rights revolution" occurring in the world. The next day, in Memphis, 450 people marched again from Clayborn Temple to downtown. Thousands of people filed by Larry Payne's body as a funeral home prepared him for burial. Daily marches and organizing among the workers and their allies resumed. On April 3, despite strong opposition from his staff, King came back to Memphis. He vowed to lead a mass nonviolent march regardless of a court injunction on behalf of the city that would put him in jail for doing so. Despite violent storms late that night, King at Mason Temple called on people to exercise "dangerous unselfishness" on behalf of the poor. He urged his audience to continue down the dangerous Jericho Road taken by the Good Samaritan despite all fears and difficulties. He electrified his audience with his ringing conclusion, "I may not get there with you, but I want you to know tonight that we as a people will get to the Promised Land!"

On March 28, when he could not get to any other place to stay because of the riot spreading through the city, King had stayed at the Rivermont Hotel. With FBI prompting, Memphis newspapers called him a hypocrite for not staying at a black-owned hotel. This time, to avoid such criticism, he stayed at the black-owned Lorraine Motel. He had stayed there so many times that its owners, Walter and Lorraine Bailey, reserved a room for him and did not charge him to stay. They cooked him collard greens and brought food to his room. The newspapers and television news published his room number, 306. The room faced an open-air balcony. It provided no security.

Investigative reporters later discovered that a plainclothes unit of the Military Intelligence Division of the U.S. Army, which had an office in downtown Memphis, roamed the streets and watched King's every move. The FBI and the Memphis Police Department worked hand in glove to infiltrate the ranks of the strikers and the Invaders, a group that now demanded payments from SCLC in order for them to cooperate with building a nonviolent demonstration. Security forces tracked King's every move, and several officers watched King's room in secret from a firehouse across the street from the Lorraine. Police cars circled the area for miles around. Yet no one was assigned to guard King. Higher-ups in the police department had removed several black police officers who had previously considered it their duty to protect King. And because of their record of attacking the movement, white police officers were not particularly welcomed by SCLC.

On April 4, King's aides and lawyers went into court and Rev. Lawson argued that the city would be better off having King lead a legal march on April 8 than to have him arrested for breaking an injunction against marching, which could set off another upheaval in the streets. The court approved a march to be held on April 8. King and his entourage were in a happy mood, getting ready to go to dinner. As King stood on the balcony of the Lorraine Motel bantering with his colleagues in the parking lot below, a bullet slammed through his jaw.

Within an hour, Martin Luther King was dead. That night riots began in Memphis, and for the next three days, riots consumed the nation. When hotel co-owner Lorraine Bailey learned King was shot, she had a heart attack, and would die five days later. Coretta Scott King was grief-stricken, but not surprised. "We knew that FBI director J. Edgar Hoover had labeled my husband a public enemy, a threat to the United States of America. How could we not know were living on borrowed moments?" She later wrote, "For most of our married lives, Martin and I knew that one day there would be a scene like this. . . ."

Robert F. Kennedy and Jacqueline Kennedy reached out to comfort her and help bring her husband's body back to Atlanta. Coretta

Scott King and her husband's family had a long haul ahead. King's brother A. D. would drown in a swimming pool a year later, and on June 30, 1974, a madman would shoot King's revered mother to death while she was playing "The Lord's Prayer" on the organ at Ebenezer Church. Daddy King would end up without his sons and his wife, helping to raise Martin and Coretta's four fatherless children.

Later, people wondered how James Earl Ray, an escapee from federal prison, could go unnoticed when he purchased a Gamemaster rifle powerful enough to bring down a charging bull. The law did not require that he register the weapon or be checked for criminal background. A poor white brought up in a dysfunctional family, Ray could have been a candidate for the Poor People's Campaign. Instead, in his life of petty and bungled thievery and imprisonment, he chose to follow George Wallace and subscribe to KKK publications. Rumors circulated of a supposed reward for King's death from an unidentified businessman in St. Louis, the area Ray came from. On the evening of April 3, Ray took a room in a boarding house where the bullet that killed King seemed to have come from across from the Lorraine Motel. After the shooting, on April 4, he fled Memphis.

King's assassination was one of a string of murders of public officials and movement leaders and grassroots activists throughout the 1960s. Time after time when a hopeful leader appeared, that leader was killed. After King's murder, the FBI apprehended Ray as he was trying to board a plane from London to the white supremacist republic of Rhodesia (now Zimbabwe). Ray pleaded guilty to King's murder but later recanted his plea. Because of that guilty plea, the evidence against him was never presented in a trial, leaving unanswered questions about who killed King. A congressional inquiry later cast doubt on who killed King and why. A civil jury in a court hearing, conducted by attorney William Pepper, decided that other people may have killed King but was widely derided for faulty methodology and bias. Ray had every reason to want to kill King, and his alibis seemed like fabrications. But whether Ray or someone else pulled the trigger, Andrew Young later wrote, the issue was not *who* killed King, but *what* killed King. And *why* did it happen? Young thought the answers to those questions went to the heart of a society built on slavery and segregation.

Right-wing and racist hate had plagued King all of his life. He said hardly a day went by that he didn't get a death threat. As Stokely Carmichael later put it, "Every Klan and Nazi group had a bounty on his head. Martin Luther King was the number one target for every racist with a rifle, shotgun, or stick of dynamite." Is it any wonder that he had strong premonitions of death when he gave his "Promised Land" speech? His colleague and companion Ralph Abernathy wrote that King had many fears but refused to give in to them. Had he not been a brave man, "none of the rest of us would have followed him and we might still be riding in the back of buses and eating in segregated restaurants."

While most people today see King as a prophet, many whites reviled him in his time. Strike sympathizers recorded many of the gross jokes they heard in the streets and shops of Memphis after King's death. A survey of Memphis State University white students in three classes found 20 percent approved of King's murder, and 19 percent didn't care one way or another. A reader wrote in a letter to the *Commercial Appeal* what many white people said on the streets and in their living rooms, that King was "the biggest Communist in the nation." Others said the problem was black people themselves. "No matter what else there is, you just can't overlook that black skin," a neighbor told one Southwestern College professor. Rev. Lawson remarked that hatred of King symbolized white America's "moral blindness." He did not think America could really change unless Euro-Americans came to understand King's message.

After the murder of King on April 4, National Guard troops reoccupied Memphis. Nationwide, riots led to more than 20,000 arrests, at least forty-three deaths and $100 million in damages. The federal government called out some 50,000 troops, responding to riots in perhaps as many as 130 cities. It was the largest use of federal force to suppress domestic rebellion since the Civil War. The 14th Street corridor in Washington, D.C., remained burned out for years to

The Memorial March for Dr. Martin Luther King Jr. on April 8, 1968, makes its way down Main Street. Mourners include a mixture of civil rights activists, members of the clergy, and union leaders. It included James Lawson, Cornelia Crenshaw, Jerry Wurt, T. O. Jones, May and Walter Reuther, Coretta King and three of her children (not shown).

Marchers in Memphis on April 8 honored King by
demanding union rights and an end to racism.

come. In Memphis, amid drawn bayonets, walking past tanks and soldiers in jeeps with their rifles prominently displayed, the sanitation workers marched on.

On April 8 people came from all over the nation to hold a completely silent march from Clayborn Temple through downtown Memphis. Hate mail and phone calls threatening death had inundated James Lawson throughout the strike, and in the middle of the night on April 7, someone called to say tell him that when he reached Main Street, "You'll be cut down." Lawson, thinking he too would not live much longer, walked at the front of the march, along with Coretta King, union leaders Jerry Wurf of AFSCME and Walter Reuther of UAW, Harry Belafonte—one of King's strongest supporters—and other King associates.

According to wildly varying estimates, on April 8 in Memphis somewhere between 19,000 and 42,000 people demonstrated their respect for King and their refusal to give in to violence. Even the Invaders helped to provide marshals to maintain nonviolent discipline for the event. Through her composure and her heartfelt statements, Coretta Scott King drove home her husband's message of nonviolence even unto death. On April 6 she had issued a statement: "The day that Negro people and others in bondage are truly free, on the day want is abolished, on the day wars are no more, on that day I know my husband will rest in a long-deserved peace." On April 8, at the Memphis demonstration, she declared, "his campaign for the poor must go on." But she also cried out, "How many men must die before we can really have a free and true and peaceful society? How long will it take?" Yet she still believed that "this nation can be transformed into a society of love, of justice, peace, and brotherhood."

A domestic worker in the audience named Luella Cook said, "If Mrs. King had cried a single tear, this whole city would have give way." There had been some fires and destruction right after King's death, but this nonviolent rally put an end to it. "Memphis was in fact the quietest place in the nation," AFSCME's Bill Lucy later recalled. Students from Hamilton High School, where police attacks had set off a frenzied student response on March 28, also attended, among them Alice Wright, granddaughter of a striking sanitation worker, and Ernestine Johnson, who had cried herself to sleep on April 4, and said she felt hopeless until she heard Mrs. King speak. Then, "I got the courage to go on with life and struggle . . . to make something of myself." Others inclined to violence decided to honor King that day with nonviolence.

April 8 also symbolized the union- and civil-rights coalition King had long sought to build. Union members all over the country stopped work and held memorial gatherings. The AFL-CIO sent a check for $20,000 and mailed a letter to member unions that raised thousands of additional dollars to support the strikers. UAW President Walter Reuther brought a $50,000 check for the strike fund to the Memphis memorial. The International Longshoremen's and Warehousemen's Union (ILWU) led by Harry Bridges shut down a number of West Coast ports for twenty-four hours, as did unionized black workers in some Mississippi Gulf ports. The cry went up among union- and civil-rights supporters for a national holiday to honor King. Members of the unions King worked with, including District 65 RWDSU, which demanded a King holiday in all of its contracts, 1199 Hospital Workers, which began a major educational campaign around labor and civil rights, and the United Electrical Workers Union (UE), National Education Association and American Federation of Teachers, AFSCME, the United Furniture Workers Union, the Screen Actors Guild, and steel, packinghouse, auto, longshore, rubber workers and many other unionists memorialized King as a labor hero. On April 8 in Memphis, "The town was full of labor people," said Bill Ross.

On April 9 in Atlanta, between 100,000 and 150,000 people from all walks of life marched through the streets following a mule-drawn wagon honoring King's struggle to launch the Poor People's Campaign. The funeral there played the "Drum Major" sermon that King had given at Ebenezer Baptist Church on February 4, exactly two months before his death. He had said that when the time for his funeral came, he wanted people to remember that

"Martin Luther King, Jr., tried to give his life serving others. I'd like for somebody to say that day, that Martin Luther King, Jr., tried to love somebody. I want you to say that day, that I tried to be right on the war question. . . . I want you to say that I tried to love and serve humanity."

* * *

ASTONISHINGLY, TO AFSCME president Jerry Wurf, the Memphis workers continued marching but Mayor Henry Loeb still refused to sign a contract. White and black ministers, over one hundred of them, confronted Loeb the day after King's death, demanding that he settle the strike. But talking to Loeb, many said, was like talking to a wall. He would seem to listen, but his opinions never changed. National companies started to cancel contracts to hold meetings in Memphis. Cornelia Crenshaw, Dorothy Evans, Tarlese Matthews and others picketed stores and told shoppers to boycott downtown businesses in the biggest shopping days before Easter.

After weeks of contentious debate, on April 4 the U.S. Senate passed the Fair Housing Act banning discrimination in the rental, sale, and financing of housing by race, religion, national origin, or gender. The House of Representatives passed it on April 10, and President Johnson signed it on April 11. King had at last won one of the major demands of the Chicago demonstrations, a national law banning housing discrimination. President Johnson also sent James Reynolds, the U.S. Labor Department's top negotiator, to Memphis. In his response to the Memphis tragedy, Senator Eastland took the National Rifle Association's position and blocked a gun registration law that might have prevented the purchase of the gun, or at least readily identified who purchased the gun, that killed King.

Ultimately, the Memphis City Council settled the sanitation workers' strike without Loeb's help. The complicated negotiations required private donations to pay the cost of tiny wage increases; provided a memo of agreement, not a contract; and, because of Tennessee's right-to-work law, workers could not be required to join the union or pay dues. "All we did get was a premise for staying alive," Wurf later explained. But in the first clause in the contract it signed, the City of Memphis recognized AFSCME Local 1733 as a collective bargaining agent; that word "recognition" was the key to the demand of "I *Am* a man." The city also allowed workers to voluntarily have union dues deducted from their paychecks; guaranteed they could not be fired for joining a union or talking about it at work; opened up promotion to higher-paying jobs; set up grievance procedures; and included a nondiscrimination clause—the kind CIO unions had fought for since the 1940s. The workers gained a few cents an hour in wage increases, but of all these provisions, Wurf said, the most important was to make union membership "a basic right in a free society."

On April 16, at Clayborn Temple, after sixty-five days on strike, the sanitation workers stood up, to a man, and approved the agreement. They whooped, cheered, and cried. Tears streaming down his face, T. O. Jones said, "We have been aggrieved many times, we have lost many things. But we have got the victory." A general celebration ensued. White AFL-CIO Memphis president Tommy Powell said he hoped black and white workers could now join to elect some decent politicians; Cornelia Crenshaw called for organizing hospital and domestic workers; Rev. Lawson pledged a lasting alliance between civil rights and labor. People joined hands and swayed together, singing "We Shall Overcome," including the verse, "Black and white together."

Their movement came out of two tragedies, the loss of Echol Cole and Robert Walker that set off the strike and the death of Dr. King that ended the strike. Taylor Rogers, who became Local 1733 president for twenty years, told me that this struggle was not in vain. King, he said, "went where he was needed, where he could help poor people. . . . He didn't get all accomplished he wanted accomplished, but I don't think he died in vain. Because what he came here to do, that was settled." As King's mentor Benjamin Mays said on April 9 in Atlanta, King "believed especially that he was sent to champion the cause of the man furthest down. If death had to come, I am sure there was no greater cause to die for than fighting to get a just wage for garbage collectors."

* * *

IN THE AFTERMATH of King's death, donations to the Poor People's Campaign soared. The national AFL-CIO never endorsed the campaign, but King's close union allies and the UAW invested thousands of dollars in it and members of various other unions participated. On April 27, Coretta Scott King spoke at a mass antiwar rally in New York City, reading from "Ten Commandments on Vietnam," a note found in her husband's coat after the assassination. The tenth was "Thou shall not kill." Mrs. King addressed women especially, saying, "The woman power of this nation can be the power" to make the nation whole by ending racism, poverty, and war. On May 2, 1968, she placed a wreath outside room 306 at the Lorraine Motel, beginning a caravan that would travel down to Marks, Mississippi, and through Alabama and Georgia to Washington, D.C.

Many of the people King had spoken to in February and March would follow a mule-drawn carriage through the South and onward to the nation's capital. Other caravans started on the West Coast, including Native Americans fresh from fishing-rights struggles in Washington State, and Chicanos demanding land rights in the Southwest. On May 12 Coretta Scott King walked with Ethel Kennedy, the wife of Senator Robert Kennedy, in the front row of a Mother's Day march of the National Welfare Rights Organization through the streets of D.C. She wrote, "We highlighted the plight of poor women and children . . . from rural Appalachia to the urban ghettos," demonstrating women's power in the fight for "decent medical care," a life without hunger, and against welfare "reforms" that made life harder on recipients and their children.

The Poor People's Campaign brought together many of the people King had struggled to organize from various parts of the country. Participants included unionists, religious people, students, and others, and even armed self-defense advocates like Charles Cabbage of the Invaders in Memphis and Bobby Seale of the Black Panther

Party in Oakland, California. Most important, the poor them-selves turned out and established an encampment of 2,500 people on the national mall, and called it "Resurrection City." Mexican Americans, Native Americans, poor whites, Puerto Ricans, and African Americans all came to Washington. Freedom singers Jimmy Collier and Brother Frederick Douglass Kirkpatrick, as well as a Poor People's University created a sense of collective and interracial purpose. Although the campaign did not produce new legislation or the attention to poverty King desired, according to historian Gordon Mantler, "Its organizers and participants made great strides in producing, at least at times, a unified multiracial voice for the poor."

Police in Detroit, cheered on by Donald Lobsinger and his Breakthrough right-wing activists, had beaten up PPC travelers when they came through. Police also harassed people in Marks before and after the campaign. On June 5, Robert Kennedy won the California primary, virtually assuring that he would be the Democratic Party's next presidential candidate. At the end of a celebration that night, a Palestinian Arab nationalist named Sirhan Bishara Sirhan, seeking revenge for Kennedy's support for Israel's military actions in the Mideast, shot him with a handgun and Kennedy died on June 6. UAW organizer Paul Schrade was among the wounded, and former SNCC chairman John Lewis was in a room next to where Kennedy was shot. He fell to the floor sobbing, having lost his two model leaders, King and Kennedy. Followers of both men would line the railroad tracks as a train returned Kennedy's body to the nation's capital.

The Poor People's Campaign carried on. Walter Reuther came to speak at a mass interracial rally of tens of thousands on June 19, 1968, called Solidarity Day, where Coretta Scott King called on participants to continue to teach and organize around the power of love and nonviolence. Despite this high point, however, devastating rains beset the shantytown called Resurrection City in honor of King; delegations to Congress demanding action for poor people got little support. Police in July demolished the poor people's encampment, and forced its residents to leave. Two years

Demonstrators from across the country converge
on the National Mall in Washington, D.C., during the Poor
People's Campaign on June 19, 1968.

Coretta Scott King supported Local 282 of the United Furniture
Workers Union, which continued to organize in Memphis,
as workers remembered King on April 4.

later, on May 7, 1970, Walter Reuther and his wife May died in a plane crash. Many of the people who supported King's labor–civil rights agenda passed. The media and most historians cast the Poor People's Campaign as a failure.

However, in that campaign people learned skills and crossed cultural boundaries, and many of them began a journey for economic justice that they continued for the rest of their lives. King had told his staff when they worried about the campaign's possible effectiveness that failure consists of people not trying to bring about a change; failure consists of good people remaining silent in the face of injustice. From Montgomery to Albany, St. Augustine to Atlanta, Birmingham to Selma and Chicago, the March Against Fear in Mississippi, the Poor People's Campaign, and the Memphis sanitation strike, every campaign Martin Luther King worked on involved both failures and successes. King, Lawson, and others understood that the struggle doesn't stop. Put simply in the civil rights anthem, "Freedom Is a Constant Struggle."

Yet, in his last days, King had feared that racial prejudice and the legacy of slavery remained America's greatest obstacles to becoming a functioning democracy that would benefit all its people. In an article published posthumously in *Look* magazine on April 16, 1968, King wrote that he even feared that resurgent racism could lead to a form of American fascism. In a series of Christmas sermons aired on the Canadian Broadcasting system in 1967, he had explained, "There is such a thing as being too late." And he warned, "Disinherited people all over the world are bleeding to death from deep social and economic wounds. They need brigades of ambulance drivers who will have to ignore the red lights of the present system until the emergency is solved." In this broadcast, King said that pursuing the American Dream required a renewed commitment to economic justice for both the unemployed and the working poor. "It is murder, psychologically, to deprive a man of a job or an income. . . . You are in a real way depriving him of life, liberty, and pursuit of happiness, denying in his case the very creed of his society. Now millions of people are being strangled in that way. The problem is international in scope. And it is getting worse. . . ."

People in Memphis remember King every year on April 4.

King dreamed of much more than obtaining civil rights and voting rights. In his fight for a phase two of the movement, for economic justice, he remained uncertain whether the deeper tentacles of racism would be uprooted. And he feared time was not on his side. AFSCME's William Lucy told me, "Dr. King really highlighted the great contradiction. . . . If you relieve the civil rights shackles or barriers, that does not necessarily guarantee that your economic situation will change. There is something wrong with the social structure. There is something wrong with the economic structure."

* * *

EVEN AS WE fight to stop regression and rollback of fundamental rights in our own times, the achievements of phase one of the freedom struggle cannot be fully undone. American apartheid is gone; there is no putting it back. Memphis provides one example of that. Many people there as elsewhere carried on "the long civil rights movement" into the 1970s and beyond. In Memphis in 1974, Harold Ford, the first black congressman in the Deep South since Reconstruction, replaced the reactionary congressman Dan Kuykendal, who had excoriated King as a troublemaker during the Memphis strike. After many years of electoral struggle by black voters and a few white allies, in 1991 Memphians elected Willie Herrenton as their first black mayor; he continued in office for sixteen years with good and bad results. African Americans and Latinos and women joined a unionized police force and it became less like an occupying army; interracial friendships and sexual relations became acceptable to many. AFSCME, elected officials, and civic activists turned the decrepit Lorraine Motel into the National Civil Rights Museum. Along with Memphis music and civil rights tourism, a widespread and multiracial sense of civic engagement keeps the "spirit of Memphis" alive. As economic historian Gavin Wright documented in *Sharing the Prize*, by taking steps toward integrating workplaces, education, skilled jobs, and political office holding, the civil rights revolution to a significant degree raised incomes and benefited both blacks and whites. With the election of America's first black president, Barack Obama, in 2008, some thought phase one of the freedom movement for legal and voting rights had triumphed. Even as efforts have accelerated to turn back voting and civil rights, it will be hard for anyone to fully turn back the results of phase one of the freedom movement.

However, King's demand for a phase two of the freedom movement, for economic justice, stalled. From the 1980s onward, even while incomes of the top one percent skyrocketed the loss of union jobs and wages undermined the strongest sector of both the black and white middle class—unionized workers. In Memphis, the unionized Firestone, International Harvester, and RCA plants all closed. Union density plummeted; wages cratered; working families frayed or collapsed; drug use, family violence, criminalization of the poor, and mass incarceration escalated. As the sociologist William Julius Wilson wrote in a study of Chicago in the 1980s, this is what happens "when work disappears." Retired Memphis union member Evelyn Bates told me, "This is pitiful how you can go by all of these factories, and the windows are all broke out. The building just sitting there, just going to waste. *No jobs.* Nothing to look forward to" for the younger generation. Deindustrialization especially damaged working families dependent on laboring jobs. Black and Latino incomes on average got stuck at only about 60 percent of those of whites.

Memphis in some ways is a poster child for a much greater degree of civic engagement and spirit since the 1960s. But it also serves as an example of the hit taken by the interracial American working class. The near-meltdown of the American economy in 2007–2008, spiraling health insurance costs, the collapsing housing market, and the loss of good jobs hit black Memphis especially hard. This city, now of 600,000, has one of the highest poverty and infant and maternal mortality rates of any city of its size. The issue of labor and race remains at the heart of a continuing crisis for many black workers, and for white workers as well. And across the nation, employer and politician demands for low wages, low taxes on the wealthy, and no unions have returned, as the low-wage economic model of the South has gone national. In 2010, the Republican attack against public employee unions and wages from Governor Scott Walker in Wisconsin ramified across the country, with right-to-work laws popping up in previous northern union strongholds like Wisconsin and Michigan. As taxes and incomes and federal funding declined, "cost cutting" became a strategy everywhere. The City of Memphis and other governments sought to freeze wages, cut health benefits, mechanize jobs and contract out work to private companies. A return to cheap wages and privatization threatens the very existence of AFSCME Local 1733 and of public-employee unionism. "If they can dig up the root, they can topple that tree," said long-time union activist Gail Tyree.

Private sector unions, now representing less than ten percent of the American workforce, also remain under attack. In 2013, the Kellogg Company, a profitable national megacorporation, locked out its union workers in Memphis, put nonunion workers in their place, and demanded a two-tiered wage system that would impoverish the next generation. Union members picketed for sixteen months, and lost cars, homes, and health care. Families broke up. The Kellogg workers ultimately won their jobs back through appeals to the courts and the National Labor Relations Board, but the company put a second tier of lower-wage workers in place. In Memphis as elsewhere, when people at the local level tried to raise wages and taxes to support social policies and help the community, Republican state legislatures passed laws taking away local power to enact these policies. Integrated schools exist, but under such precarious political and economic conditions that many flee to private schools. And climate change and ferocious weather have put infrastructure and housing at risk for people of all ethnicities everywhere.

Perhaps a third of African Americans in Memphis count themselves as "middle class," but two-thirds are not. Most African Americans are only a few paychecks away from falling, like about another third of blacks, into poverty. Those with jobs are no longer primarily unskilled laborers and domestic workers but employed in service, education, distribution, and health economies, where the great majority still lack union rights and control over their economic future. Although higher wages for working-class people clearly benefit a consumer-based economy, the low-wage, antiunion model is back in style, not only in Memphis but nearly everywhere. And government for the benefit of the rich and powerful to the detriment of the rest for us has returned with a vengeance.

* * *

ON APRIL 8, 1968, when Coretta Scott King and thousands of others in Memphis had honored King in a silent, nonviolent march, many carried picket signs reading, "Honor King: End Racism," and "Union Justice Now." Mrs. King continued supporting worker-organizing in numerous campaigns, as an honorary member of 1199 Hospital Workers and AFSCME. She led a campaign to obtain a national holiday in honor of Dr. King and the things he stood for. When President Ronald Reagan signed it into law on November 2, 1983, Mrs. King commented that it was the first holiday to honor "an American who gave his life in a labor struggle." She continued throughout her life to support union rights, to speak loudly against war, and to embrace lesbian, gay, and transgender rights. James Lawson too carried on the nonviolent organizing tradition, including among Latino immigrants and service economy workers in Los Angeles after he moved there in 1974 to pastor Holman United Methodist Church. Nonviolence, he continued to teach, remains the most potent weapon for creating positive social change.

More than fifty years since his death, King's message of agape love, or love for all, lives on. In his last book, Dr. King pointed out that all of us live in a "world house," and that what affects one of us directly affects us all indirectly. While most of us think that "self preservation is the first law of life," King objected that, actually, "other-preservation is the first law of life." Ending racism, poverty and war in a global economy and a global climate requires everyone to develop an "overriding loyalty to mankind as a whole." Humankind, he wrote, has "a last chance to choose between chaos and community," and to choose love over hate.

During thirteen years of struggle, he preached a reordering

of values and a strategy for change that does not inflict harm. In his fight for equal rights and economic justice, King left behind a theory and a practice of nonviolence available to all. Almost anyone can express his or her beliefs by writing a letter and speaking out. One does not need a PhD or a minister's eloquence to go out on the picket line, to go to jail for a just cause, or to organize people for positive change. King emphasized that "everyone can be great, because everyone can serve."

From Memphis to Seattle and beyond, people still march and unionists and organizers everywhere still draw inspiration by remembering King as a hero to the American working class, the poor, and the oppressed. King stressed that "either we go up together or we go down together." As he told the AFL-CIO in 1961, the key ideal for humanity is solidarity, "a dream of a nation where all our gifts and resources are held not for ourselves alone but as instruments of service for the rest of humanity." Are we moving in that direction? Many are still asking, as King did in his last year, "Where do we go from here?"

ACKNOWLEDGMENTS

I owe special thanks to Clayborne and Susan Carson, who have been guiding lights and dear friends in the world of King and freedom-movement scholarship for many years. The Martin Luther King, Jr., Papers Project and the MLK Research and Education Institute at Stanford University, led by senior editor Clayborne Carson, associate director Tenisha Armstrong, and others associated with the Institute helped me to find documents and always provided friendship and solidarity in studying the life and legacy of Dr. King. This is a unique group and a special place.

Grateful thanks to Alane Salierno Mason, my editor at W. W. Norton, who read this manuscript several times and saw it through to completion, to Ashley Patrick and Kyle Radler at Norton, and to Roz Foster, my agent at the Sandra Dijkstra Literary Agency, who provided marvelous support.

Special thanks to Nancy Bristow, who helped me to get this manuscript to the finish line, Will Jones, Keona Ervin, David Black, Martha Allen, Joseph Rosenbloom, and Roz Foster, friends and colleagues who read all or nearly all of the manuscript and offered much help in how to tell this story. Thanks to Erik Gellman, Aram Goudsouzian, Alan Draper, Kenneth O'Reilly, Anthony D'Costa, Robert Korstad, Ray Glantz, Jill Twist, David Smith, Beth Stevens, and Patti Krueger, who read parts of it and offered comments at various stages, and to Charles McKinney. Special thanks as well to colleagues and friends Nelson Lichtenstein and Eileen Boris, David Roediger, Robin D. G. Kelley, Paul Ortiz, Ray Arsenault, Dennis Dickerson, James Gregory, Nancy MacLean, Alice Kessler-Harris, Martha

Biondi, Eric Arnesen, Joseph McCartin, Joe Trotter, David Bacon, Lisa Brock, Thavolia Glymph, Kwame Hassan Jeffries, Ira Berlin, Barbara Fields, Marcus Rediker, David Chappel, Nell Irvin Painter, Jacqueline Dowd Hall, Tera Hunter, Keith Miller, Thomas Jackson, Kieran Taylor, John Lear, and others who helped me to think about this history. Friendships and discussions with freedom-movement veterans Jack O'Dell and James Lawson have deeply informed my study of King and nonviolence, as have Kent Wong and his colleagues at the UCLA Labor Center. Beloved mentors and colleagues David Montgomery, Otto Olsen, Henry Rosemont, Jr., Robert Zieger, James Green, Carl and Anne Braden, Lyle Mercer, and faculty and fellow students who taught me at Oakland University, Howard University, and Northern Illinois University history departments all set the stage.

Thanks to the National Civil Rights Museum for its marvelous way of carrying on the freedom-movement story and providing a continuing connection to the Memphis community. Thanks to colleagues and friends Mark Allen and Cheryl Cornish, Steve Lockwood and Mary Durham, David Ciscel, and Anthony Siracusa, who continue to make Memphis a second home; to Daphene McFerrin and Elena Delavega at the Ben Hooks Institute, Wanda Rushing, David Ciscel (emeritus), Wendy Thomas, and Otis Sanborn at the University of Memphis for their research insights; and to Kevin Bradshaw, Tom Smith, A. C. Wharton, Gail Tyree, Mar Perrusquia, and Kay Davis for generous insights on labor and civil rights in Memphis today.

Thanks for generous research help on this project from Suzanne Klinger, our extraordinary history librarian at the University of Washington Tacoma, and to students and former students Olga Subbotin, Richard Agee, Kelvin Wong, Daniel Twigg, Lucas Dambergs, Adam Nolan, Kyle Veldhuizen, and to Keith Ward and Randy Hightower. And to Turan Kayaoglu, and my many colleagues at the University of Washington Tacoma who continue to support research, teaching, and community outreach. Special thanks to the family of Fred and Dorothy Haley and to the Haley professorship for making a continuing life of research and writing possible. Grateful thanks to Kathy Cowell and the Arthur and Helen Riaboff Whiteley Center and UW Marine Labs in Friday Harbor, Washington, for supporting my writing retreats, and to Ray Glantz and Sandy Rabinowitz for their loving hospitality. The Harry Bridges Chair and Center for Labor Studies has provided a wonderful home for me at the University of Washington, and I thank all my friends and union allies, particularly members of the International Longshore and Warehouse Union (ILWU), the University of Washington Faculty Forward, and American Association of University Professors. I am thankful also for a Guggenheim fellowship that provided time to think about this project as I wrote my book about John Handcox, the Sharecroppers' Troubadour.

The Martin Luther King, Jr., Papers at the Martin Luther King, Jr., Center for Nonviolent Social Change, Atlanta, Georgia; the Walter Reuther Archives of Labor and Urban Affairs at Wayne State University, Detroit; the FBI records on Martin Luther King, Jr., and the Memphis sanitation strike; the AFL-CIO Papers, now at the University of Maryland, College Park; the Sanitation Strike Collection at the Mississippi Valley Collection at the University of Memphis McWherter Library; clipping files and manuscript collections of the Memphis Public Library, with generous help by Wayne Dowdy; the James Lawson Papers at Vanderbilt University; and the A. Philip Randolph Papers at the Library of Congress Manuscripts Collection all have been important sources for my research.

Richard Copley, Bob Fitch, and others have provided extraordinary photos. My thanks also to friends and colleagues in the Labor and Working Class History Association, the Southern Historical Association, the Organization of American Historians, and the Southern Labor Studies Association. There are many more people to thank for making real the possibility of being a freedom movement and labor-history scholar.

Special thanks to my partner in life, Patti Krueger, whose steadfast love makes all things possible; to my brother Charles Honey and sister Maureen Honey; and to all the people in our extended Krueger, Allen, and Miner families whose love and solidarity keep us all strong.

SOURCE NOTES

A world of scholarship exists on Martin Luther King, Jr., and freedom- and labor-movement history. Citations below are not meant to survey that historiography but to indicate where I focused my research and lead readers to additional sources. Notes follow more or less as items appear in my narrative. The quotes from Dr. King on the opening page of this book, and many subsequent quotes, appear in Michael K. Honey, ed., *All Labor Has Dignity* (Boston: Beacon Press, 2011). I found these speeches in 1994, in series 3 of King's "Speeches, Sermons, and Statements, etc., and/or About Labor Unions or Labor Groups," in the Martin Luther King, Jr., Center for Nonviolent Social Change Library (now designated online as the King Center). Its archives may be found in digitized form on the Center's website (http://www.thekingcenter.org/archive), although my references are to the paper copies I used, designated as MLKP Atlanta.

Introduction: PROMISED LAND

Under the direction of senior scholar Clayborne Carson and his coeditor Tenisha Armstrong, the Martin Luther King Papers Project at Stanford University has published seven volumes of the King Papers as of this writing. I list references to its documents as MLKP Stanford. Stanford's Martin Luther King, Jr., Research and Education Institute also provides extensive online resources: https://kinginstitute.stanford.edu.

Sources on King I used in this book include: Clayborne Carson, *Martin's Dream: My Journey and the Legacy of Martin Luther King, Jr., A Memoir* (New York: Palgrave Macmillan, 2013); Keith D. Miller, *Martin Luther King's Biblical Epic: His Final, Great Speech* (Jackson: University Press of Mississippi, 2012), and *Voice of Deliverance: The Language of Martin Luther King, Jr., and Its Sources* (New York: Free Press, 1992); David L. Chappell, *A Stone of Hope: Prophetic Religion and the Death of Jim Crow* (Chapel Hill: University of North Carolina Press,

2004), and *Waking from the Dream: The Struggle for Civil Rights in the Shadow of Martin Luther King, Jr.* (New York: Random House, 2014); Jennifer J. Yanco, *Misremembering Dr. King: Revisiting the Legacy of Martin Luther King, Jr.* (Bloomington: Indiana University Press, 2014); Martin Luther King, Jr., *The Radical King,* ed. Cornel West (Boston: Beacon, 2015); Michael Eric Dyson, *April 4, 1968: Martin Luther King, Jr.'s Death and How it Changed America* (New York: Basic Books, 2008); Tavis Smiley, *Death of a King: The Real Story of Dr. Martin Luther King Jr.'s Final Year* (New York: Little, Brown, 2014); William P. Jones, *The March on Washington: Jobs, Freedom, and the Forgotten History of Civil Rights* (New York: W. W. Norton, 2013); Vincent Harding, *Martin Luther King, The Inconvenient Hero* (New York: Orbis, 1996); Harvard Sitkoff, *King: Pilgrimage to the Mountaintop* (New York: Hill and Wang, 2008); Adam Fairclough, *To Redeem the Soul of America: The Southern Christian Leadership Conference and Martin Luther King, Jr.* (Athens: University of Georgia Press, 1987); David J. Garrow, *Bearing the Cross: Martin Luther King, Jr., and the Southern Christian Leadership Conference* (New York: William Morrow, 1986); Taylor Branch, *Parting the Waters: America in the King Years, 1954–63* (New York: Simon and Schuster, 1988), *Pillar of Fire: America in the King Years, 1963–65* (1998), and *At Canaan's Edge: America in the King Years, 1965–68* (2006); Stewart Burns, *To the Mountaintop: Martin Luther King Jr.'s Sacred Mission to Save America, 1955–1968* (San Francisco: Harper Collins, 2004); and David Levering Lewis, *King: A Biography* (Urbana: University of Illinois Press, 1978).

Thomas F. Jackson, *From Civil Rights to Human Rights: Martin Luther King, Jr., and the Struggle for Economic Justice* (Philadelphia: University of Pennsylvania Press, 2007), provides the definitive account of King's thinking on economic justice and identifies him as a "democratic socialist." I have relied heavily on my research in Michael K. Honey, *Going Down Jericho Road: The Memphis Strike, Martin Luther King's Last Campaign* (New York: W. W. Norton, 2007), and *All Labor Has Dignity,* cited above. Over the years I have done numerous interviews with James Lawson. Most useful on economic justice were a personal interview on May 6, 2005, in Santa Barbara, California, and see "Forty Years Since King: The Memphis Sanitation Strike," *Labor: A Journal of Working-Class Studies of the Americas,* vol. 5, No. 1 (Spring 2008): 9–13.

Also, see my film, "Love and Solidarity: James M. Lawson and Nonviolence in the Search for Workers' Rights," 2016, available from Bullfrog Films; and Kent Wong, Ana Luz Gonzalez, and Rev. James Lawson, Jr., eds., *Nonviolence and Social Movements: The Teachings of Rev. James M. Lawson, Jr.* (Los Angeles: UCLA Labor Center, 2016). David

Halberstam, *The Children* (New York: Random House, 1998) begins his book with a short biography of Rev. Lawson.

On the United Negro Protest Committee picketing the Mine Safety Appliance Company in Homewood, Pa., "UNPC's Pickets March for Jobs at Mine Safety: Future Hiring is Issue" and "'Hands Off' by CHR on UNPC-Union Tiff," *Pittsburgh Courier,* Oct. 5 and 26, 1963, ProQuest Historical Newspapers.

Guides to freedom-movement history include: Harvard Sitkoff, *Toward Freedom Land* (Lexington: University Press of Kentucky, 2010); Jacquelyn Dowd Hall, "The Long Civil Rights Movement and the Political Uses of the Past," *Journal of American History* (March 2005): 1233–67; Talitha LaFlouria, *Chained in Silence: Black Women and Convict Labor in the New South* (Chapel Hill: University of North Carolina Press, 2015); Steven Hahn, *A Nation Under Our Feet: Black Political Struggles in the Rural South from Slavery to the Great Migration* (Cambridge, MA: Harvard University Press, 2005); Peniel E. Joseph, *Waiting 'Til the Midnight Hour: A Narrative History of Black Power in America* (New York: Henry Holt, 2006), and "The Black Power Movement: A State of the Field," *Journal of American History* (December 2009): 751–76; Joshua Bloom and Waldo E. Martin, *Black Against Empire. The History and Politics of the Black Panther Party* (Berkeley: University of California Press, 2013); Jacquelyn Jones, *Labor of Love, Labor of Sorrow: Black Women, Work, and the Family from Slavery to the Present* (New York: Basic Books, 1985). A collective memoir of black women in the freedom movement is Faith S. Holsaert, *Hands on the Freedom Plow: Personal Accounts by Women in SNCC* (Urbana: University of Illinois Press, 2010); see also Laurie Beth Green, *Battling the Plantation Mentality: Memphis and the Black Freedom Struggle* (Chapel Hill: University of North Carolina Press, 2007); Belinda Robnett, *How Long? How Long? African American Women in the Struggle for Civil Rights* (New York: Oxford University Press, 1997); and Barbara Ransby, *Ella Baker and the Black Freedom Movement: A Radical, Democratic Vision* (Chapel Hill: University of North Carolina Press, 2003).

Chapter 1. "WE THE DISINHERITED OF THIS
     LAND," 1929-1956

Opening epigrams are from Dr. King's letter to Coretta Scott, 125–26, and King, "Thou Fool," transcript of a sermon at Mt. Pisgah Baptist Church, Chicago, n.d., 1967, MLK Speech files, MLKP Atlanta, ser. 3,.

I rely in chapter 1 on Clayborne Carson, et al., eds., *The Papers of*

Martin Luther King., Jr., vol. 6, *Advocate of the Social Gospel, September 1948–March 1963* (Berkeley: University of California Press, 2007), and *The Papers of Martin Luther King, Jr.*, vol. 1, *Called to Serve, January 1929–June 1951* (1992); Carson, "Martin Luther King, Jr., and the African-American Social Gospel," ed. Paul E. Johnson, in *African-American Christianity* (Berkeley: University of California Press, 1994); and Martin Luther King, Jr., *The Autobiography of Martin Luther King, Jr.*, ed. Carson (New York: Grand Central, 1998); Martin Luther King, Sr., *Daddy King: An Autobiography* (New York: Morrow, 1980); Coretta Scott King, *My Life With Martin Luther King, Jr.* (New York: Holt, Rinehart and Winston, 1969), and Scott King, as told to Rev. Dr. Barbara Reynolds, *My Life, My Love, My Legacy* (New York: Henry Holt, 2017). Adam Daniel Williams, 1861–1931, and Alberta Williams, 1903–1974: http://kingencyclopedia.stanford.edu/encyclopedia/encyclopedia/enc.

Cornel West, "The Religious Foundations of the Thought of Martin Luther King, Jr.," in Peter J. Albert and Ronald Hoffman, eds., *We Shall Overcome: Martin Luther King, Jr., and the Black Freedom Struggle* (New York: Pantheon, 1990), quotes on 116, 117, 119; King's speech, "There are three major social evils," to District 65, Retail, Wholesale, and Department Store Union (RWDSU) on September 8, 1962, appears in Honey, ed., *All Labor Has Dignity, 55–65.*

"Racial capitalism" refers to America's capitalism organized by race, while "Jim Crow capitalism" refers to postemancipation capitalism under segregation in the South. M. F. Ashley Montague, *Man's Most Dangerous Myth: The Fallacy of Race* (New York: Columbia University Press, 1942); William McKee Evans, *Open Wound: The Long View of Race in America* (Urbana: University of Illinois, 2009); Jacquelyn Jones, *A Dreadful Deceit: The Myth of Race from the Colonial Era to Obama's America* (New York: Basic Books, 2013); George Frederickson, *White Supremacy: A Comparative Study of American and South African History* (Oxford: Oxford University Press, 1981); W. E. B. Du Bois, *Black Reconstruction in America: An Essay Toward a History of the Part Which Black Folk Played in the Attempt to Reconstruct Democracy in America* (1935; repr. New York: Oxford, 2007); David Roediger, *The Wages of Whiteness: Race and the Making of the American Working Class* (London: Verso, 2007), and *Seizing Freedom: Slave Emancipation and Liberty for All* (London: Verso, 2015); Ira Berlin, *Generations of Captivity: A History of African-American Slaves* (Cambridge, MA: Belknap Press of Harvard University Press, 2003); Eric Foner, *Reconstruction: America's Unfinished Revolution, 1863–1877* (New York: Harper and Row, 1990); Michael Honey, "Class, Race, and Power in the New South," in *Democracy Betrayed: The Wilmington Race Riot of 1898 and Its Legacy*, ed. Timothy Tyson and

David Cicelski (Chapel Hill: University of North Carolina Press, 1998), 163–84; Lawrence Goodwyn, *The Populist Moment* (New York: Oxford, 1978); Peter Rachleff, *Black Labor in the South: Richmond, Virginia, 1865–1890* (Urbana: University of Illinois Press, 1984); Talitha LeFlouria, *Chained in Silence: Black Women and Convict Labor in the New South* (Chapel Hill: University of North Carolina Press, 2015); Jordan T. Camp, *Incarcerating the Crisis: Freedom Struggles and the Rise of the Neoliberal State* (Berkeley: University of California Press, 2016); Alex Lichtenstein, *Twice the Work of Free Labor: The Political Economy of Convict Labor in the New South* (London: Verso, 1996); Danielle McGuire, *At the Dark End of the Street: Black Women, Rape, and Resistance* (New York: Knopf, 2010). Patrick Phillips, *Blood at the Root: A Racial Cleansing in America* (New York: W. W. Norton, 2017), documents the grim legacy of horrendous racial violence close to King's home town of Atlanta.

Daddy King, as many referred to him, changed his name from Michael to Martin Luther King, as did his son. Carson, et al., *The Papers of MLKP*, vol. 1, 30–31. Malcolm X, *The Autobiography of Malcolm X*, ed. Alex Haley (New York: Grove Press, 1965); author interview with C. T. Vivian, Atlanta, Georgia, November 8, 1997.

Scholars have debated the reasons for King's plagiarism in his graduate school research papers. Keith Miller has shown that King never left the mode of Protestant preachers who borrowed freely from each other without attribution to popularize basic themes of Christianity in "Becoming Martin Luther King, Jr.—Plagiarism and Originality: a Round Table," *Journal of American History* 78, No. 1 (June 1991): 11–123; Miller, *Voice of Deliverance: The Language of Martin Luther King, Jr., and Its Sources* (New York: Free Press, 1992).

On American traditions of nonviolence, Leilah Danielson, *American Gandhi: A. J. Muste and the History of Radicalism in the Twentieth Century* (Philadelphia: University of Pennsylvania Press, 2014); King's comments on capitalism, Martin to Coretta Scott, July 18, 1952, King Papers, vol. 6, 123–26. Coretta Scott King's memoirs cited above provide moving insights into King family history.

On the red scare against labor and civil rights: Kenneth O'Reilly, *Hoover and the Un-Americans: The FBI, HUAC, and the Red Menace* (Philadelphia: Temple University Press, 1983); Anne Braden, *HUAC: Bulwark of Segregation* (National Committee to Abolish HUAC, 1964), Braden Papers, Wisconsin Historical Society, Madison; Curtis S. McDougal, *Gideon's Army*, vol. 3 (New York: Marzani and Munsell, 1965); John Egerton, *Speak Now Against the Day: The Generation Before the Civil Rights Movement in the South* (New York: Knopf, 1994); Robert H. Zieger, Timothy J. Minchin, and Gilbert J. Gall, *American Workers,*

American Unions: The Twentieth and Early Twenty-First Centuries, 4th ed. (Baltimore: Johns Hopkins University Press, 2014); Nelson Lichtenstein, *State of the Union: A Century of American Labor,* rev. ed. (Princeton: Princeton University Press, 2013); Glenda Elizabeth Gilmore, *Defying Dixie: The Radical Roots of Civil Rights, 1919–1950* (New York: W. W. Norton, 2008); Robin D. G. Kelley, *Hammer and Hoe: Alabama Communists During the Great Depression* (Chapel Hill: University of North Carolina Press, 1990); Mark I. Solomon, *The Cry Was Unity: Communists and African Americans, 1917–1936* (Jackson: University Press of Mississippi, 1998); Michael K. Honey, *Southern Labor and Black Civil Rights: Organizing Memphis Workers* (Urbana: University of Illinois Press, 1993), and *Black Workers Remember* (Berkeley: University of California Press, 1999); Robert Rogers Korstad, *Civil Rights Unionism: Tobacco Workers and the Struggle for Democracy in the Mid-Twentieth-Century South* (Chapel Hill: University of North Carolina Press, 2003). Communists and Socialists were in conflict over sharecropper organizing but both left an interracial organizing legacy: Michael K. Honey, *Sharecroppers' Troubadour: John L. Handcox, the Southern Tenant Farmers' Union, and the African-American Song Tradition* (New York: Palgrave Macmillan, 2013); Erik Gellman and Jarod Roll, *The Gospel of the Working Class: Labor's Southern Prophets in New Deal America* (Urbana: University of Illinois Press, 2011).

On postwar southern organizing: Michael K. Honey, "Operation Dixie, the Red Scare, and the Defeat of Southern Labor Organizing," in *American Labor and the Cold War,* ed. Robert W. Cherny, William Issel, and Kieran Walsh Taylor (New Brunswick, NJ: Rutgers University Press, 2004), 216–44; Barbara S. Griffith, *The Crisis of American Labor: Operation Dixie and the Defeat of the CIO* (Philadelphia: Temple University Press, 1988); Lichtenstein, *State of the Union,* 114–22; Robert H. Zieger, *The CIO, 1935–1955* (Chapel Hill: University of North Carolina Press, 1995), ch. 9; Honey, *Southern Labor and Black Civil Rights,* chs. 8 and 9; author interview with Myles Horton, New Market, Tennessee, June 1–2, 1981; Ellen Schrecker, *Many Are the Crimes: McCarthyism in America* (Boston: Little, Brown, 1998); Robert O'Harrow, Jr., and Shawn Boburg, "The man who showed Donald Trump how to exploit power and instill fear," *Washington Post,* June 17, 2016; Alex Heard, *The Eyes of Willie McGee: A Tragedy of Race, Sex, and Secrets in the Jim Crow South* (New York: Harper, 2010); Gerald Horne, *Communist Front? The Civil Rights Congress, 1946–1956* (Rutherford, NJ: Fairleigh Dickinson, 1988); Horace Huntley, "The Red Scare and Black Workers in Alabama: The International Union of Mine, Mill, and Smelter Workers, 1945–53," in *Labor Divided: Race and Ethnicity in United States Labor Struggles, 1835–1960,* ed. Robert Asher and Charles Stephenson (Albany: SUNY Press, 1990), 129–50; Korstad, *Civil Rights Unionism*; Ellen Schrecker, "McCarthyism and the Labor Movement: The Role of the State," in *The CIO's Left-led Unions,* ed. Steve Rosswurm (New Brunswick, NJ: Rutgers University Press, 1992), 139–58; Robert Korstad and Nelson Lichtenstein, "Opportunities Found and Lost: Labor, Radicals, and the Early Civil Rights Movement," *Journal of American History* 75, No. 3 (December 1988): 786–811. Eric Arnesen defends left anticommunism, "'No Graver Danger': Black Anticommunism, the Communist Party, and the Race Question," *Labor: Studies in Working-Class History of the Americas* 3, no. 4 (Winter 2006): 13–52; Martha Biondi, "Response to Eric Arnesen," 59–64, sees anticommunism as a disaster for the labor and civil rights movements. See also Biondi, *To Stand and Fight: The Struggle for Civil Rights in Postwar New York City* (Cambridge, MA: Harvard University Press, 2003), and Harvey A. Levenstein, *Communism, Anti-Communism, and the CIO* (Westport, CT: Greenwood Press, 1981).

The Montgomery bus boycott: *The Papers of MLK*, vol. 6, Introduction, and quotes on 6, 73, 125–26; Scott King, *My Life With Martin Luther King,* 127–30; Troy Jackson, *Becoming King: Martin Luther King, Jr. and the Making of a National Leader* (Lexington: University Press of Kentucky, 2008); Jeanne Theoharris, *The Rebellious Life of Mrs. Rosa Parks* (Boston: Beacon Press, 2013); Timothy Tyson, *The Blood of Emmett Till* (New York: Simon and Schuster, 2017), 133, 191, 210–11; Neil McMillen, *The Citizen's Council: Organized Resistance to the Second Reconstruction, 1954–64* (1971, repr. Urbana: University of Illinois Press, 1994); Dan T. Carter, *The Politics of Rage: George Wallace, the Origins of the New Conservatism, and the Transformation of American Politics* (New York: Simon and Schuster, 1995); David J. Garrow, *Bearing the Cross: Martin Luther King, Jr., and the Southern Christian Leadership Conference* (New York: William Morrow, 1986), 55–61. Black southerners used armed self-defense as a matter of course to protect themselves: Timothy B. Tyson, *Radio Free Dixie: Robert F. Williams and the Roots of Black Power* (Chapel Hill: University of North Carolina Press, 2001); Charles E. Cobb, Jr., *"That Nonviolent Stuff'l Get You Killed": How Guns Made the Civil Rights Movement Possible* (New York: Basic Books, 2014); Martin Luther King, Jr., *Where Do We Go From Here: Chaos or Community?* (Boston: Beacon Press, 2010), accepted the necessity for self-defense on a personal level, pp. 27, 57. Racist handbills distributed in Montgomery, dated February 10, 1956, are in the A. Philip Randolph Collection, Library of Congress Manuscripts Collection (LOC). On Bayard Rustin's early work with King, Garrow, *Bearing the Cross,* 64–73, 83; John D'Emilio, *Lost Prophet: The Life and Times of Bayard Rustin* (New

York: Free Press, 2003), 265–98; Thomas Jackson, "Recasting the Dream: Race and Poverty in the Social Thought of Martin Luther King, Jr.," Stanford University seminar paper, June 1989. With drafts written by Rustin, Dr. King clearly explained nonviolence in *Christian Century* 74 (February 6, 1957) and in King, *Stride Toward Freedom: The Montgomery Story* (1958; repr. Boston: Beacon Press, 2010), 196–99; Barbara Ransby, *Ella Baker and the Black Freedom Movement: A Radical, Democratic Vision* (Chapel Hill: University of North Carolina Press, 2003).

Chapter 2. "WE HAVE A POWERFUL INSTRUMENT,"
1957–1963

Epigraph, "There are three major social evils," in Michael K. Honey, ed., *All Labor Has Dignity* (Boston: Beacon Press, 2011), 55–64. Sources for this chapter include *Time*, Feb. 18, 1957; David J. Garrow, *Bearing the Cross: Martin Luther King, Jr., and the Southern Christian Leadership Conference* (New York: William Morrow, 1986), 79–80, 83, 89. On Iola Curry's anticommunist obsession, Thomas F. Jackson, *From Civil Rights to Human Rights: Martin Luther King, Jr., and the Struggle for Economic Justice* (Philadelphia: University of Pennsylvania Press, 2007), 92; Hugh Pearson, *When Harlem Nearly Killed King: The 1958 Stabbing of Dr. Martin Luther King, Jr.* (New York: Seven Stories Press, 2002); Coretta Scott King, as told to Rev. Dr. Barbara Reynolds, *My Life, My Love, My Legacy* (New York: Henry Holt, 2017), 88; James Melvin Washington, ed., *A Testament of Hope: The Essential Writings of Martin Luther King, Jr.* (San Francisco: Harper, 1986), 41; Mary Dudziak, *Cold War Civil Rights: Race and the Image of American Democracy* (Princeton: Princeton University Press, 2000); King, "A Look to the Future," in Honey, ed., *All Labor Has Dignity*, 3–18; Guy and Candie Carawan, *Sing for Freedom: The Story of the Civil Rights Movement Through Its Songs* (Bethlehem, PA: Sing Out, 1990), and David Spener, *We shall not be moved/No nos moverán: Biography of a song of struggle* (Philadelphia: Temple University Press, 2016), on southern freedom songs heard around the world. Author interview with W. E. "Red" Davis, St. Louis, January 26–28, 1983, on his travels with King after Highlander. The Defenders of State Sovereignty and Individual Liberties in Richmond, Virginia, and others distributed the Georgia Education Commission slander on King, *Aryan Views and White Folk News* (Waco, Texas, July 1963), Randolph Papers, box 30, "smear literature," Library of Congress Manuscripts Collection; Jeff Woods, *Black Struggle, Red Scare: Segregation and Anti-Communism* (Baton Rouge: Louisiana State University Press, 2004), 105–7, ch. 3. Jane Mayer, *Dark Money: The*

Hidden History of the Billionaires Behind the Rise of the Radical Right (New York: Doubleday, 2016), 28–33, 38, 39, 43–44; Daniel Schulman, *Sons of Wichita: How the Koch Brothers Became America's Most Powerful Dynasty* (New York: Grand Central, 2014). Author interview with Myles Horton, New Market, Tennessee, June 1–2, 1981; Richard Gid Powers, *Secrecy and Power: The Life of J. Edgar Hoover* (New York: Free Press, 1987); Honey, *Southern Labor and Black Civil Rights*, ch. 8. The Southern Conference Educational Fund's monthly newspaper, 1945–1970, documents the persistence of the red scare; Braden and Wilkinson clemency petition dated June 7, 1961, in the Braden Collection, Wisconsin Historical Society, Madison; Andrew Manis, *A Fire You Can't Put Out: The Civil Rights Life of Birmingham's Fred Shuttlesworth* (Tuscaloosa: University of Alabama Press, 2010); Anne Braden, *The Wall Between* (New York: Monthly Review, 1958); Catherine Fosl, *Subversive Southerner: Anne Braden and the Struggle for Racial Justice in the Post-War South* (New York: Palgrave Macmillan, 2002); see also Michael K. Honey, *Going Down Jericho Road: The Memphis Strike, Martin Luther King's Last Campaign* (New York: W. W. Norton, 2007), 28–29; John D'Emilio, *Lost Prophet: The Life and Times of Bayard Rustin* (New York: Free Press, 2003), 266.

King, "The Future of Integration" speech, Chicago, October 2, 1957, is in MLKP Atlanta, ser. 3. *The Packinghouse Worker* newspaper and the United Packinghouse Workers of America collection 118, Wisconsin Historical Society, documents the union's powerful civil rights efforts. On Russell Lasley, Pat Kinney, "Civil Rights Hero had Waterloo Roots," Waterloo-Cedar Falls *Courier*, February 17, 2013, http://wcfcourier.com/news/local/civil-rights-hero-had-waterloo-roots/article_71a9ac9e-c986-5b9b-89a7-e55d71b24794.html. See also Rick Halpern and Roger Horowitz, *Meatpackers: An Oral History of Black Packinghouse Workers and Their Struggle for Racial and Economic Equality* (New York: Twayne Publishers, 1996); Halpern, *Down on the Killing Floor: Black and White Workers in Chicago's Packinghouses, 1904–54* (Urbana: University of Illinois Press, 1994); and Horowitz, *"Negro and White, Unite and Fight!": A Social History, Industrial Unionism in Meatpacking, 1930–90* (Urbana: University of Illinois Press, 1997). Ralph Helstein rallied black workers and defended labor's left while conceding to the CIO and AFL-CIO that Communists could not hold top positions: author interview with Les Orear, Chicago, August 1, 1981; and Cyril D. Robinson, *Marching With Dr. King: Ralph Helstein and the United Packinghouse Workers of America* (Santa Barbara, CA: Praeger, 2011). Kim Scipes, *AFL-CIO's Secret War Against Developing Country Workers: Solidarity or Sabotage?* (Lanham, MD: Lexington, 2010); Stephen Kinzer and Stephen

Schlesinger, *Bitter Fruit: The Story of the American Coup in Guatemala*, rev. ed. (Boston: Harvard University Press, 2005).

On SCLC, SNCC, and King: Barbara Ransby, *Ella Baker and the Black Freedom Movement: A Radical, Democratic Vision* (Chapel Hill: University of North Carolina Press, 2003), 184, 188; Septima Clark, *Ready from Within: Septima Clark and the Civil Rights Movement* (Navarro, CA: Wild Tree Press, 1986); Dorothy F. Cotton, *If Your Back's Not Bent: The Role of the Citizenship Education Program in the Civil Rights Movement* (New York: Aria Books, 2012); Katherine Mellen Charron, *Freedom's Teacher: The Life of Septima Clark* (Chapel Hill: University of North Carolina Press, 2009); Clayborne Carson, *In Struggle: SNCC and the Black Awakening of the 1960s* (Cambridge, MA: Harvard University Press, 1981); Wesley Hogan, *Many Minds, One Heart: SNCC's Dream for a New America* (Chapel Hill: University of North Carolina Press, 2007); Charles Payne, *I've Got the Light of Freedom: The Organizing Tradition and the Mississippi Freedom Struggle* (Berkeley: University of California Press, 1995); Kevin Boyle, *The UAW and the Heyday of American Liberalism* (Ithaca, NY: Cornell University Press, 1995), quote on 227; Raymond Arsenault, *Freedom Riders: 1961 and the Struggle for Racial Justice* (New York: Oxford University Press, 2006).

Randolph's "Dear Brother," letter to unionists, December 8 and April 1960, Committee to Defend Martin Luther King, box 24, A. Philip Randolph Papers, Library of Congress. Erik S. Gellman, *Death Blow to Jim Crow: The National Negro Congress and the Rise of Militant Civil Rights* (Chapel Hill: University of North Carolina Press, 2012); Cornelius Bynum, *A. Philip Randolph and the Struggle for Civil Rights* (Urbana: University of Illinois Press, 1971); Herbert Hill, "Racism Within Organized Labor: A Report of Five Years of the AFL-CIO, 1955–60," in MLKP Atlanta, box 140:31, Trade Unions. F. Ray Marshall, *The Negro and Organized Labor* (New York: Wiley, 1965), 46–48, 53–85, 177–207; Philip S. Foner, *Organized Labor and the Black Worker, 1619–1981* (New York: International Publishers, 1981); Robert H. Zieger, *For Jobs and Freedom: Race and Labor in America Since 1865* (Lexington: University Press of Kentucky, 2014); Eric Arnesen, ed. *The Black Worker: Race, Labor, and Civil Rights Since Emancipation* (Urbana: University of Illinois Press, 2007). SCLC Press Release, Statement in Defense of Randolph, October 13, 1961, MLKP Stanford. King, "If the Negro Wins, Labor Wins," in Honey, ed., *All Labor Has Dignity*, 31–46; Ira Katznelson, *When Affirmative Action Was White: An Untold Story of Racial Inequality in Twentieth-Century America* (New York: W. W. Norton, 2005). Pete Daniel, *Dispossession: Discrimination Against African American Farmers in the Age of Civil Rights* (Chapel Hill: University of North Carolina Press, 2015). James

C. Cobb, *The Selling of the South: The Southern Crusade for Economic Development, 1936–1980* (Baton Rouge: Louisiana State University Press, 1983). AFL-CIO, *Proceedings of the Fourth Constitutional Convention of the AFL-CIO,* vol. 1 (Miami Beach, FL, December 7–13, 1961). On survival of the black vote and its effect in Memphis: David M. Tucker, *Memphis Since Crump: Bossism, Blacks, and Civic Reform, 1949–1986* (Knoxville: University of Tennessee Press, 1980), 54–60; Elizabeth Gritter, *River of Hope: Black Politics and the Memphis Freedom Movement, 1865–1954* (Lexington: University Press of Kentucky, 2014), 177–87ff. On union racial divisions: Bruce Nelson, *Divided We Stand: American Workers and the Struggle for Black Equality* (Princeton: Princeton University Press, 2001). "Dr. King's Statements on 1199, 1959–68," MLKP Stanford, shows a long, deep connection between King and 1199 Hospital Workers Union. Inventories of District 65 RWDSU Papers at the Tamiment Library, and Lisa Phillips, *A Renegade Union: Interracial Organizing and Labor Radicalism* (Urbana: University of Illinois Press, 2013), document King's long-standing connection to RWDSU. On 1199 see Leon Fink and Brian Greenberg, *Upheaval in the Quiet Zone: A History of Hospital Workers' Union, Local 1199* (Urbana: University of Illinois Press, 1989).

On FBI repression: David J. Garrow, *The FBI and Martin Luther King, Jr.: From "Solo" to Memphis* (New York: W. W. Norton, 1981), 44–49, and throughout; Kenneth O'Reilly, *Racial Matters: The FBI's Secret File on Black America, 1960–1972* (New York: Free Press, 1989), 38–39, 41–77, 157–58ff; Jeff Woods, *Black Struggle, Red Scare: Segregation and Anti-Communism* (Baton Rouge: Louisiana State University Press, 2004). A few weeks before King's death, a CIA memo uncovered through a FOIA inquiry said, "According to the FBI, Dr. King is regarded in Communist circles as a 'genuine Marxist-Leninist who is following the Marxist-Leninist line'"; Garrow, "The FBI and Martin Luther King," *Atlantic Monthly,* July/August 2002, 80–88, quote on 88. The FBI began wiretapping Levison on March 20 and its "Communist Infiltration" investigation of SCLC began on October 23, 1962: Adam Fairclough, *To Redeem the Soul of America: The Southern Christian Leadership Conference and Martin Luther King, Jr.* (Athens: University of Georgia Press, 1987), 482. FBI files on King are now available online. On Nazi and racist threats: George Lincoln Rockwell, *White Power* (Dallas: Ragnarok Press, 1967)—a reader wrote on a library copy of this book at the University of Washington, "This man should be ashamed to be a human being." William H. Schmaltz, *Hate: George Lincoln Rockwell and the American Nazi Party* (Washington: Brassey's, 1999), quotes on 326, 271. For chilling images of whites screaming for King's blood, see Henry Hampton and Steve Fayer, "Eyes on the Prize II: America at the Racial Crossroads, 1965–1985,"

WGBH and Public Broadcasting System. John Harold Redekop, *The American Far Right: A Case Study of Billy James Hargis and Christian Crusade* (Grand Rapids: William B. Eerdmans Publishing, 1968), 22–39, and Hatfield's warnings, i–iii; Lori L. Bogle, "The U.S. Military, the Radical Right, and Harding College's National Education Program: Propaganda Partners of the Cold War, 1958–1962," Organization of American Historians national conference in Chicago, Illinois, March 29, 1966, paper in author's possession, quote on pp. 14–15. Michael C. Pierce, "The Racist Origins of Right to Work," *Labor Notes* #463 (October 2017), 4–5. Elizabeth Jacoway *Turn Away Thy Son: Little Rock, the Crisis that Shocked the Nation* (New York: Free Press, 2007).

King quote on "right to work" laws in the ILWU *Dispatcher*, March 2017, p. 2. James Baldwin, *The Fire Next Time* (New York: Dial Press, 1963), 5. On "Bombingham," Angela Y. Davis, *Angela Davis: An Autobiography* (New York: Random House, 1974), and Diane McWhorter, *Carry Me Home: Birmingham, Alabama, the Climactic Battle of the Civil Rights Revolution* (New York: Simon and Schuster, 2001), 101–3ff. On civil rights martyr William Moore, Mary Stanton, *Freedom Walk: Mississippi or Bust* (Jackson: University Press of Mississippi, 2003). "Letter from Birmingham Jail" in Martin Luther King, Jr., *Why We Can't Wait* (New York: Harper and Row, 1963). Horace Huntley and David Montgomery, eds., *Black Workers' Struggle for Equality in Birmingham* (Urbana: University of Illinois Press, 2004), quote on 24. When southern AFL-CIO leaders adhered to national AFL-CIO equal rights doctrine many rank-and-file whites resisted, undermining both unions and democracy: Alan Draper, *Conflict of Interests: Organized Labor and the Civil Rights Movement in the South, 1954–1968* (Ithaca, NY: ILR Press, 1994), and Michael Goldfield, *The Color of Politics: Race and the Mainsprings of American Politics* (New York: New Press, 1997).

"Emancipation March on Washington for Jobs and Freedom" flyer, Randolph Papers, box 26, Library of Congress; King quotes, Detroit speech, "Now is the time," in Honey, ed., *All Labor Has Dignity,* 76–86. On UAW support for the civil rights movement, Nelson Lichtenstein, *The Most Dangerous Man in Detroit: Walter Reuther and the Fate of American Labor* (Basic Books, 1995); John Bernard, *Walter Reuther and the Rise of the Auto Workers* (Boston: Little, Brown, and Company, 1983); and Boyle, *The UAW and the Heyday of American Liberalism.* King to O'Dell, July 3, 1963, and O'Dell to King, Jan. 29, 1963, MLKP Atlanta, ser. 1, Primary Correspondence; author interview with Jack O'Dell, Seattle, Feb. 5, 2010; Jack O'Dell, *Climbin' Jacob's Ladder: The Black Freedom Movement Writings of Jack O'Dell,* ed. Nikhil Pal Singh (Berkeley: University of California Press, 2010). William P. Jones, *The March on*

Washington: Jobs, Freedom, and the Forgotten History of Civil Rights (New York: W. W. Norton, 2013), quote on 52, and "The Unknown Origins of the March on Washington: Civil Rights Politics and the Black Working Class," in *Labor: Studies in Working-Class History of the Americas* 7, no. 3: 33–52. Emilie Raymond, *Stars for Freedom: Hollywood, Black Celebrities, and the Civil Rights Movement* (Seattle: University of Washington Press, 2015). King's eulogy, in *A Call to Conscience: The Landmark Speeches of Dr. Martin Luther King, Jr.,* ed. Clayborne Carson and Kris Shepard (New York: Warner Books, 2003), 81–87, 96; Scott King, *My Life, My Love, My Legacy,* 109, 115, 117.

Chapter 3. "NORTHERN GHETTOS ARE THE PRISONS OF FORGOTTEN MEN," 1964-1966

"Martin Luther King, Jr.: Never Again Where He Was," *Time,* January 3, 1964; Hoover's surveillance: Adam Fairclough, *To Redeem the Soul of America: The Southern Christian Leadership Conference and Martin Luther King, Jr.* (Athens: University of Georgia Press, 1987), 484; King, *Why We Can't Wait* (1964; repr. Boston: Beacon Press, 2010). Mississippi freedom movement: John Dittmer, *Local People: The Struggle for Civil Rights in Mississippi* (Urbana: University of Illinois, 1994); Chris Meyers Asch, *The Senator and the Sharecropper: The Freedom Struggles of James O. Eastland and Fannie Lou Hamer* (Chapel Hill: University of North Carolina Press), 225–27. Nancy Maclean, "The Civil Rights Act of 1964: The Difference a Law Can Make," and symposium on Title VII, in *Labor: a Journal of Working-Class History of the Americas* 11, no. 3 (Fall 2014): 19–48, and MacLean, *Freedom Is Not Enough: Opening the American Work Place* (Cambridge, MA: Harvard University Press, 2006), 73–74ff; Timothy Minchin, *Color of Work* (Chapel Hill: University of North Carolina Press, 2001), and *Fighting Against the Odds: A History of Southern Labor Since World War II* (Gainesville: University of Florida Press, 2005). Wharlest Jackson Civil Rights Cold Case Project, http://coldcases.org/cases/wharlest-jackson-case.

On the war and electoral shifts: Marilyn Blatt Young, *The Vietnam Wars, 1945–1990* (New York: Harper Collins, 1991); Alan Draper, "Labor and the 1966 Elections," *Labor History* 30, no. 1 (1989): 76–92; Rick Perstein, *Before the Storm: Barry Goldwater and the Unmaking of the American Consensus* (New York: Hill and Wang, 2001). King wrote, "The Civil Rights Act is a reality, Goldwaterism has been soundly defeated and we have embarked on the prodigious journey into the Great Society. It would seem that we are well on the way to equality. . ." *Saturday Review* draft titled "The Movement: Prospects for '65," MLK Research and Education Institute, Stanford. On the FBI and the Nobel Prize: Fairclough, *To Redeem the Soul of America*, 219–21; Dorothy F. Cotton, *If Your Back's Not Bent: The Role of the Citizenship Education Program in the Civil Rights Movement* (New York: Aria Books, 2012), 8–22.

On the Scripto strike: Hartwell and Susan Hooper, "The Script Strike: Martin Luther King's 'Valley of Problems': Atlanta, 1964–65," *Atlanta History: A Journal of Georgia* 43, no. 3 (1999): 5–34; Tera Hunter, *To 'joy My Freedom: Southern Black Women's Lives and Labors After the Civil War* (Cambridge, MA: Harvard University Press, 1997); Leonard Dinnerstein, *Jews in the South* (Baton Rouge: Louisiana State University Press, 1973); Vartanig G. Vartan, "Civil Rights Group Backs Scripto Strike in Atlanta," *New York Times*, December 17, 1964, p. 46, ProQuest; Paul Good, "Dr. King's Group Enters Labor Dispute in Atlanta," *Washington Post*, December 5, 1964, p. A12, ProQuest; author interview with C. T. Vivian, Atlanta, November 8, 1997; "SNCC wins SCLC support in boycott of Scripto Co," *Baltimore Afro-American*, December 19, 1964, p. 16, ProQuest Historical Newspapers; G. S. Carlson, "King Says Prepare For World Boycott of Scripto Products," United Press International in *Chicago Daily Defender*, December 22, 1964, p. 1, ProQuest; David J. Garrow, *Bearing the Cross: Martin Luther King, Jr., and the Southern Christian Leadership Conference* (New York: William Morrow, 1986), 368–69; Kathryn Johnson, "Memoir Recalls MLK, family and the movement," Associated Press in *Broward* [Florida] *Times*, Jan. 21– 27, 2016; "Atlanta's Dinner For Dr. King Gains," *New York Times*, December 31, 1964, 10, ProQuest. "Union and Freedom," a film by the International Chemical Workers Union, 1964, George Meany Memorial Archive at the University of Maryland-College Park Library manuscript; The Scripto Strike: A Guide to Records, Georgia State University Library, Atlanta. Scripto news stories accessed through ProQuest Historical Newspapers include: *Baltimore Afro-American*, September 23, 1933, October 19, 1946, December 5, 12, and 19, 1964, January 2, 9, and 30, 1965; *Chicago Daily Defender*, November 30, December 14, 21, 22, and 24, 1964, October 12, 1968; *Los Angeles Times*, December 20, 1964; *Washington Post*, December 5, 11, and 15, 1964; *New York Amsterdam News*, December 19, 1964, October 19, 1968; *Wall Street Journal*, December 1, 1964; *New York Times*, November 16 and 28, December 21, 22, 25, 29, and 31, 1964, and January 10, 1965. "King Calls Secret Ballot 'Our Secret Weapon' In Integration Struggle," *Chicago Daily Defender*, October 25, 1962. Thanks to Richard Agee and Suzanne Klinger for helping me research the Scripto story.

On Selma: Coretta Scott King, as told to Rev. Dr. Barbara Reynolds, *My Life, My Love, My Legacy* (New York: Henry Holt, 2017, 131–34, 140, emphasis in the original; Manning Marable, *Malcolm X: A Life of Reinvention* (New York: Viking, 2011). King called Malcolm X's strategy one of "reciprocal bleeding" and "a desperate course of action": "Dr. King's statement on Malcolm X," March 16, 1964, MLKP Atlanta, ser. 1-1, 15:16. John Lewis with Michael D'Orso, *Walking with the Wind: A Memoir of the Movement* (New York: Simon and Schuster, 1998), 187. Freedom singer Bettie Mae Fikes told me in 2009 that she still suffered from post-traumatic stress from being arrested and locked up during the Selma movement as a teenager. Hasan Kwame Jeffries, *Bloody Lowndes: Civil Rights and Black Power in Alabama's Black Belt* (New York: New York University Press, 2009), 81–82; death statistics: Fairclough, *To Redeem the Soul of America,* 266; Gary May, *The Informant: The FBI, the Ku Klux Klan, and the Murder of Viola Liuzzo* (New Haven: Yale University Press, 2005); and Mary Stanton, *From Selma to Sorrow: The Life and Death of Viola Liuzzo* (Athens: University of Georgia Press, 1998). "Leaders Flock to Detroit for Mrs. Liuzzo Funeral," *Chicago Daily Defender,* March 30, 1965, ProQuest. William Oliver to King, June 1, 1965, sent $2,755 collected from workers at plant gates in Michigan and New York, MLKP Atlanta, ser. 1-1, 24:4.

Labor alliances and black worker challenges: King to Reuther, September 1965, thanked him for a $5,000 donation and enclosed an SCLC memo "To All Union Representatives," suggesting unions train civil rights activists to organize unions. SCLC records, box 245:2, MLKP Atlanta, and see also Reuther's correspondence files, UAW President's Office, Walter P. Reuther Archives of Labor and Urban Affairs, Library, Wayne State University, Detroit. Meany to King, June 3, 1964, and NAACP flyer, "Vote No on State Question 409," National Labor College Archive M 28 Civil Rights Department 9-00, University of Maryland College Park Library manuscripts; Honey, ed., *All Labor Has Dignity,* 23–24. Black workers at Atlantic Steel in Atlanta and elsewhere used Title VII to sue the United Steelworkers union for workplace discrimination: Bruce Nelson, *Divided We Stand: American Workers and the Struggle for Black Equality* (Princeton: Princeton University Press, 2001), documents, 227–50; Dennis Dickerson, *Out of the Crucible: Black Steelworkers in Western Pennsylvania, 1875–1980* (Albany: SUNY Press, 1986); Ruth Needleman, *Black Freedom Fighters in Steel: The Struggle for Democratic Unionism* (Ithaca, NY: ILR Press, 2003); "Struggles in Steel," California Newsreel, 1996. A. S. Miller to King, March 30, 1964, and King to Quill, March 25, 1964, box 13, folder 9, ser. 1-4, 4-6, MLKP Atlanta. When King endorsed the Philadelphia chapter of the American Federation of Teachers in an election, the National Education Association objected, leading to months of controversy. King-Hoffa correspondence also showed complications. Primary

Correspondence and Administrative Records 1955–68, SCLC President's Office, MLKP Atlanta.

On voting rights, Steven F. Lawson, *Running for Freedom: Civil Rights and Black Politics in America Since 1941* (Hoboken, NJ: Wiley, 2014), and Ari Berman, *Give Us the Ballot: The Modern Struggle for Voting Rights in America* (New York: Farrar, Straus and Giroux, 2015). Fairclough, *To Redeem the Soul of America,* 486; Gerald Horne, *Fire This Time: The Watts Uprising and the 1960s* (Charlottesville: University Press of Virginia, 1995). UAW Region 6 Statement to the Governor's Commission on the LA Riots, file 6.6.1.4, Kenneth Hahn Papers, box 317, folder 3, Huntington Library, Pasadena, California. *Newsweek,* August 20, 1965, reported on the antagonism toward King. Reuther invested heavily in his "Citizens Crusade Against Poverty," and King and Reuther sought to organize alliances. President's files, MLKP Atlanta, 6:10–13, and UAW President's Office, correspondence, Walter P. Reuther Archives of Labor and Urban Affairs, Reuther Library.

Manning Marable, "The Crisis of the Black Working Class: An Economic and Historical Analysis," *Science and Society,* vol. 46, no. 2 (Summer 1982): 130–61; Charles Killingsworth, "Negroes in a Changing Labor Market," 68, quote on 73, and Vivian W. Henderson, "Region, Race, and Jobs," 80, in Arthur M. Ross and Herbert Hill, *Employment, Race, and Poverty* (New York: Harcourt, Brace, 1967), 18–19, 3–48, 55. Jacquelyn Jones, *Labor of Love, Labor of Sorrow: Black Women, Work, and the Family from Slavery to the Present* (New York: Basic Books, 1985), 256–57; Paula Giddings, *When and Where I Enter: The Impact of Black Women on Race and Sex in America* (New York: William Morrow, 1984), 245–46, 256; Gavin Wright, *Old South, New South: Revolutions in the Southern Economy Since the Civil War* (New York: Basic Books, 1986), 243, 247, 255, on cotton mechanization and unemployment; F. Ray Marshall, "Industrialization and Race Relations in the Southern States," in Guy Hunter, ed., *Industrialization and Race Relations: A Symposium* (New York: Oxford University Press, 1965), 91, on decline in median income. Clarence Coe quoted in Michael K. Honey, *Black Workers Remember: An Oral History of Segregation Unionism, and the Freedom Struggle* (Berkeley: University of California Press, 1999), 360.

Labor-civil rights divergence: Kim Philips-Fein, *Invisible Hands: The Making of the Conservative Movement From the New Deal to Reagan* (New York: W. W. Norton, 2009); Kevin Boyle, *The UAW and the Heyday of American Liberalism* (Ithaca, NY: Cornell University Press, 1995); Nelson Lichtenstein, *The Most Dangerous Man in Detroit: Walter Reuther and the Fate of American Labor* (Basic Books, 1995), and *State of the Union: A Century of American Labor,* rev. ed. (Princeton: Princeton University Press, 2013), ch. 5; Peter Levy, *The New Left and Labor in the 1960s* (Urbana: University of Illinois Press, 1993). Andrew Young speaking notes, September 16, 1965, before District 65, King Labor Speeches, MLKP Atlanta. King, "Labor Cannot Stand Still," convention of the Illinois AFL-CIO, October 7, 1965, in Honey, ed., *All Labor Has Dignity*, 112–20. *A "Freedom Budget" for all Americans: Budgeting Our Resources, 1966–75 to Achieve "Freedom From Want"* (New York: A. Philip Randolph Institute, Oct. 1966); Paul Le Blanc and Michael D. Yates, *A Freedom Budget for All Americans: Recapturing the Promise of the Civil Rights Movement in the Struggle for Economic Justice Today* (New York: Monthly Review Press, 2013), 95–96; D'Emilio, *Lost Prophet: The Life and Times of Bayard Rustin* (New York: Free Press, 2003), 396–403 and ch. 17; King, "Beyond the Los Angeles Riots," *Saturday Review,* Nov. 13, 1965, 33–35; Daniel Levine, *Bayard Rustin and the Civil Rights Movement* (New Brunswick, NJ: Rutgers University Press), 174, quote on 187.

"Its towering housing project," Scott King, *My Life, My Love, My Legacy,* 143; James Ralph, *Northern Protest: Martin Luther King, Chicago, and the Civil Rights Movement* (Cambridge, MA: Harvard University Press, 1993), 46, 48, 103–5, 112. Mary Lou Finley, Bernard Lafayette, Jr., James R. Ralph, Jr., and Pam Smith, eds., *The Chicago Freedom Movement: Martin Luther King, Jr., and Civil Rights Activism in the North* (Lexington: University Press of Kentucky, 2015). Martin L. Deppe, *Operation Breadbasket: An Untold Story of Civil Rights in Chicago, 1966–1971* (Athens: University of Georgia Press, 2017). Aram Goudsouzian, *Down to the Crossroads: Civil Rights, Black Power, and the Meredith March Against Fear* (New York: Farrar, Straus, and Giroux, 2014), 171–76; John Lewis with Michael D'Orso, *Walking with the Wind: A Memoir of the Movement* (New York: Simon and Schuster, 1998), 369–73; Donna Cooper and Charles V. Hamilton, *The Dual Agenda: The African-American Struggle for Civil and Economic Equality* (New York: Columbia University Press, 1997); D'Emilio, *Lost Prophet,* 426–29; Joseph Peniel, *Stokely: A Life* (New York: Basic Books, 2014); Peniel E. Joseph, "The Black Power Movement, Democracy, and America in the King Years," *American Historical Review,* vol 114, no. 4 (October 1, 2009): 1001–16. William Julius Wilson, *When Jobs Disappear: The World of the New Urban Poor* (New York: Vintage, 1997); Heather Thompson, *Whose Detroit? Politics, Labor, and Race in a Modern American City* (Ithaca, NY: Cornell University Press, 2001); Thomas J. Sugrue, *The Origins of the Urban Crisis: Race and Inequality in Post-war Detroit* (Princeton: Princeton University Press, 1996), and *Sweet Land of Liberty: The Forgotten Struggle for Civil Rights in the North* (New York: Random House, 1962). Erik S. Gellman,

"'The Stone Wall Behind,' The Chicago Coalition for United Community Action and Labor's Overseers, 1968–1973," in David Goldberg and Trevor Griffey, eds., *Black Power at Work: Community Control, Affirmative Action, and the Construction Industry* (Ithaca, NY: Cornell University Press, 2010), 112–243; Gellman, "In the Driver's Seat: Chicago's Bus Drivers and Labor Insurgency in the Era of Black Power," *Labor: Studies in Working-Class History of the Americas*, vol. 11, no. 3 (2014): 49–76. Milton Derber, *Labor in Illinois: The Affluent Years, 1945–1980* (Urbana: University of Illinois Press, 1989). On the "malignant kinship," Thomas F. Jackson, *From Civil Rights to Human Rights: Martin Luther King, Jr., and the Struggle for Economic Justice* (Philadelphia: University of Pennsylvania Press, 2007); Carson quote in Mary Lou Finley, et al., *The Chicago Freedom Movement*, xi. "SCLC 10th Convention Urges Labor-Civil Rights Alliance," *The Mine-Mill Union*, vol. 25, no. 9 (September 1966); Alan Draper, "Labor and the 1966 Elections," *Labor History*, vol. 30, no. 1 (1989); Bayard Rustin, "Civil Rights at the Crossroads," *American Federationist*, vol. 73, no. 11(November 1966): 16–20. David J. Garrow, *Bearing the Cross: Martin Luther King, Jr., and the Southern Christian Leadership Conference* (New York: William Morrow, 1986), 536, 532.

Chapter 4. "IN GOD'S ECONOMY," 1967-1968

Epigraph, King speech, February 15, 1968, Mississippi Leaders on the Washington Campaign, St. Thomas AME Church, Birmingham, Alabama, MLKP Atlanta, ser. 3; author interview with Jack O'Dell, Seattle, December 17, 2012; Coretta Scott King, as told to Rev. Dr. Barbara Reynolds, *My Life, My Love, My Legacy* (New York: Henry Holt, 2017), 87–88, 149, 150; Christian Appy, *Working-Class War: American Combat Soldiers and Vietnam* (Chapel Hill: University of North Carolina Press, 2000); King, "A Time to Break Silence," April 4, 1967, in James Melvin Washington, ed., *A Testament of Hope: The Essential Writings of Martin Luther King, Jr.* (San Francisco: Harper, 1986), 232–33. Apparently unlike America's leaders at the time, King had read the history of Vietnam's oppression by French, Japanese, and American military occupations and concluded that there was no justification for continuing it; Taylor Branch, *At Canaan's Edge: America in the King Years, 1965–68* (New York: Simon and Schuster, 2006), 324–31.

King, "Civil Rights at the Crossroads," Address to the Shop Stewards of Local 815, Teamsters and Allied Trades Council, Americana Hotel, New York, May 2, 1967, in Michael K. Honey, ed., *All Labor Has Dignity* (Boston: Beacon Press, 2011), 121–36. King was correct that the federal government had subsidized white ethnics and the middle class at the expense of African Americans: Ira Katznelson, *When Affirmative Action Was White: An Untold Story of Racial Inequality in Twentieth-Century America* (New York: W. W. Norton, 2005). "An American Tragedy, 1967 Detroit," *Newsweek,* August 7, 1967, 18–27; "An Army Expert in Guerrilla War Sees a New Vietnam Developing in Our Ghettoes," *I. F. Stone's Weekly,* February 5, 1968, 3; "Detroit's Economic Disaster," *Newsweek,* August 7, 1967, 57–58; Heather Thompson, *Whose Detroit? Politics, Labor, and Race in a Modern American City* (Ithaca, NY: Cornell University Press, 2001); Telegram, King to LBJ, quoted in Gordon Mantler, *Power to the Poor: Black-Brown Coalition and the Fight for Economic Justice, 1960–1974* (Chapel Hill: University of North Carolina Press, 2013), 92. King, *Where Do We Go from Here: Chaos or Community? (New York: Harper and Row, 1967),* 24, 4, 5, 211, 214, 218; King, "Where Do We Go from Here?" SCLC presidential address, 1967, in Washington, ed., *A Testament of Hope,* 245–52.

New York Times and *Washington Post* quotes in David J. Garrow, *Bearing the Cross: Martin Luther King, Jr., and the Southern Christian Leadership Conference* (New York: William Morrow, 1986), 553–54, and Louisville incident, 561; Richard Lentz, *Symbols, the News Magazines, and Martin Luther King* (Baton Rouge: Louisiana State University Press, 1990), documents jaded media representations condemning King's antiwar speech and his antipoverty crusade; King at the National Conference quoted in Sylvie Laurent, "Martin Luther King, Jr., Beyond Race: The 1968 'Poor People's Campaign,' Class, and Justice," 79, unpublished manuscript in author's possession; Adam Fairclough, *To Redeem the Soul of America: The Southern Christian Leadership Conference and Martin Luther King, Jr.* (Athens: University of Georgia Press, 1987), 344, 357–58, 362, 466 n. 41; King, *Where Do We Go from Here?,* 87. Philip S. Foner, *U.S. Labor and the Vietnam War* (New York: International Publishers, 1989); King, "Domestic Impact of the War in Vietnam," Labor Leadership Assembly for Peace, November 11, 1967, in Honey, ed., *All Labor Has Dignity,* 137–52. David J. Garrow, *The FBI and Martin Luther King, Jr.: From "Solo" to Memphis* (New York: W. W. Norton, 1981), 214, 215, and *Bearing the Cross,* 532–35, 576, 580–82, 590–600; Mantler, *Power to the Poor,* 96–97ff.

On the Poor People's Campaign: Andrew Young observed that "once we moved North . . . the private sector turned against us," that "the working poor were not among the members of the big unions," and that SCLC had more experience with middle-class people, making the Poor People's Campaign very difficult indeed: Young, *An Easy Burden: The Civil Rights Movement and the Transformation of America* (New York: Harper Collins, 1996), 440–47. Fairclough, *To Redeem the Soul of America*, ch. 14. King, "What Are Your New Year's Resolutions?" January 7, 1968; Press conference; "Why We Must Go to Washington," January 16, 1968, and "See You in Washington," January 17, 1968, all at Ebenezer Baptist Church; "To Minister to the Valley," February, 23, 1968, Ministers Leadership Training Program, Miami, Florida, all in MLKP Atlanta. Not wild ideas: Robert Reich, *Saving Capitalism: For the Many, Not the Few* (New York: Knopf, 2015); Hedrick Smith, *Who Stole the American Dream?* (New York: Random House, 2012). Horton quote in transcript of Myles Horton interviews for Frank Adams, *Unearthing Seeds of Fire: The Idea of Highlander* (Winston-Salem, NC: J. F. Blair, 1975), in Highlander Folk School archive, box 17, folder 23, MLK, Wisconsin Historical Society.

"MLK and Welfare" transcript, Chicago, January 5, 1968, MLKP Atlanta; Nick Kotz, *Judgment Days: Lyndon Baines Johnson, Martin Luther King, Jr., and the Laws That Changed America* (Boston: Houghton Mifflin, 2005), 76ff; King speech, Waycross, Georgia, transcript, March 22, 1968, MLKP Atlanta. King said, "We've had the privilege of working very closely over the last few weeks" with the Welfare Rights Organization, speech transcript, Jackson, MS, March 20, 1968, MLKP Atlanta. Women were the largest group signing up: Registration forms, box 180:2, SCLC Papers, E-8, PPC, MLKP Atlanta; Thomas F. Jackson, *From Civil Rights to Human Rights: Martin Luther King, Jr., and the Struggle for Economic Justice* (Philadelphia: University of Pennsylvania Press, 2007), 507–8. Premilla Nadasen, *Welfare Warriors: The Welfare Rights Movement in the United States* (New York: Routledge, 2005). Kotz, *Judgment Days*, 79. On February 7: King, "In Search for a New Sense of Direction," Vermont Ave. Baptist Church, Washington, DC, February 7, 1968, and comment in "Why We Must Go to Washington," SCLC Conference, Ebenezer Baptist Church, Atlanta, January 15, 1968, MLKP Atlanta. War on Poverty statistics from Nelson Lichtenstein, *State of the Union: A Century of American Labor* (Princeton: Princeton University Press, 2002), 194. King speech transcript, February 15, 1968, Mississippi Leaders on the Washington Campaign, St. Thomas AME Church, Birmingham, Alabama, ser. 3, MLKP Atlanta. "Speaks to a Mass Meeting, Montgomery, Alabama," transcript, February 16, 1968; "Pre-Washington Campaign," mass meeting, Selma, February 16 and 19, 1968; "That argument should never have come up," King to Mississippi Leaders on the Washington Campaign, St. Thomas AME Birmingham, February 15, 1968; King, "To Minister to the Valley," February 23, 1968, Ministers Leadership Training Program, Miami, Florida, all in MLKP Atlanta; Garrow, *Bearing the Cross*, 590–91; Young, *An Easy Burden*, 444; Mantler, *Power to the Poor*, 91, 109–11; Myles Horton, *The Long Haul* (New York: Doubleday,

1990), 118. Donald Lobsinger interview, June 23, 2016, Detroit Historical Society, https://detroit1967.detroithistorical.org/items/show/287; Jude
Huetteman, "Remembering King's Visit," *Grosse Pointe News,* January
5, 2017.

Chapter 5. "ALL LABOR HAS DIGNITY," 1968

King, March 18, 1968, AFSCME speech in Michael K. Honey, ed., *"All
Labor Has Dignity"* (Boston: Beacon Press, 2011), 167–78. Author interviews with James Robinson, Alzada and Leroy Clark, Clarence Coe,
George Holloway, and Leroy Boyd in Honey, *Black Workers Remember:
An Oral History of Segregation Unionism, and the Freedom Struggle*
(Berkeley: University of California Press, 1999). For extensive documen-
tation for this chapter, see Honey, *Going Down Jericho Road: The Memphis Strike, Martin Luther King's Last Campaign* (New York: W. W. Norton, 2007), and Joan Beifuss, *At the River I Stand* (Memphis, TN: B & W,
1985). Beifuss led a team of researchers under a National Endowment for
the Humanities grant to create the Sanitation Strike Collection, Mississippi Valley Collection, McWherter Library, University of Memphis (SSC).
Jesse Epps interview, SSC. Author interview with Taylor Rogers and Bessie Rogers, in Honey, *Black Workers Remember,* 293–301. For details on
early Memphis, see Honey, *Southern Labor and Black Civil Rights: Organizing Memphis Workers* (Urbana: University of Illinois Press, 1993), chs.
1 and 2. "Something is going to take place," in Honey, *Going Down Jericho Road,* 40. On Memphis elections, Elizabeth Gritter, *River of Hope:
Black Politics and the Memphis Freedom Movement, 1865–1954* (Lexington: University Press of Kentucky, 2014); Papers of Henry Loeb III, and
news clipping files, Memphis Public Library; David M. Tucker, *Memphis
Since Crump: Bossism, Blacks, and Civic Reformers, 1948–1968* (Knoxville: University of Tennessee Press, 1980); G. Wayne Dowdy, *Crusades
for Freedom: Memphis and the Political Transformation of the American
South* (Jackson: University Press of Mississippi, 2010); and Laurie Beth
Green, *Battling the Plantation Mentality: Memphis and the Black Freedom Struggle* (Chapel Hill: University of North Carolina Press, 2007).
Ezekial Bell and T. O. Jones interviews in SSC. Beifuss, *At the River I
Stand,* 32–34. Paul Winfield, David Appleby, Allison Graham, and Steven
Ross, "At the River I Stand," California Newsreel film, 2004. "The people
just booed him right down," *Commercial Appeal,* February 14, 1968; Epps
and Lucy interviews, SSC; Beifuss, *At the River I Stand,* 55; Joseph G.
Goulden, *Jerry Wurf, Labor's Last Angry Man: A Biography* (New York:
Atheneum, 1982); S. B. "Billy" Kyles interview, SSC; Ortha B. Strong

Jones said the union slogan meant "we had somebody who would protect us if we needed help," quoted in Honey, *Going Down Jericho Road*, 502; Steve Estes, *I Am a Man! Race, Manhood, and the Civil Rights Movement* (Chapel Hill: University of North Carolina Press, 1972), examines this gendered slogan as an appeal for human dignity. The "Dignity" photo taken by Richard Copley is in Honey, *Black Workers Remember*.

The *Commercial Appeal* cartoon is of T. O. Jones, February 24, 1968. Richard Lentz documented the Memphis commercial media's overwhelming bias, "Sixty-five Days in Memphis" (master's thesis, Southern Illinois University, 1976); on the wider issue of media racism see Lentz, *Symbols, the News Magazines, and Martin Luther King* (Baton Rouge: Louisiana State University Press, 1999). The black-owned, Sengstacke family's *Tri-State Defender* provided an informative weekly alternative, and WLOK and WDIA played to black audiences. Kimberly L. Little, *You Must Be From the North: Southern White Women in the Memphis Civil Rights Movement* (Jackson: University Press of Mississippi, 2009). William Lucy and George "Rip" Clark and Jesse Epps interviews, SSC. Author interview with Tommy Powell, August 6, 2004, Memphis. Beifuss, *At the River I Stand*, 107–8; *Commercial Appeal*, March 12, 15, and 16, 1968. Goulden, *Jerry Wurf, Labor's Last Angry Man*, ch. 5. The UAW at a national level had a long battle with Local 988 in Memphis to get it to desegregate facilities and advance black workers: Local 988 records under UAW Local Regions, UAW President's Office records, Reuther Library.

Despite larger estimates of the March 18 turnout, Mason Temple could have only held 3,500 to 5,000, according to a seat count by Keith D. Miller, *Martin Luther King's Biblical Epic: His Final, Great Speech* (Jackson: University Press of Mississippi, 2012). Lucy's comments on King's speech in Henry Hampton and Steve Fayer, *Voices of Freedom: An Oral History of the Civil Rights Movement from the 1950s through the 1980s* (New York: Bantam, 1991), 459–60. The media failed to report: *Commercial Appeal*, March 19, and Beifuss, *At the River I Stand*, 201–2. King and Levison: Adam Fairclough, *To Redeem the Soul of America: The Southern Christian Leadership Conference and Martin Luther King, Jr.* (Athens: University of Georgia Press, 1987), 372, and David J. Garrow, *Bearing the Cross: Martin Luther King, Jr., and the Southern Christian Leadership Conference* (New York: William Morrow, 1986), 606. Memphis music provided a powerful elixir blasted daily from WLOK and WDIA, and African Americans had been tuning in to it for years. Charles L. Hughes, *Country Soul: Making Music and Making Race in the American South* (Chapel Hill: University of North Carolina Press, 2015); Robert Gordon, *Respect Yourself: Stax Records and the Soul Explosion* (New

York: Bloomsbury, 2013); Pete Daniel, *Lost Revolutions: The South in the 1950s* (Chapel Hill: University of North Carolina Press, 2000); Brian Ward, *Just My Soul Responding: Rhythm and Blues, Black Consciousness, and Race Relations* (Berkeley: University of California Press, 1998).

Chapter 6. "DANGEROUS UNSELFISHNESS"

"I literally cried," quoted in Amy Nathan Wright, "The 1968 Poor People's Campaign, Marks, Mississippi, and the Mule Train," in Emily Crosby, ed., *Civil Rights History from the Ground Up: Local Struggles, a National Movement* (Athens: University of Georgia Press, 2011), and on conditions in Marks, 109–43. Stokely Carmichael with Ekwueme Michael Thelwell, *Ready for Revolution: The Life and Struggles of Stokely Carmichael (Kwame Ture)* (New York: Scribners, 2003), 512–13. Poor People's Campaign tour, rally speech, Grenada, MS, March 18; Laurel, MS, and Eutaw, AL, March 20; Clarksdale, MS, February 15; "Mississippi Leaders on the Washington Campaign," St. Thomas AME Church, Birmingham, AL, and Albany, GA, March 22, 1968, in MLKP Atlanta, ser. 3. On the mysterious white donor, Taylor Branch, *At Canaan's Edge: America in the King Years, 1965–68* (New York: Simon and Schuster, 2006), 720. On King's tour in Mississippi and New York and last days in Memphis, David J. Garrow, *Bearing the Cross: Martin Luther King, Jr., and the Southern Christian Leadership Conference* (New York: William Morrow, 1986), 608–24.

For details on the March 28 events in Memphis, see Honey, *Going Down Jericho Road: The Memphis Strike, Martin Luther King's Last Campaign* (New York: W. W. Norton, 2007), and Joseph Rosenbloom, *Redemption: Martin Luther King Jr.'s Last 31 Hours* (Boston: Beacon Press, 2018). "According to their strategy," author interview with Charles Cabbage, August 4, 2004, Memphis, TN. Adam Fairclough, *To Redeem the Soul of America: The Southern Christian Leadership Conference and Martin Luther King, Jr.* (Athens: University of Georgia Press, 1987), 367–69; Gordon Mantler, *Power to the Poor: Black-Brown Coalition and the Fight for Economic Justice, 1960–1974* (Chapel Hill: University of North Carolina Press, 2013), 93; Kenneth O'Reilly, *Racial Matters: The FBI's Secret File on Black America, 1960–1972* (New York: Free Press, 1989); and Michael Friedly and David Gallen, eds., *Martin Luther King, Jr.: The FBI File* (New York: Carroll and Graf, 1993). King, "Honoring Dr. DuBois" on the one-hundredth anniversary of his birth, reprinted in Esther Cooper Jackson, ed., *Freedomways Reader: Prophets in Their Own Country* (Boulder, CO: Westview Press, 2000),

31–39. Like King, James Lawson suffered from daily racist and right wing threats during the Memphis strike: Lawson Papers, Vanderbilt University. Media and FBI-orchestrated attacks on King on March 28, in Honey, *Going Down Jericho Road*, 367–73. "Martin Luther King Warned," Natchez [Mississippi] *Democrat,* April 8, 1968, essentially blamed King for his own death. King spoke at the Washington Cathedral, "Remaining Awake Through a Great Revolution, March 31, 1968, in James Melvin Washington, ed., *A Testament of Hope: The Essential Writings of Martin Luther King, Jr.* (San Francisco: Harper, 1986), 268–78. Andrew Young, *An Easy Burden: The Civil Rights Movement and the Transformation of America* (New York: Harper Collins, 1996), 470–71. A report by Lt. E. H. Arkin, a special agent of the Memphis Police Department, revealed combined police and FBI surveillance: "Civil Disorders, Memphis, Tennessee," February 12 to April 16, 1968, Beudoin Collection, Misssissippi Valley Collection, McWherter Library, University of Memphis. The FBI often knew of threats against King but failed to alert him: Files on the Memphis Sanitation Strike, Memphis Field Office, 157-1092, and FBI files on King, 100-106670, FBI Reading Room, Washington, DC. Honey, *Going Down Jericho Road*, 401–7, 445–46ff.; Coretta Scott King, as told to Rev. Dr. Barbara Reynolds, *My Life, My Love, My Legacy* (New York: Henry Holt, 2017), 154, 160. William F. Pepper, *An Act of State: The Execution of Martin Luther King* (London: Verso, 2003), believed government agencies collaborated in killing King; see also *The Final Assassinations Report, House Select Committee on Investigations* (New York: Bantam, 1979). But Gerald Posner, *Killing the Dream: James Earl Ray and the Assassination of Martin Luther King, Jr.* (New York: Random House, 1998), and Hampton Sides, *Hellhound on His Trail: The Stalking of Martin Luther King, Jr., and the International Hunt for his Assassin* (New York: Doubleday, 2010), document Ray as the trigger man. See also Honey, *Going Down Jericho Road*, 407–8, 435, 460. The National Civil Rights Museum annex displays evidence in the King murder. Young, *An Easy Burden,* 470-72; Carmichael with Thelwell, *Ready for Revolution*, quote on 512; Ralph David Abernathy, *And the Walls Came Tumbling Down: An Autobiography* (New York: Harper and Row, 1989), 492. Anecdotes and racist comments collected after King's death, Honey, *Going Down Jericho Road*, 444–46, 463–64, 478–82, Lawson quote on 454. Judith Smith, *Becoming Belafonte: Black Artist, Public Radical* (Austin: University of Texas Press, 2014), documents Belafonte as one of King's most dedicated supporters and fund-raisers.

King, "The Drum Major Instinct," in Washington, ed., *A Testament of Hope,* 267; Scott King, *My Life, My Love, My Legacy*, 178–79, quote on 180. On continuation of the Poor People's Campaign: Mantler, *Power to the Poor,* ch. 4, quote on 152. Charles Cabbage showed up as a marshal in the list of participants, MLKP Atlanta; Bobby Seale remembered going to the PPC as his salute to King, in a talk at the University of Puget Sound, April 5, 2017, Tacoma, WA. John Lewis, with Michael D'Orso, *Walking with the Wind: A Memoir of the Movement* (New York: Simon and Schuster, 1998). King, "Showdown for Nonviolence," *Look,* April 16, 1968, 23–25, and "Trumpet of Conscience," Washington, ed., *A Testament of Hope,* 647–48. Author interview with William Lucy in Honey, *Black Workers Remember,* 318. "Love and Solidarity: James M. Lawson and Nonviolence in the Search for Workers' Rights," Michael Honey, producer and director, Bullfrog Films; and Lawson and Kent Wong, *Nonviolence and Social Movements* (Los Angeles: UCLA Labor Center, 2016). "Mrs. King Gives Aid to Unionization," *Commercial Appeal,* April 30, 1977, and see Honey on Memphis Furniture organizing, in *Black Workers Remember,* 343–47, 366–67. Some of King's favorite unions obtained a King holiday through contract demands before declaration of the national holiday; Honey, ed., *All Labor Has Dignity,* 197–99. David Chappell, *Waking from the Dream: The Struggle for Civil Rights in the Shadow of Martin Luther King, Jr.* (New York: Random House, 2014), ch. 4, quote on 101; Scott King, *My Life, My Love, My Legacy,* wrote that six million people signed petitions for the King holiday, 272.

"Even as we fight": Sharon D. Wright, *Race, Power and Political Emergence in Memphis* (New York: Garland Publishing, 2000); Gavin Wright, *Sharing the Prize: The Economics of the Civil Rights Revolution in the South* (Cambridge, MA: Harvard University Press, 2013). Peter T. Kilborn, "Memphis Blacks Find Poverty's Grip Strong," *New York Times,* October 5, 1999. Author interviews with Kevin Bradshaw, February 8; Gail Tyree, February 9; A. C. Wharton, February 9; Otis Sanborn, Daphine McFerrin, and Elena Delavega, February 11, all in Memphis, 2016; and Kay Davis, phone interview, July 9, 2016. Michael Honey and David Ciscel, "Memphis Since King: Race and Labor in the City," *Poverty and Race* 18, no. 2 (March/April 2009): 8–11. Michael Powell, "Blacks in Memphis Lose Decades of Economic Gains," *New York Times,* May 30, 2010. David H. Ciscel and Michael Honey, "Memphis 50 Years Since King: The Unfinished Agenda," *Poverty & Race* (July-September 2016). Elena Delavega, "2015 Memphis Poverty Fact Sheet," Mid-South Family and Community Empowerment Institute, University of Memphis. Honey, "Black Workers Matter: The Continuing Search for Racial-Economic Equality in Memphis,"in Aram Goudsouzian and Charles McKinney, eds., *An Unseen Light: Black Struggles for Freedom in Memphis, Tennessee* (Lexington: University Press of

Kentucky, 2018). Rev. William J. Barber II, *The Third Reconstruction: Moral Mondays, Fusion Politics, and the Rise of a New Justice Movement* (Boston: Beacon Press, 2016), is calling for a new Poor People's Campaign. King, *Where Do We Go from Here: Chaos or Community?* (New York: Harper and Row, 1967), "The World House," 195–223.

IMAGE CREDITS

iv   King speaking to strikers and supporters on March 18, 1968. *Memphis Press-Scimitar* newspaper morgue, courtesy of the Special Collections Department, University of Memphis Libraries.

18   *Montgomery Bus Boycott*, 1956. Burton Silverman (born 1928). Graphite on paper, composition: 10 5/8 × 9 1/16 in. (27 × 23 cm). Delaware Art Museum, Gift of the Robert Lehman Foundation Inc., 1994. © Burton Philip Silverman/ Licensed by VAGA, New York, NY. Digital image provided by Burton Silverman.

46   King at Highander Library in 1957 with (left to right) Pete Seeger, Charis Horton, Rosa Parks, and Ralph David Abernathy. Photo reprinted with permission of the Highlander Research and Education Center.

51   "King at a Communist Training School." Photo reprinted with permission of the Highlander Research and Education Center.

82   King with a photo of Mahatma Gandhi at the Southern Christian Leadership Conference office in Atlanta, 1966. Courtesy of the Department of Special Collections, Stanford University Libraries. Photo by Bob Fitch by permission.

112 Martin and Coretta Scott King in the March Against Fear in Mississippi, July 1966. Courtesy of the Department of Special Collections, Stanford University Libraries. Photo by Bob Fitch by permission. Copyright 1966 Dr. Martin Luther King Jr. Copyright renewed 1994 Coretta Scott King.

134 I Am A Man; Striking members of Memphis Local 1733 hold signs whose slogan symbolized the sanitation workers' campaign in 1968. © Richard L. Copley, reprinted with permission.

139 Scab sanitation workers empty garbage in a sanitation truck, guarded by police during the Memphis sanitation workers strike. *Memphis Press-Scimitar* newspaper morgue, courtesy of the Special Collections Department, University of Memphis Libraries.

160 Dr. Martin Luther King, Jr. takes a moment for sober reflection before delivering his speech "The Other America" to the audience at Grosse Pointe High School. The Tony Spina Collection, Walter P. Reuther Library, Archives of Labor and Urban Affairs, Wayne State University.

165 After a police attack and a riot on March 28, 1968, the Tennessee National Guard occupied Memphis, but members of AFSCME Local 1733 continued to march. *Memphis Press-Scimitar* newspaper morgue, courtesy of the Special Collections Department, University of Memphis Libraries.

177 After King's assassination on April 4, 1968, Walter Reuther, James Lawson, and tens of thousands of others demonstrated in Memphis on April 8. Walter P. Reuther Library, Archives of Labor and Urban Affairs, Wayne State University.

178 Marchers with signs reading "Honor King: End Racism!" and "Union Justice Now!" *Memphis Press-Scimitar* newspaper morgue, courtesy of the Special Collections Department, University of Memphis Libraries.

185 On June 19, 1968, an interracial mass march demonstrated support of the Poor People's Campaign on the National Mall in Washington, D.C. © Jim Pickerell, courtesy of the Walter P. Reuther Library, Archives of Labor and Urban Affairs, Wayne State University.

186 Crowd with "Local 282 UFWA-AFL-CIO Remembers Dr. Martin Luther King, Jr." banner and other signs. *Memphis Press-Scimitar* newspaper morgue, courtesy of the Special Collections Department, University of Memphis Libraries.

188 Woman in front of Lorraine Motel with sign reading "Dr. King Died So You Might Live." *Memphis Press-Scimitar* newspaper morgue, courtesy of the Special Collections Department, University of Memphis Libraries.

QUOTATION CREDITS

INDEX

Page numbers in *italics* indicate photographs or illustrations.

Walker, Robert, 135–36, 142, 182
Walker, Scott, 191
Walker, Wyatt T., 69
Wallace, George, 39, 171, 175
Wallace, Henry, 30–31, 34
Wall Street Journal, 118
Walton, Sam, 70, 71
War on Poverty, 86–87, 100, 114, 129
Washington, D.C., riots (1968), 176
Washington Post, 118
Watts Riots (1965), 99–100, 103
WDIA (Memphis), 147
wealth gap, 101–2
welfare rights movement, 126–28, 183
Wells-Barnett, Ida B., 138
"We Shall Overcome" (song), 50
Wesley, Cynthia Diane, 80
West, Cornel, 24–25
Where Do We Go From Here (King), 117–19
White, James, 148
"white backlash," 72, 102–3, 119, 121
White Citizens Council, 39, 41, 75
white-collar work, 101
"white primary," 94
white supremacists, 21–22, 69–70, 80
Why We Can't Wait (King), 84
Wiley, George, 126
Wilkins, Roy, 150
Wilkinson, Frank, 54
Williams, Adam Daniel, 20, 23–24
Williams, Alberta, 24, 25, 175
Williams, Aubrey, 50
Williams, Carol, 127
Williams, Jennie C. Parks, 24, 26–27
Williams, Lucrecia (Creecy), 20
Williams, Robert F., 40
Williams, Willis, 20, 24–25

Wilson, William Julius, 190
wiretaps, 2, 67, 68, 84, 157
WLOK (Memphis), 147
women
  in freedom-movement scholarship, 14–15
  March on Washington, 79–80
  Memphis sanitation strike, 145–47
  Poor People's Campaign, 127–28
  Scripto strike, 88–89
  social justice movements, 183
  welfare rights movement, 127–28
Women's International League for Peace and Freedom, 114
Women's Political Council (WPC), 38
Women Strike for Peace, 114
Woods, Jeff, 52
World War II, 32–33, 89
Wright, Alice, 180
Wright, Gavin, 189
Wurf, Jerry, 144, 149, 150, 179, 181, 182
Wyatt, Addie, 56

X, Malcolm, 27, 78, 95

Young, Andrew
  on civil rights movement as middle-class movement, 128
  on King's condition before final trip to Memphis, 164
  on King's death, 175–76
  Poor People's Campaign, 123, 126
  and SCLC, 58
  on Watts riot, 103
Young Communist League, 41, 42

Zinn, Howard, 67

ABOUT THE AUTHOR

Michael K. Honey is the author of the Robert F. Kennedy Book Award–winning *Going Down Jericho Road: The Memphis Sanitation Strike, Martin Luther King's Last Campaign* (2007), which also received the Liberty Foundation Legacy Award from the Organization of American Historians (OAH), the H. L. Mitchell Award from the Southern Historical Association (SHA), and University Association of Labor Educator and International Labor Research Association best book awards. Honey's other books include *Sharecropper's Troubadour: John L. Handcox, the Southern Tenant Farmers Union, and the African American Song Tradition* (2013); *Black Workers Remember: An Oral History of Segregation, Unionism, and the Freedom Struggle* (1999), winner of the Lillian Smith Book Award from the Southern Regional Council and the H. L. Mitchell Award (SHA); and *Southern Labor and Black Civil Rights: Organizing Memphis Workers* (1993), winner of the Charles S. Sydnor Award (SHA) and the James A. Rawley Prize (OAH). He edited a volume of Martin Luther King, Jr.'s speeches, *"All Labor Has Dignity"* (2011); produced and performed "Links on the Chain" with Pete Seeger and other musicians; and wrote and produced the film *Love and Solidarity: James M. Lawson and Nonviolence in the Search for Workers' Rights* (2016). He has received Guggenheim, Rockefeller Foundation, National Endowment for the Humanities, and other research fellowships.

A former southern civil liberties and community organizer in Memphis (1970–76), Honey is the Fred and Dorothy Haley Professor of Humanities and teaches labor and civil rights history at the University of Washington Tacoma, and is past president of the Labor and Working-Class History Association and Harry Bridges Chair of Labor Studies for the University of Washington. He lives in Tacoma, Washington, with his wife Patti Krueger.

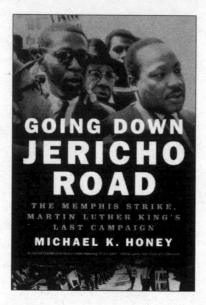